NORMANDY

BREACHING THE ATLANTIC WALL

FROM D-DAY TO THE BREAKOUT AND LIBERATION

Dominique François

ZENITH PRESS

First published in 2008 by Zenith Press, an imprint of MBI Publishing Company,
400 1st Avenue North, Minneapolis, MN 55401 USA.

Zenith Press titles are also available at discounts in bulk quantity for industrial
or sales-promotional use. For details write to Special Sales Manager at MBI
Publishing Company, 400 1st Avenue North, Minneapolis, MN 55401 USA.

To find out more about our books, join us online at www.zenithpress.com.

Library of Congress Cataloging-in-Publication Data

François, Dominique, 1962-
  Normandy : breaching the Atlantic Wall: from D-day to the breakout and
liberation / by Dominique François.
     p. cm.
  ISBN 978-0-7603-3327-3 (hbk.)
  1. World War, 1939-1945—Campaigns—France—Normandy. 2. World War,
1939-1945—Campaigns—France—Normandy—Pictorial works. I. Title.
  D756.5.N6F74 2008
  940.54'21421—dc22

                                              2008006485

Editor: Steve Gansen
Designer: Lois Stanfield
Jacket Design: John Barnett, 4Eyes Design

Front cover: National Archives and Records Administration, Washington, D.C. (NARA)
Back cover, main image: NARA; *inset maps:* Philip Schwartzberg, Meridian Mapping, Minneapolis
Endpaper map: Philip Schwartzberg
Frontispiece: NARA
Title pages: NARA

Printed in China

This book is dedicated to my grandfather
Joseph François, a cavalry officer in
World War I, who was killed on June 6, 1944,
at Saint-Marcouf, France.

CONTENTS

MAPS

Cartography by Philip Schwartzberg, Meridian Mapping, Minneapolis

ACKNOWLEDGMENTS

THIS BOOK IS THE FRUIT of more than ten years of writing and research in France and the United States. On the eve of its publication, my thoughts go first to friends, all of them veterans of the Normandy Campaign, who are no longer among us, but who encouraged and helped me in earlier stages of this project: my deepest gratitude goes to Col. Louis Mendez, 508th PIR, 82nd Airborne Division (ABN); Lou Horn, 507th PIR, 82nd ABN; O. B. Hill, 508th PIR; Marcus Heim, 505th PIR, 82nd ABN; Capt. David Brummit, 507th PIR; and many others whose friendship and stories permitted me to better understand the daily life of the frontline soldiers who fought the Battle of Normandy.

The work could never have been accomplished without the conversations, interviews, factual information, and original documents that many veterans have generously supplied. I here thank Maj. Gen. Paul Smith, Col. Francis Naughton, Col. Gordon K. Smith, Capt. Roy Creek, Jack Schlegel, Herb Suerth, Ray Naggell, Roy Harold, James Carroll, Chaplain Kuehl, Albert Larson, Aldo Valentini, and many others too numerous to mention who shared their experiences and photographs with me. Many families of veterans have, in turn, helped to preserve and transmit the memories of their loved ones: for this, I particularly thank Ray and Soley Boland, Jane Mendez, Skip MacGrath, Denny Roussey, and Gene and Jack Williams, but many others also come to mind.

I also express my gratitude to my agent and translator, Dr. Gayle Wurst of Princeton International Agency for the Arts, who translated this work from the French and patiently took me through the steps of publishing it in the United States. My hearty thanks and compliments go to Richard Kane, my publisher at Zenith Press, to my editor, Steve Gansen, and to the rest of the team for their support of this project and the splendid volume they have produced. Thanks as well to Phil

Schwartzberg of Meridian Mapping, who has done a fantastic job of producing the fine maps that enrich these pages.

A very large and special thank you goes to my friend Bud Parker, who helped to finance my research for this book at the National Archives in Washington, D.C. His friendship for the veterans and his generous support of projects that preserve the history of World War II have done much to keep the memory of the war and the men who fought it alive. I also wish to thank my friend Doug Bekke, historian and conservator at the Minnesota Military Museum, for sharing his considerable knowledge and photographs.

To the librarians and archivists who helped to identify and furnish the photographs in this book, I owe a debt of gratitude: they include Madame Marie Claude Berthelot, Mémorial de Caen; Madame Nathalie Riou, l'Etablissement de Communication et de Production Audiovisuelle de la Défense Française; Z. Frank Hanner, director of the National Infantry Museum at Fort Benning; the archivists at the National Archives and Record Administration in College Park, Maryland; and Mrs. Marilyn Ashmore, Col. Patrick Bartness, and the rest of the team at the Museum of Aviation at Warner Robins, who generously received me and opened up the treasures of their archives.

Finally, this book would probably never have seen the light of day if it had not been for my father, Fernand François, whose stories about World War II and passionate gratitude to our liberators awakened my interest in the period.

These pages would be incomplete without the mention of my wife Gaëlle and my children, Aurélien, Corentin, and Eilean. They put up with the many absences my research occasioned, and with long periods of writing and reflection that did not permit me to be present at their sides. Without their understanding and support, this book would not have been possible.

My grandfather, Joseph François, a cavalry officer in World War I. After the war, he settled in Saint-Marcouf and became a farmer. *Dominique François*

INTRODUCTION

THE MAN IN THE DONKEY cart rode past the artillery battery that the Germans had built on his land, casting a scowl of contempt at the occupying soldiers. He and his family had been forced to live with their hated presence ever since 1940, when the Germans had requisitioned his land, half of his horses, and even part of his own house. A cavalry officer who had fought at the Somme in World War I, he had now been reduced to watching the enemy construct the immense Crisbecq battery, with its imposing cannons pointed toward the sea, just a few hundred meters from his home.[1] Food rationing, curfews, and requisitions had transformed him from a free man to a captive. Like many Frenchmen, he kept his mouth shut and waited for the Allied invasion. After four long years of occupation, the Germans were losing on all fronts. Surely, freedom was soon to come!

As he arrived at the farm, it began to rain. The month of June had started badly, with heavy rains that would delay the harvest. The man found his three children in the kitchen of the old house along with his niece, whom he had adopted after her parents had died in the exodus of 1940. The young girl helped around the house, trying her best to perform the chores of his wife, who had died the previous year.

After dinner, the man sent the children to bed. He planned on getting up early the next morning to cut hay, providing the weather cooperated. At 10:15 p.m. by the old Norman clock, he heard a rumbling in the sky. Opening his door, he saw a formation of airplanes in the distance, heading toward the village. As the noise increased, he realized that they were probably coming to bomb the battery so uncomfortably close to his house. He called to the children to hurry downstairs and into the shelter he had built behind the garden.

---

[1] Crisbecq: German name given to the battery at Saint-Marcouf. Commanded by 1st Lt. Zee Walter Ohmsen, the battery had three 210mm Skoda cannons and a range of twenty-seven kilometers.

In the next instant, the first bomb exploded with a thunderous sound, ripping into part of the house and immediately killing the man in the kitchen. The next two bombs knocked down what was left of the walls. Shortly after, two of the children, dazed but only slightly injured, stumbled out of the wreckage. But one of the children and the niece remained trapped in the ruins.

Panicked, the two who were able to extricate themselves found refuge in the village as bombs continued to explode in the surrounding countryside. Early the next morning, the petrified villagers came out of their shelters and discovered that the bombs had partially destroyed their village. Saint-Marcouf was in ruins. As the civilians began to sift through the rubble, soldiers with blackened faces appeared, moving cautiously through the streets. As the villagers later learned, these were paratroopers from the 82nd Airborne Division, who had landed far outside their drop zones.

In the ruins of the house, the two children, helped by their neighbors, found their brother unconscious but alive. Deeper down in the rubble, they discovered the bodies of their father and cousin, crushed under a ton of debris. That man was my grandfather, Joseph François, and one of the children was none other than my father, Fernand François.

At dawn on June 6, 1944, as the Battle of Normandy began, the Allies who landed on the coast of France began the liberation that my grandfather and many others had so longed to see. Like many Frenchmen, my grandfather dreamt of revenge, of washing away the stain of the French defeat in 1940, and of freedom. But he never lived to see that long-awaited day, the day his country was liberated from the Germans.

My grandfather with my father, aged eight, in 1943 in front of the church at Saint-Marcouf. A recent widower, my grandfather was bringing up three children with the help of his niece. France had been occupied for three years, and German restrictions had considerably changed the life of the ordinary citizen. *Dominique François*

In June 1940, Mont-Saint-Michel, the symbol of Normandy and the jewel of its architecture, was invaded and occupied by the German army. Four years would pass before the French and Norman flags would again fly over its walls. *Dominique François*

I probably began to write this book because I never had a grandfather to tell me stories about the war. For many years now, I have been fascinated by the history of World War II, and particularly by the conflict that ravaged my native Normandy.

It has taken me a dozen years to gather and study the material necessary to write this book. I have spent hundreds of hours in military archives in France and the United States, poring over documents from the period. But throughout my research, my greatest pleasure has been meeting the veterans who participated in the dramatic days of the war. Sharing their memories and photographs with me, they recreated the very essence of combat as they relived their fears and joys and recounted the myriad personal stories that compose the grand history of the Battle of Normandy.

★ ★ ★ ★ ★

After much planning and preparation, on May 15, 1944, General Eisenhower presented the final details of Operation Overlord to King George VI, Winston Churchill, and Allied commanders in Saint Paul's School in London.

Along four thousand kilometers of the facing shoreline, between La Frise in the Netherlands and the Pyrenees in southwestern France, the Germans were feverishly working around the clock to complete the Atlantic Wall. The men in charge, Field Marshal Erwin Johannes Eugen Rommel and Gen. Field Marshal Karl Rudolf Gerd von Rundstedt, argued about the best way to proceed in the highly probable case that the Allies would try to invade the continent.

In Spring 1944, France was at the heart of the debate, for it was here, on French soil, that decisive operations would begin on D-Day. Discussions about D-Day were nevertheless not confined to the Allied invasion: the world had already been at war for four years. In France, these years saw suffering, treachery, bravery, famine, and black markets, and an atmosphere of simultaneous indifference and solidarity, courage and cowardice, resistance and collaboration. The Allies had made previous attempts, both successful and failed, at getting a foothold on the continent: the raids of 1940 and 1941; the landings at Dieppe and North Africa in 1942; lightning raids by Allied commandoes; the invasions of Sicily and Italy in 1943; and, finally, Operation Tiger in April 1944 in the south of England.

Without the example of British resistance, the Allied invasion would never have taken place. The British populace had demonstrated incredible courage and self-sacrifice throughout the German blitzkrieg, as bombs killed 60,000 British civilians and wounded another 240,000, destroying two million homes in cities and villages throughout the country.

The awakening of America after the infamous Japanese attack on Pearl Harbor brought about crucial changes. A "Victory Program" mobilized millions of young Americans from all over the country, assembling a formidable modern army that could deliver the military potential the Allies had so far lacked.

Even before June 5–6, 1944, when the paratroopers dropped and the Allied infantry disembarked on French shores, even before the French resistance helped prepare the way, providing information that was indispensable on D-Day, many had died in preparatory operations. The death toll already stood at twelve thousand dead, wounded, and missing. Their numbers included many young men who had crossed the Atlantic Ocean or English Channel to liberate the countries from which their ancestors had emigrated only decades before.

During the long summer of 1944, 1.85 million Allied soldiers followed the tens of thousands who had crossed the English Channel on the night of the Allied invasion. German soldiers baptized this period "das Stalingrad der Normandie"—Normandy's Stalingrad. The name was apt: in just two months, the ferocious campaign cost the lives of 130,000 soldiers and caused another 340,000 to be wounded. Normandy lost twenty thousand civilians in a war of snipers and carpet bombings, hedgerows, trenches, artillery barrages, and tanks.

But before the landings, the French defeat of 1940 had brought about four years of occupation, shame, repression, and deprivation.

CHILDHOOD MEMORIES OF D-DAY

FERNAND FRANÇOIS WAS only six years old when the Germans invaded his village of Saint-Marcouf, and ten when the Allied landings took place, but he has vivid memories of both these arrivals, as he here recounts.

"The first Germans arrived on motorcycles. They wore green leather coats and goggles, and looked rather frightening. They quickly requisitioned our farmhouse for living quarters. Four soldiers who were posted at the construction site for the Crisbecq Battery lived in our house. They all were older soldiers who regretted the war and wanted nothing more than to return home to their own children. They were nice to us, but my father had a lot of trouble swallowing the presence of German soldiers on our land and in our home.

"One day, some SS soldiers came to deliver a message to one of the Germans who lived with us. They got into a quarrel, and the one who lived with us took out his pistol and threatened the SS soldier. I don't know what they were arguing about. We lived through four years of restrictions. The most difficult thing for us was the shortage of food— things like sugar and chocolate—but leather had also been requisitioned and was now impossible to find, so we were forced to wear wooden *sabots* when our shoes wore out.

"On June 6, 1944, the Americans arrived and our house was bombed. My brother Joseph and I hid in a shelter in the village until the bombing stopped. We left the shelter at dawn and discovered an American paratrooper near the village pump. He was wounded in the stomach, and trying to drag himself to the pump. The poor man died in the next few minutes.

"We then went back to the house with some of the villagers to try to find our father, brother, and cousin Aline. After what seemed like a very long time, we found our father's body. Buried beneath him was our brother Jules, who was unconscious but still breathing. Later, Aline's body was also discovered. Our mother had already died in 1943 of a sudden attack of peritonitis, and now here we were on June 6, 1944, and we had lost our father too.

"Luckily, in the following days, we had some wonderful experiences which helped us to forget our sad situation."

Image credit: Fernand François

Part I

FOUR YEARS OF GERMAN OCCUPATION

★ ★ ★ ★ ★

The West Wall is impregnable.
We will crush the invaders at the fortifications
stretching from Holland to the Pyrenees.

—ADOLF HITLER[2]

[2] Albin Michel, *Hitler parle à ses généraux*, (1964), p. 201.

In April 1940 it was *une drôle de guerre*, or "phony war," to use the famous term. In lieu of a *blitzkrieg*, or "lightning war," the Germans found a *sitzkrieg*, or "sitting war," as they mockingly dubbed it. France and England sought to buy time, in the belief they needed to catch up to the Germans in troops and matériel. Both sides eyed each other but did not make a move. In a few weeks, the Germans would go on the offensive. *Dominique François*

1
JUNE 1940:
THE DEFEAT OF FRANCE

★ ★ ★ ★ ★

On May 10, 1940, Hitler launches the western offensive, invading Holland, Belgium, and Luxembourg in the space of a few days. The blitzkrieg has begun. *Dominique François*

FRANCE ENTERED THE WAR DEVOID of patriotic fervor, at a time when the country was more than ever a victim of political division. Ever since 1918, when France had emerged victorious from World War I, political instability had toppled one government after another, as right- and left-wing majorities replaced each other in rapid succession. The country was largely rural, with an archaic economic structure. The Popular Front, the coalition of the left which had offered such hope in 1936, had been stopped in its tracks, only to become a contributor, along with the economic crisis, to the prevailing national malaise.

At the beginning of the war, France mobilized five million men but had no means to arm them, while the German Reich was able to arm twelve to thirteen million. The confused mixture of pessimism and pacifism that reigned in France caused the country to fare no better psychologically than militarily.

Unlike the French, the Germans believed in going on the offensive. Their officers were young, their command structure was perfectly centralized, and their army was very modern, enthralled by the concept of blitzkrieg. Literally translated as "lightning war," the doctrine maintained that a swift, combined attack by air and land forces, the latter fortified with tanks, was the surest way to penetrate and decisively defeat the enemy.

The Wehrmacht (armed forces) had already demonstrated the concept in Poland, which fell to the Germans in less than a month, in spite of Polish heroism: 200,000 Poles died and 450,000 were taken prisoner. Though vanquished, Poland nevertheless continued to show the brave face of resistance, sending its government into exile while Germany and the Soviet Union divided the war-torn country up among themselves.

Rommel's Seventh Army thrusts west. His tanks and reconnaissance units would encounter no opposition, and he soon would arrive in Normandy. *Dominique François*

North African infantrymen from Algeria and Morocco, more familiar with desert warfare, were unused to the kind of combat they encountered in Normandy. Many endured five years of captivity as POWs.

Dominique François

Some German units used bicycles to follow the passage of first-wave troops. Here, arriving troops will settle into an administrative building at Caen. *Dominique François*

Hitler no longer showed any fear of waging war on two fronts. But France, unable to react, failed to shoulder arms for eight months after a weak offensive in the Sarre. It was *une drôle de guerre*, or "phony war" to use the famous term. In lieu of a blitzkrieg, the Germans found a *sitzkrieg*, or "sitting war," as they mockingly dubbed the French response (or lack of it). Meanwhile, both the French and the English tried to buy time, in the belief it first was necessary to remedy their deficit of men and matériel. Sitting idle for so long, the entire French army wound up demoralized.

On May 10, 1940, the Wehrmacht went on the offensive on the western front, invading the Netherlands, Belgium, and Luxembourg with 145 divisions, including ten tank divisions and five thousand planes. For their part, the Franco-British Allies had 127 divisions, with very inferior air support, as the British would engage only a part of the Royal Air Force on the Continent. The Allies immediately advanced on Belgium, their left flank. However, the Wehrmacht's main offensive occurred in the Ardennes, completely taking French commanders by surprise. The Maginot Line proved totally useless, for it stopped at Sedan, and it was here the Germans crossed the Meuse River and entered France.

From this point on, the blitzkrieg developed with lightning speed: once they had broken through the front lines, the Germans massed their forces and surged toward the Atlantic, isolating Franco-British divisions, which then pulled back into Belgium. On May 19, Gen. Maxime Weygand, who had replaced Gen. Maurice Gamelin as commander of the French armed forces, tried in vain to cut through the thinly stretched German lines,

French colonial troops from North Africa, sub-Saharan Africa, and Indochina, like troops from metropolitan France, would be crushed. These soldiers would soon be part of one of the many long columns of German POWs. *Dominique François*

The Germans cross the Loire after violent fighting that cost the lives of many French soldiers. When the French blew the bridges, German engineers built pontoon bridges that permitted their troops to continue the advance. *Dominique François*

A classic scene of the Battle of France in 1940. The French have been routed and their columns destroyed. Soon, the roads would be full of fleeing civilians and convoys of prisoners. *Dominique François*

Soldiers in retreat, or attempting to organize defenses, mix with the great civilian exodus in the Battle of France. Fleeing civilians paid a heavy price to the Luftwaffe, which strafed them by machine gun in the roads.
Dominique François

At Cherbourg, French troops attempted to slow down Rommel's advance by creating traffic jams at the entrance points to the Cotentin Peninsula. Constrained to cease fighting, Vice Admiral Le Bigot rendered his arms to Rommel on the afternoon of June 19. *Dominique François*

Facing Gen. Erwin Rommel, Vice Admiral Le Bigot, surrounded by his general staff, surrenders his arms in a barracks at Cherbourg on June 19. Normandy will be occupied for four long years. *Dominique François*

On June 19, 1940, the Nazi flag flies above the Fort du Roule at Cherbourg. Its citizens will soon be subjected to humiliation, restrictions, and requisitioning.
Dominique François

The inhabitants of many villages flee the areas where the fighting is still continuing. Their numbers will swell the columns of soldiers in retreat. *Dominique François*

but it was too late. The English had already retreated toward ports in Pas-de-Calais. On May 28, the Belgian army surrendered, and, from May 29 to June 4, 350,000 British and French soldiers were evacuated from Dunkirk under bombardment.

The Germans also broke through the front at the Somme and Aisne Rivers. After crossing the Seine River near Rouen on June 7, they entered Paris and declared the French capital an "open city" on June 14, 1940.

In Normandy, and especially in Cherbourg, no one seemed to know if they should fight or surrender. For Vice Admiral Le Bigot, responsible for the defense of the Cotentin Peninsula, the answer was to stand and fight. But with what? In mid-May 1940, before the recent, unfortunate turn of events, an old plan of defense dating from 1905 had been dug up from the archives. This served as the inspiration for a new plan of defense, which in principle created, at best, two lines of resistance: one to bar access to the peninsula, and the other to stop an enemy attack on Cherbourg.

Two thousand French soldiers spread out among a dozen positions from Saint-Côme-du-Mont to Saint-Lô d'Orville, armed with a few machine guns and antiquated 75mm cannons. With this wisp of straw, the French proposed to resist Rommel's Seventh Army. The Germans left Aigle on the morning of June 17 and broke through French frontier defenses by the end of the afternoon. At 8:00 p.m., the Germans were spotted at Villedieu. Fifteen minutes later they arrived in Coutances, where several inhabitants, believing they were English troops, applauded them as they marched past. A little later they had reached Lessay. Toward 10:00 p.m., the first vehicles crossed La Haye-du-Puits and

Many French civilians were forced to leave their ruined villages on foot in search of more hospitable surroundings. Lodged in farms throughout the countryside, they were soon referred to as "the refugees." *Dominique François*

drove down the road toward Barneville. There was not a moment to waste: Hitler had given Rommel the order to take Cherbourg before an armistice could be signed.

And yet, at places, the wisp of straw did hold. At Denneville and Saint-Côme-du-Mont, German grenadiers encountered their first engagements and prudently retreated, preferring to wait until the following day to begin a new attack. Cherbourg took full advantage of this precious respite to reassemble retreating French and British soldiers, dockyard engineers, technicians, and submarines—anyone and anything that could help to rally the British ports.

By June 18, the Germans had arrived on the outskirts of Cherbourg. Fighting would still take place at Martinvast, Roule, and the fort at Querqueville, as workers sabotaged several submarines under repair at the Arsenal, the maritime factory on the Cherbourg docks. On the 19th, after having come within a hair's breadth of disaster, a bombardment of the city, and after a last-ditch stand, the Cherbourg garrison surrendered its arms. At 2:30 p.m., the end of hostilities was officially declared. The people of Cherbourg, who had fled the city en masse during the preceding days, began to return to their homes.

The regional authorities counted their dead: a thousand citizens of the Department of La Manche died during the German campaign to take France. Another four thousand were wounded, and twenty thousand who had mobilized to defend the region were taken prisoner. At Cherbourg, as in the rest of Normandy, the occupation had begun.

The rest of France was in total collapse. Millions of civilians, fleeing along the roads in utter chaos, disrupted the movements of the few troops who still were fighting or at least attempting to make an orderly withdrawal.

In the Department of La Manche, one thousand French civilians were killed and four thousand wounded in the Battle of France. *Dominique François*

War does not spare children: many little ones like these were part of the great exodus. Cities established shelters to care for children who became separated from their parents, or whose parents were killed on the road.

Dominique François

MARSHAL PHILIPPE PÉTAIN (1856—1951)

HERO OF WORLD WAR I, victor at the crucial Battle of Verdun in 1916, commander in chief of French forces after the loss at Chemin des Dames (Second Battle of the Aisne) in 1917, Pétain succeeded in boosting the morale of French troops and led them to victory in 1918. Minister of war in 1934 and ambassador to Madrid in 1939, he became president of France after the Battle of France in 1940 and signed the armistice with Germany on June 22, 1940. At eighty-four years of age, he became head of state of the French government at Vichy and was given full powers of the presidency by the National Assembly.

Pétain's collaborationist policies led him to create French militias that enforced German rules and decrees during the occupation and permitted the deportation of French Jews. He was arrested after the Liberation and condemned to death. His sentence was commuted to life imprisonment because of his advanced age and his achievements during World War I. He died on the Isle of Yeu on July 23, 1951.

Image credit: Dominique François

The government was torn between two opposing lines of thought on whether to continue the war. One the one hand was Paul Reynaud, who had replaced Maurice Daladier in March as prime minister. Reynaud was supported by Winston Churchill, who himself had just succeeded Neville Chamberlain as the head of the British government, and by Gen. Charles de Gaulle, whom Reynaud had appointed undersecretary of defense. De Gaulle held that France should continue to fight in North Africa, at the time an integral part of France, and continue its alliance with Great Britain. Opposing Reynaud, General Weygand and Marshal Philippe Pétain, revered as France's greatest hero in World War I, felt that following de Gaulle would necessarily force the French metropolitan army to capitulate. This outcome they considered dishonorable, even though they themselves were imploring the government to ask for an armistice. This was signed on June 22, 1940.

During this terrible time, General de Gaulle sounded the clarion call for honor and hope. Speaking by radio from London on June 18, he issued an appeal to the French people: "*Il faut que la France continue la lutte. Rien n'est perdu.*" ("France must continue the fight. Nothing has been lost.") Although this appeal later became famous, at the time, very few French could have heard it.

In five weeks, the French suffered 120,000 dead (including 92,000 soldiers) and 250,000 wounded. The draconian terms of the armistice only allowed for an army of one hundred thousand men and a disarmed navy. The armistice divided France into an

GENERAL CHARLES DE GAULLE (1890–1970)

AN OFFICER DURING World War I, de Gaulle wrote several political works and works on military strategy, in which he recommended the use of tanks. Serving as brigadier general during the Battle of France in 1940, and undersecretary of state for national defense in the cabinet of Prime Minister Paul Reynaud, he refused the armistice. On June 18, he broadcast from London his now-famous appeal to the French people to resist the German occupation.

Asserting his position bit by bit, and despite many obstacles, de Gaulle emerged as the leader of the Free French. He moved his headquarters from London to Algiers in May 1943 and created the French Committee of National Liberation (FCNL), the future provisional government of the French Republic, which was installed in France in August 1944, under his presidency.

As president of the FCNL, General de Gaulle took command of the military in April 1944. As such, his first concern was to organize and equip enough armed forces to effectively fight the Germans. His objective was to establish a battle corps of 230,000 men (including four tank divisions), a navy of 350,000 tons, and an air force of five hundred planes—modest numbers compared to Allied forces, but nevertheless terribly ambitious for the Gaullists. All were to be equipped by the Americans, who in turn required that de Gaulle's forces follow the table of organization of their own army, where support troops in the service branches greatly outnumbered combat troops on the lines.

De Gaulle was far from appreciating the American stance, which forced him to endure the constant humiliation of deliberate exclusion from deliberations and meetings of the highest level. Kept out of the Teheran Conference in December 1943, he was also not informed of the secret decisions of the Combined Chiefs of Staff committee headed by Churchill and Roosevelt. De Gaulle attached great importance to the French expeditionary corps fighting in Italy. His position was strengthened as a result of the battle at Monte Cassino between the forces of French-Algerian Gen. Alphonse Juin and the Tenth Army of German Gen. Field Marshal Albrecht (Albert) von Kesselring. The Allied leaders were favorably impressed by the solid comportment of the French troops. On June 5, Free French Forces (FFL) marched down the streets of Rome, now declared an open city.

Awaiting D-Day, de Gaulle endeavored to coordinate the actions of the Resistance and other networks operating in France. In March 1944, he created the Interior French Forces (FFI). On May 16, 1944, he signed a directive called the "Caiman Plan" from Algiers, consisting of a number of plans to carry out acts of sabotage throughout occupied France. Finally, his ultimate and perhaps principal preoccupation was to prepare himself and his most trusted colleagues to take over the administration of the liberated French territories.

The founder of the Fifth Republic in 1958, de Gaulle became its first president, serving in that office from 1959 to 1969. He was the only grand master of the Order of the Liberation, the French order uniquely awarded to heroes of the liberation of France in World War II. *Image credit: NARA*

On June 14, 1940, the Germans enter Paris, declared to be *une ville ouverte*, or "open city," and march down the Champs Elysées. The armistice was signed on June 22, instituting an era of occupation and collaboration.

National Archives and Records Administration, Washington, D.C. (NARA)

occupied zone and an unoccupied zone. The first constituted three-fifths of all of France, including the northern half of the country and the Atlantic coast. The French government, which was to administer the unoccupied zone, chose Vichy as its seat.

The 1.6 million prisoners of war would not be repatriated. They remained in stalags and oflags (camps reserved for officers) until 1945.

Again, the French fell to bickering among themselves. On one side were those who thought that, however difficult the terms, the armistice had kept the country from further death and destruction, and saved it from "Polandization": in other words, simple annexation to the Reich. On the other side, a smaller camp considered the armistice a dishonor; in their view, maintaining a French government, far from a diplomatic victory, was a long-time guarantee of forced collaboration with the occupiers.

Throughout the occupation, new restrictions and other official measures by the German military and the Vichy government were announced by public notice. *Mémorial de Caen*

2

FRANCE UNDER THE OCCUPATION

★ ★ ★ ★ ★

DEFEATED, FRANCE ENTERED INTO COLLABORATION, although Pétain continued to think of himself as the "shield of France," acting to ward off the worst. His unilateral request for an armistice left Great Britain to fight alone. His policies turned French agriculture into the "milking cow" of Germany and permitted the Service du Travail Obligatoire (STO, or Obligatory Work Service) to transport prisoners of war and hundreds of thousands of French workers to Germany in direct support of the war effort of the Third Reich. Under Pétain, the French militia also tracked down, tortured, and shot thousands of French Resistance fighters. Moreover, he did nothing to impede either the deportation of political opponents of the Reich or the genocide perpetrated against French Jews.

A new political order swept down on occupied Europe, everywhere imposing organized pillage and forced labor. The German SS, enjoying unlimited power, exercised a campaign of ferocious repression, arresting, torturing, shooting, and deporting people to concentration camps.

In the months that immediately followed the armistice, the Germans instituted a series of restrictions and requisitions, including curfews, rationing, and the requisition of farm animals and food, all imposed by the occupational authority. France, deprived of its male population, was forced to make do as it could. Towns and villages were forced to issue *cartes d'alimentation*, or ration cards, whereby each age segment of the population was assigned a letter: E (*enfant*, or child), J1, J2, J3 (*jeune*, or adolescents and young adults, divided into three categories), A (*adulte*, or adult), T (*travailleur*, or worker), and V (*vieux*, or elderly). The cards, in multiple colors, required various *vignettes*, or stamps, and shopkeepers became virtuosos with scissors and glue, cutting and pasting the required vignettes throughout the occupation, and even for a period after liberation.

German mountain troops march through a Norman village. These specialized gebirgjäger units were stationed in mountainous areas, where their presence soon incited the organization of Resistance groups. *Dominique François*

A German soldier scrutinizes the sea off the coast of Normandy at Saint-Vaast-la-Hougue. At the completion of his Normandy campaign, Hitler planned to launch the invasion of England, Operation Seelôwe (Operation Sea Lion). *Dominique François*

Two German soldiers on leave look over the capital of Lower Normandy from the ramparts of the Château de Caen. *Archives du Calvados*

Propaganda poster published by the Vichy government accusing the English of using Jews and Freemasons to propagate lies about the intentions of the Reich and its troops. *Mémorial de Caen*

Hitler had given the German people a choice between guns and butter, and they had chosen guns. After the French defeat in 1940, he could offer them butter as well, exacted from the villages of Normandy.

The people of Normandy quickly took the measure of the German boot on their neck. First of all, there were things they had to do, and those they had better not do, or could do no longer. The country ran on German time, and the curfew had to be respected. In town, pedestrians had to step aside to allow German officers to pass. In Cherbourg, local inhabitants were not even permitted to walk on the left-hand sidewalk, which was strictly reserved for Germans. It was forbidden to listen to the British Broadcasting Company (BBC) or to hide or even possess any guns or homing pigeons. No parties or festive gatherings of any kind were permitted. It was obligatory to obtain an official pass to leave the city. Needless to say, these were very unhappy times, subject to all the indignities and sacrifices that follow upon defeat.

Despite the dark days at the beginning of the occupation, the numerous arrests and deportations to German work camps, and increasingly savage executions, the Resistance began to organize. Although few French volunteered to work in secret immediately following the armistice, an underground network of intelligence sources quietly gathered strength. Not until spring 1944 did the Resistance take on the full character of an army.

From this point on, the armed struggle formed a focus of debate and in practice became as important as intelligence activity and propaganda. Several large *maquis*, or underground networks, were formed in the former Southern Zone and Brittany. Many people opposed to the deportation of forced labor to Germany rapidly filled the ranks of the maquis. However, although recruits were numerous, arms were as lacking as ever. The Resistance prepared plans to sabotage communication and transport systems. Selective operations, often taken on the initiative

Propaganda poster published by the French Resistance praising Allied unity and military power. *Mémorial de Caen*

Propaganda poster published by de Gaulle supporters calling for the French to join the ranks of the Free French. *Mémorial de Caen*

Propaganda poster published by the Vichy government inciting French citizens to contribute to the war against Bolshevism by volunteering to work in Germany. *Mémorial de Caen*

BEKANNTMACHUNG

Nach eingehender Beobachtung des Verhaltens der französischen Bevölkerung im besetzten Gebiet habe ich festgestellt, dass der Grossteil der Bevölkerung in Ruhe seiner Arbeit nachgeht. Man lehnt die von englischer und sowjetischer Seite gegen die deutsche Besatzungstruppe angezettelten Attentate, Sabotageakte usw. ab, weil man genau weiss, dass sich die Folgen dieser Handlungen ausschliesslich auf das friedliche Leben der französischen Zivilbevölkerung auswirken.

Ich bin gewillt, der französischen Bevölkerung mitten im Kriege weiter unbedingt Ruhe und Sicherheit bei ihrer Arbeit zu gewährleisten. Da ich aber festgestellt habe, dass den Attentätern, Saboteuren und Unruhestiftern gerade von ihren engeren Familienangehörigen vor oder nach der Tat Hilfe geleistet wurde, habe ich mich entschlossen, nicht nur die Attentäter, Saboteure und Unruhestifter selbst bei Festnahme, sondern auch die Familien der namentlich bekannten aber flüchtigen Täter, falls diese sich nicht innerhalb von 10 Tagen nach der Tat bei einer deutschen oder französischen Polizeidienststelle melden, mit den schwersten Strafen zu treffen.

Ich verkünde folgende Strafen :

1.) **Erschiessung aller männlichen Familienangehörigen auf- und absteigender Linie sowie der Schwager und Vettern vom 18. Lebensjahr an aufwärts.**
2.) **Überführung aller Frauen gleichen Verwandtschaftsgrades in Zwangsarbeit.**
3.) **Überführung aller Kinder der von vorstehenden Massnahmen betroffenen männlichen und weiblichen Personen bis zum 17. Lebensjahr einschliesslich in eine Erziehungsanstalt.**

Ich rufe daher Jeden auf, nach seinen Möglichkeiten Attentate, Sabotage und Unruhe zu verhindern und auch den kleinsten Hinweis, der zur Ergreifung der Schuldigen führen kann, der nächsten deutschen oder französischen Polizeidienststelle zu geben.

Paris, am 10. Juli 1942.

Der Höhere SS- und Polizeiführer
im Bereich des Militärbefehlshabers in Frankreich.

AVIS

Après avoir observé l'attitude de la population française en zone occupée, j'ai constaté que la majorité de la population continue à travailler dans le calme. On désapprouve les attentats, les actes de sabotage, etc., tramés par les Anglais et les Soviets et dirigés contre l'armée d'occupation, et l'on sait que c'est uniquement la vie paisible de la population civile française qui en subirait les conséquences.

Je suis résolu à garantir d'une façon absolue, en pleine guerre, à la population française la continuation de son travail dans le calme et la sécurité. Mais j'ai constaté que ce sont surtout les proches parents des auteurs d'attentats, des saboteurs et des fauteurs de troubles qui les ont aidés avant ou après le forfait. Je me suis donc décidé à frapper des peines les plus sévères non seulement les auteurs d'attentats, les saboteurs et les fauteurs de troubles eux-mêmes une fois arrêtés, mais aussi, en cas de fuite, aussitôt les noms des fuyards connus, les familles de ces criminels, s'ils ne se présentent pas dans les dix jours après le forfait à un service de police allemand ou français.

Par conséquent, j'annonce les peines suivantes :

1.) **Tous les proches parents masculins en ligne ascendante et descendante ainsi que les beaux-frères et cousins à partir de 18 ans seront fusillés.**
2.) **Toutes les femmes du même degré de parenté seront condamnées aux travaux forcés.**
3.) **Tous les enfants, jusqu'à 17 ans révolus, des hommes et des femmes frappés par ces mesures seront remis à une maison d'éducation surveillée.**

Donc, je fais appel à tous pour empêcher selon leurs moyens les attentats, les sabotages et le trouble et pour donner même la moindre indication utile aux autorités de la police allemande ou française afin d'appréhender les criminels.

Paris, le 10 juillet 1942.

Der Höhere SS- und Polizeiführer
im Bereich des Militärbefehlshabers in Frankreich.

Official notice posted by the head of the German SS in France announcing the punishment for those who refuse to denounce family members who commit acts of sabotage. Adult males will be shot, adult females will be deported to concentration camps, and all children under the age of seventeen will be sent to detention centers. *Mémorial de Caen*

Propaganda poster published by the French Legion of Volunteers against Bolshevism (LVF, Légion des Volontaires Français). The LVF was absorbed by the 33rd Waffen Grenadier Division of the SS Charlemagne (1st French), which was entirely composed of Frenchmen who volunteered to fight against the USSR on the eastern front. *Mémorial de Caen*

Propaganda poster published by the Vichy government denouncing "terrorist" attacks by "the Reds." The authors of these attacks, of Armenian origin, were executed by firing squad in Paris. *Mémorial de Caen*

of local or regional leaders, had already given the partisans a foretaste of what they could achieve.

Eventually, public opinion strongly turned in favor of the Resistance. The general opinion was that the Germans had already lost. It was only a question of when the final defeat would take place. This is not to say, however, that the public unanimously embraced the cause. Exactions, real or imagined, by the underground, and the risk of retaliation, hostage taking, and brutal mass executions by the Germans and the French militia all contributed to a

Propaganda poster published by the Vichy government offering the incentive of high pay to French workers who volunteer to work in Germany. *Mémorial de Caen*

Propaganda poster published by the Vichy government denouncing the "alliance" of the Allies with the Jews. *Mémorial de Caen*

climate of such mistrust and fear that even the "halo" of Marshal Pétain was severely tarnished. The idea that Pétain was a "shield" from the Germans now lost its power to convince; only his visits to the sites of Anglo-American bombardments sustained his former power to attract large crowds.

On moonless nights, air traffic between England and France increased, as paratroopers clandestinely dropped into France, and others working with Resistance networks secretly entered the country, often flown in by light planes like the Lysander. On the coast, the clandestine comings and goings of the partisans, including commandos, multiplied. The main activity of the special services was intelligence: some would bring back samples of sand from the Normandy beaches to London. The officers of the general staff preparing the invasion wanted to know everything about the terrain, down to a scale of square meters. Resistance members from Brittany, Normandy, and Picardy long provided invaluable information in garnering this intelligence.

Propaganda poster recruiting French youth to join the Waffen-SS. *Mémorial de Caen*

France is divided into two sectors: the "Occupied Zone" in the north and the "Free Zone" in the south. In the northern zone, and especially along the coast of Normandy, German troops move in and requisition lodging for their soldiers. *Dominique François*

Throughout Normandy, the Germans requisitioned buildings and lodgings for their troops, vehicles, and animals. In some cases, cohabitation was not overly problematic, and occupiers and occupied maintained friendly terms. *Dominique François*

Gasoline rationing was the first of many restrictions that the Germans imposed in France. The French responded by inventing alternate fueling systems, like this *gazogène* vehicle fueled by coal. *Dominique François*

Many Wehrmacht soldiers, some of whom had previously fought on the eastern front, found their four years of duty in Normandy highly agreeable. Here, soldiers relax around the table on a Norman farm near Fermanville. *Dominique François*

Normandy is famous for its cider and calvados, whose effects are well known to local inhabitants but sometimes surprised the occupiers. In 1944, Allied soldiers in turn would discover the powerful effects of these traditional Norman drinks made from fermented apples. *Dominique François*

A familiar sight during the occupation was long lines of people waiting to buy food. Bread, meat, flour, and coffee were strictly rationed and could only be purchased with ration cards using a system of stamps. *Dominique François*

The town hall in Saint-André-sur-Orne, requisitioned for use by German authorities. *Dominique François*

A busload of Luftwaffe soldiers on leave readies to depart for the Caen train station. Some are headed home for a few days in Germany; others will relax in Caen or Paris. *Dominique François*

Soldiers in the countryside sometimes rediscovered the habits and pleasures of rural Germany by lending a hand with chores on Norman farms. *Dominique François*

Some car owners constructed extremely sophisticated fuelling systems to allow their vehicles, like the one shown here, to function on alternate energy sources.

Dominique François

A horse-drawn chow wagon delivers meals to soldiers stationed along the Normandy coast. *Dominique François*

A baker posts a sign all too familiar in occupied France, announcing he is out of flour and there will be no more bread until further notice.
Dominique François

Many of the French opposed to the Vichy regime and the German occupation listened clandestinely to the BBC in London on forbidden radio sets. The punishment for such disobedience was deportation to Germany. *Dominique François*

One of the restrictions the Germans imposed was the requisition of leather. The French were soon forced to return to using wooden shoes. Here a French shoemaker fits Norman schoolchildren for traditional wooden clogs, or *sabots*.
Dominique François

Crossing the line of demarcation between the northern Occupied Zone and the so-called "Free Zone," under the authority of the Vichy government and the French Milice, or Militia. *Dominique François*

The Maquis, resistance groups opposed to the Germans and the Vichy government, rapidly organized in forests and mountainous areas. Initially acting essentially as informants for the Allied secret services, they progressively branched out into sabotage and also established underground networks to aid the escape of Allied pilots shot down over France. *NARA*

Once the Allied general command realized that the Resistance, for all its political wrangling, was an important source of intelligence and military force, the Allies furnished weapons and instructors, dropped into Normandy by parachute. *NARA*

Far from the eyes of the Germans and the Milice, the Resistance built assembly and training camps in the mountains and forested countryside. Frenchmen who evaded the Service du Travail (Obligatory Work Service) and escaped prisoners of war were among the first members. Before the Allied invasion on June 6, 1944, the Resistance numbered ten thousand members; by the end of the war, the number had grown to five hundred thousand. *NARA*

The approaches to Resistance encampments were guarded by sentinels who alerted the camp if anyone approached. Here a young man from the French Alps guards a mountain pass. *NARA*

French Resistance missions fell essentially into three categories: intelligence; sabotage (trains, rail lines, construction sites for the Atlantic Wall); and underground escape networks for Allied pilots. *NARA*

On the eve of the invasion, the Resistance received coded messages over the BBC telling operatives to effectuate "le Plan Tortue" (Operation Tortoise). The plan consisted of coordinated acts of sabotage designed to slow the movement of German troops. *NARA*

Resistance members unfortunate enough to be apprehended endured long weeks of torture before they were executed. The Gestapo and the French Milice tortured thousands of French partisans before they deported or killed them. *NARA*

At the beginning of the war, all captured members of the Resistance were condemned to death, but the Germans soon realized their economic importance to the Reich as easily replaceable slave labor. *NARA*

Thousands of French Resistance fighters were deported to concentration camps, where they worked on tunnel construction or in underground factories producing secret weapons. Few among them lived to see the liberation of their country. *NARA*

Members of the French Resistance worked as slave laborers in German factories alongside Jewish children and Gypsies. All died in droves, victims of mistreatment by the SS. *NARA*

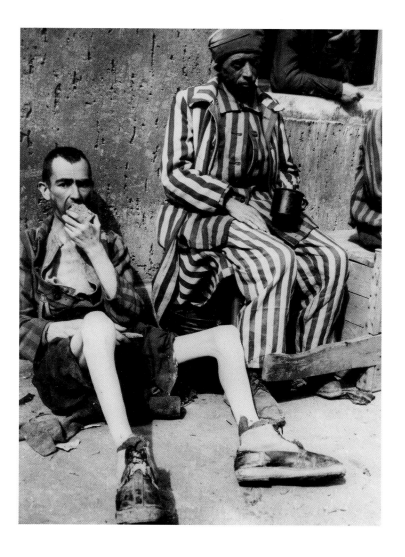

After the liberation of France, the Allies discovered the horror of the Nazi camps, which interned thousands of French citizens. The members of the French Resistance who had managed to survive deportation could now begin a new life of freedom. *NARA*

On a beach in Normandy, a soldier of the Wehrmacht looks out to sea toward England. There is no longer any doubt that the Allies will invade Europe. The only questions are when and where. *Dominique François*

3

CONSTRUCTION OF THE ATLANTIC WALL

★ ★ ★ ★ ★

HISTORY AMPLY SHOWS THAT, from time immemorial, all peoples have erected fortifications to shield themselves from attack. Some of the most obvious examples include the fortifications built by the Roman emperors to protect the city from Germanic invaders; Hadrian's Wall, erected between northern England and Scotland; or the Great Wall of China, constructed to protect the Chinese Empire from barbarian invasions from the north.

In June 1944, the Atlantic Wall, the German system of frontline defense, consisted of twelve thousand concrete structures lined up over four thousand kilometers of coast extending from northern Holland south to the Spanish border. Normandy occupied a special position in the line of fortification because of its proximity to the English Channel and its sizable coastline of approximately five hundred kilometers as the bird flies between the Bay of Mont-Saint-Michel and Tréport. It was here, along the long coast of Normandy, that the Germans constructed approximately two thousand bunkers on the eve of the Allied landings in June 1944.

Because of the general course of the war, Hitler came late to the decision to build a line of defense along the Atlantic seaboard stretching from Norway to the Pyrenees. Until the end of 1941, the German army maintained the offensive, be it on the eastern front, which was still well supplied with high-quality troops ready to do the Führer's bidding, or in Great Britain and the western Mediterranean.

The French armistice in June 1940 did not signal an end to German conquests in the West. With France defeated, Hitler ordered the Wehrmacht to prepare for an upcoming invasion of Great Britain, which still refused to accommodate Germany in exchange for peace. German plans for the invasion of England (Operation Seelöwe, or "Sea Lion"), perfected by the OKW (Oberkommando der Wehrmacht, or Supreme

Construction took several months and employed hundreds of workers from the OT as well as many residents of the island who were forced into labor. The battery was constructed to protect the western coast of the Cotentin Peninsula. *Dominique François*

Four 305mm cannons originally belonging to the Russian battleship *General Alexeiev* were shipped from Saint-Malô, then transferred to the port at Saint-Peter on the island of Guernsey, where they were unloaded and brought to the Mirus construction site.

Dominique François

The special forty-eight-wheel trailers that will serve to transport the four powerful cannons are unloaded at the port at Saint-Peter. The cannons will be transported across the island to be installed at the battery.

Dominique François

Immense cranes sent by barge to the port of Saint-Peter will be used to transfer the heavy cannons from the ship that carried them from Saint-Malô. *Dominique François*

Command of the Wehrmacht), were the cause of much German activity in Normandy throughout the summer.[3]

The Kriegsmarine, or German navy, set to work establishing numerous landing points in the principal Norman ports of Cherbourg, Le Havre, and Dieppe, which were well positioned as ports from which to attack the southern coast of England, and German infantry divisions conducted landing exercises with a view to invading the English coast. Meanwhile, the Luftwaffe, based on numerous airfields in Normandy,[4] worked to dominate the airspace, a goal the German navy deemed indispensable to an upcoming assault on Great Britain. Finally, unable to overcome British resistance, Hitler abandoned plans to invade Britain in the autumn of 1940. Germany had just suffered its first setback in the effort to bring all of Western Europe under its thumb. Victory remained incomplete in the West.

[3] The OKW was the general staff of the German armed forces, headed by Marshal Keitel, whose task was to elaborate operational plans for the war.
[4] Luftwaffe airfields in Normandy were at Querqueville, Maupertus, Lessay, Carpiquet, Saint-Gatien, Le Havre, and Saint-Andrieux.

At the end of 1941, the Germans had not yet begun to systematically establish their coastal defenses; at this point, only a few elements had been put in place. These consisted of huge batteries with long-range guns erected along the Pas-de-Calais coast, designed to protect the German fleet for a landing in Great Britain; the construction of major submarine shelters in the Atlantic ports of Brest, Lorient, and Saint-Nazaire; and several other construction projects along the Norwegian coast.

In Normandy, work on fortifications had begun at various places. The largest building sites were on the Channel islands of Jersey, Guernsey, and Alderney, where as early as February 1941, Hitler had insisted on installing coastal batteries capable of prohibiting all navigation in the vicinity. At the same time, the Luftwaffe had undertaken relatively large construction projects on the peninsula at La Hague and in the Bruneval region at Cap d'Antifer in Upper Normandy. In La Hague, the Luftwaffe had introduced diverse concrete structures around Beaumont and Jobourg to shelter powerful electro-generators and a radio control tower to direct bombing missions over England. An identical station was constructed at Dieppe, along with a facility designed to disrupt British radar along the coast. In February 1942, this chain of jamming emitters permitted Germany to achieve a great coup, when three of its largest warships set out from Brest and sailed past Pas-de-Calais, completely escaping the detection of British radar.

Finally, the German navy also began construction on a shelter for patrol boats in the port of Le Havre. On the rest of the Norman coast, as elsewhere, the occupation army did no more than fit out several open-air emplacements for heavy artillery batteries. In the autumn of 1941, roughly 1,200 pieces of German artillery were lined up along the coast

The cannons are loaded onto the trailers. They will be towed across the island by heavy tracked vehicles, much to the astonishment of its inhabitants. *Dominique François*

The Mirus Battery was operational as of summer 1942. The cannons were frequently fired on Allied objectives that came into their range, in order to test the island's defenses. The tests did not take place without incident: in June 1943, three of the four guns were damaged during firing. They were immediately repaired by specialists from Krupp. *Dominique François*

of Europe. In short, except for erecting several concrete installations, the German High Command did not believe defending the beaches was a high priority.

The decision to build a new West Wall along the coast of Europe was undertaken immediately after the United States entered the war. On the other hand, the construction of this defensive system, also known as the Siegfried Line, was only carried out piecemeal, as the Führer gradually issued the orders.

Hitler determined that fifteen thousand concrete structures would be necessary, including four thousand main structures, a thousand reinforced bunkers, and twenty thousand smaller bombproof casemates. Estimating that half a million men would suffice to hold the length of the front, he stressed that every step of construction would permit Germany to reduce the number of soldiers needed for coastal defense. The five hundred thousand men deemed necessary represented the equivalent of about forty infantry divisions: of these, three hundred thousand would man the permanent garrison of fortified coastal structures; the rest, massed in the interior, would constitute the strategic reserve of the high command. Finally, Hitler ordered the Organisation Todt (OT), charged with construction, to take charge of the concrete work, setting May 1, 1943, as the date for completing the major work. By purposely maintaining a highly accelerated pace, Hitler was able to erect the twenty-two thousand bunkers comprising the Siegfried Line in record time. Meanwhile, Nazi propaganda services publicized the grandiose *Festung Europa*, or Fortress Europe, project, while Goebbels was quick to proclaim the Atlantic Wall the most colossal fortification of all time.

Although they did not seriously slow the rhythm of construction, several developments along the western front between the autumns of 1942 and 1943 caused the Germans to considerably lengthen their coastal defenses and undertake additional work

Along the entire coast of France, the Germans built structures of reinforced concrete as part of the Atlantic Wall. In Normandy, over two thousand bunkers confronted the Allied troops who landed on D-Day. *Dominique François*

Thousands of workers in the OT were employed to build the Atlantic Wall, which stretched from northern Holland to Spain. Over twelve thousand concrete structures were completed before June 6, 1944. *Dominique François*

As soon as he had won France, Hitler ordered the Wehrmacht to prepare for the imminent invasion of England, which continued to refuse Germany's conditions for peace. The OKW's plans for the invasion, called Operation Seelöwe (Sea Lion), occasioned much activity in Normandy over the course of the summer. *Dominique François*

SS officers inspect coastal defenses at a battery in Normandy. The photo illustrates the many kinds of obstacles along the shore, including barbed wire, antitank obstacles, minefields, and trenches. *Dominique François*

On Utah Beach, a German soldier uses a pair of requisitioned horses to haul a curious structure. *Dominique François*

One of the cannons at the Gatteville Battery. This coastal battery possessed four 155mm guns. *NARA*

not foreseen in the initial plans. Operation Torch, the Anglo-American landing in French North Africa on November 8, 1942, was the first event of this sort. Immediately after the Allies seized this part of the French colonial empire, the Wehrmacht extended its rule to all of metropolitan France, putting into effect the codenamed Anton Plan. Pétain, the leader of the collaborationist Vichy government, no longer had even symbolic control over his piece of territory in the southern portion of France. At the same time, the Oberbefehlshaber West (OB West), the German ground force commanded by Field Marshal Gerd von Rundstedt, also took charge of the Mediterranean coast between the Spanish frontier and the Rhône delta.

Independently of fortifications along the southern coast of France, the priority given to constructing facilities to launch secret arms created a further source of difficulty for the OT. The last element of disruption along the western front was the fact that Italy had changed sides after signing an armistice with the Allies in late summer 1943. This decision constrained the Wehrmacht to take charge of the other part of Mediterranean France, situated between the Rhône and Nice, which up to that time had been held by the Fourth Italian Army.

In spite of these setbacks, the construction of the Atlantic Wall continued apace at other places along the French coast, thanks in large part to an abundance of free labor from occupied Eastern European countries. At the end of April 1943, 6,250 bunkers were complete or under construction. At the end of July, a total of eight thousand permanent defensive installations had been completed, or nearly so, along the whole of the western front, stretching from northern Holland to the Spanish frontier, as day by day, the Germans solidified their system of defense.

At the beginning of 1944, Field Marshal Rommel took command of Army Group B. His authority thus extended from the Loire to Lescaut, the sector most threatened by the imminent Allied invasion. Upon his arrival at the Atlantic Wall, Rommel increased his inspections and tried to inspire a new spirit in his troops. Although he commanded these troops for only a short period, his impact on the coastal defensive system was considerable. In contrast to Field Marshal von Rundstedt, Rommel believed in the worth of the Atlantic Wall. He was even accused by the general staff of OB West of making a "fetish" of the fortifications.

Rommel's main idea was that the coast would constitute the principal line of combat, and the decisive battle against the invasion would thus take place on the beaches. With this in mind, he concentrated to the maximum on the narrow coastal fringe, hardening defenses at every critical point. Although he forbade the construction of larger structures, he encouraged the erection of multiple small concrete forts interconnected by trenches, hence constructing a continuous cordon along the entire shoreline. In addition to organizing *kriegspiel*, or war games, at the level of general command, over the course of his tour he increased the firepower of the casemates, improved camouflage, planted thousands of obstacles on the shore, and buried millions of mines all along the coast.

A casemate at Pointe du Hoc. This famous battery was located six kilometers west of Omaha Beach, on the summit of a rocky cliff thirty-five meters high. It boasted six French 155mm cannons installed in open-air, concrete gun emplacements. *NARA*

The observation post of the battery at Longues-sur-Mer, situated on the summit of a picturesque cliff west of Arromanches. Its four modern 152mm guns had a range of twenty kilometers and could reach Omaha Beach to the west, as well as Gold Beach to the east. The post was located three hundred meters in front of the casemates, at the extreme edge of the cliff. *NARA*

This photo, taken at an identified site, illustrates the different types of camouflage the Germans used to hide their concrete structures from Allied aviation. After the foundations were dug, the displaced earth was carefully smoothed over and disguised so it could not be spotted by plane. The cannon seems to be a 155mm. *European Commission on Preservation and Access (ECPA)*

A very interesting photograph showing a large concrete structure perfectly camouflaged to look like a typical Norman house. The Germans became true masters at disguising their artillery positions. *ECPA*

This floodlight used during Allied air raids was hidden beneath the roof of a Norman barn. *ECPA*

Hitler was persuaded that the invasion had no chance of success if it failed to capture a major port; on January 19, 1944, he therefore ordered the fortification of all large ports on the French littoral. Situated above other defensive structures along the fortified areas, select coastal fortresses were built to resist all enemy attacks. In Normandy, only the ports of Le Havre and Cherbourg, and later the Channel Islands, were elevated to this rank of importance. These *festungen* received highest priority in the distribution of construction material, arms, and reinforcements, and were the strongest moorings in the Atlantic Wall.

At the beginning of November 1943, while Field Marshal Rommel carried out his inspections, abundant reinforcements began arriving at the western front, following Hitler's instructions. Between December 1943 and the beginning of June 1944, ten tank and infantry divisions were installed behind the concrete ramparts, amounting to a

The command post of a coastal battery disguised as a Norman house. A false tile roof and painted windows contribute to the realism of the illusion. *ECPA*

Below: On a Norman beach, a Luftwaffe unit gathered around a flak gun enjoys a moment of relaxation. *ECPA*

The interior of a radio-control station designed to guide planes on bombing missions over England. This could either be the station at La Hague on the Cotentin Peninsula or the one at Dieppe. Such equipment was also used to jam radar signals along the British coast. Their skill at disturbing enemy radar allowed the Germans to pull off a tremendous coup in February 1942, when they sailed three of their largest ships right under the noses of the British, passing undetected through Pas-de-Calais. *ECPA*

Soldiers in their barracks at a coastal battery. Artillery pieces were better protected than troops and munitions. The concrete walls and floors of troop barracks and munitions bunkers were always less than two meters thick, and most measured half a meter to a meter. *ECPA*

Antitank defenses on a Normandy beach. *ECPA*

This photo of a beach in northern Normandy illustrates the various kinds of concrete and metal obstacles the Germans planted along the shore. *ECPA*

contingent of about 150,000 men. Between January 1944 and the end of April 1944, the number of tanks increased from 752 to 1,402. These reinforcements were awarded in priority to the Fifteenth Army (Seine-Escaut); however, beginning in May 1944, Hitler ordered them to be sent to Brittany and Normandy. The origin of his sudden interest in Lower Normandy remains a mystery, but it was probably simple intuition on his part.

As the defensive capacity of the western front notably increased, a strong disagreement developed between the two main commanders in the West concerning the best strategy for repelling an invasion. More precisely, the disaccord centered on where to place the reserves. While Rommel wanted them near the coast, von Rundstedt, who favored a more flexible defense, wanted to avoid premature engagements with tank units during secondary operations and preferred to station reinforcements in the interior of the country, far from aerial bombardments. Hitler, in an effort to split the difference, considerably weakened the ability of his armored units to respond to an attack.

In spite of all of Rommel's efforts, the defensive work proceeded because of an increase in Allied aerial raids beginning in spring 1944. Systematic bombing of the railroad, the main means of German transport, hampered the delivery of construction material for the wall. For lack of cement, work at numerous construction sites ground to a halt after May 1.

A German soldier installs a network of concrete antipersonnel mines on a beach. Over two million mines and two hundred thousand obstacles were buried behind the beaches by D-Day. *ECPA*

An agonizing question further added to the paralyzing effects of the Allied bombings: when and where would the Allies strike? From the moment Hitler issued his directive of November 1943, the German army stationed on the beaches had lived in a state of permanent tension. "Everything leads us to believe that the enemy is preparing to launch a western offensive next spring at the latest," Hitler wrote.

Diverse German reports mentioned that soldiers guarding the coasts seemed very nervous. Any ship spotted on the open sea immediately provoked a commotion, at least until a reconnaissance detail reported that the vessel was only a fishing boat or an unannounced German convoy.

On the eve of the invasion, the wall along the coast of Normandy was an imposing structure, although its strength was far from uniform. Extending from Couesnon to Bresle, fully five hundred kilometers of coastline, were 2,011 concrete structures: of these, 1,643 were completed; another 79 were near completion; and 289 were still under construction. On average, there were four bunkers per kilometer. In front of the ramparts, along 242 kilometers of beach, Rommel had planted nearly two hundred thousand obstructions,

Rommel's beach defenses included a whole range of obstacles that would seriously impede the Allies on D-Day and result in many Allied deaths. Beach obstacles included these wooden stakes topped with mines; the famous "Rommel's asparagus," long, sharpened poles, also often mined, which were planted in likely landing zones or drop zones; and voluntarily flooded areas. *NARA*

Two German soldiers dressed in white work uniforms install barbed wire on the dunes of a Norman beach. The obstacles were of varying importance, but all were designed to slow down the Allies on the beaches and enable German defenders to push them back to the sea. Von Rundstedt believed it was better to allow the Allies to land and then destroy their beachhead; Rommel, to the contrary, insisted that they must not be given the opportunity to pierce coastal defenses and should be stopped dead on the beaches before reinforcements could arrive. *Dominique François*

Birth of a battery: Immediately after they arrived in Cherbourg on June 1940, the Germans began preparing to invade the Channel Islands, and thus ensure complete control over the Manche. In 1942 they began construction on the Mirus Battery on Guernsey, which would host the largest artillery guns on the coast. Its four 305mm cannons could attain a distance of forty-two kilometers. The immense building site was run by the Organisation Todt (OT), the construction enterprise headed by Fritz Todt, which combined government firms, private companies, and the Reichsarbeitsdienst (Reich Labor Service). In addition to its own workers, the OT conscripted inhabitants of Guernsey to work on the site. *Dominique François*

A delegation of top German officers visits the Atlantic Wall. Field Marshal Rommel took command of Army Group B, which consisted of the Fifteenth Army and the Seventh Army. Rommel immediately increased inspections at the wall and tried to inspire the troops in charge of coastal defenses with a new spirit. Unlike von Rundstedt, Rommel believed in the effectiveness of the wall. *ECPA*

amounting to a density of eight hundred obstacles per kilometer. Behind the bunkers and along the coastline of three departments, La Manche, Calvados, and Seine-Inférieure, the Germans had buried more than two million mines and planted several thousand pieces of "Rommel's asparagus."[5]

As late as June 1944, the facts belied the seeming impenetrability of the wall. The system of fortification was very imposing around the big ports, which the Germans had turned into veritable fortresses. It would also serve as a deterrent around ports of secondary importance and impede attacks on important military installations. But everywhere else, the fortifications were mediocre and remained unfinished. Nowhere, except at Omaha Beach, could the wall resist an enemy attack; its vaunted reputation as a great and impenetrable fortification was largely the work of mere propaganda.

[5] Sharpened wooden spikes, several meters tall and sometimes tied together with barbed wire. Rommel had these planted these in fields that might serve as drop zones or landing zones. Their tips could impale a falling paratrooper, and they effectively obstructed glider landings.

A Junkers Ju-87, or Stuka, is ready to take off from an airfield in Normandy. These German dive-bombers famously went into steep attack dives, dropped their bombs right on top of their targets, and then soared straight up with dizzying speed. *Dominique François*

4

GERMAN FORCES IN NORMANDY ON THE EVE OF THE ALLIED INVASION

ON MARCH 1, 1944, THE GRAND total of German forces stationed in the West numbered 1.4 million men: 850,000 ground troops, 326,000 Luftwaffe, 102,000 in the navy, and 102,000 in the Waffen-SS and police.

GROUND FORCES

On the eve of the landing, ground forces based in the West were distributed over fifty-eight divisions: forty-eight infantry divisions, nine tank divisions, and one panzergrenadier (armored infantry) division. All were dedicated to ensuring the defense of five thousand kilometers of coastline, which averages out to one division for every eighty-six kilometers—a number deemed insufficient by all German authorities, especially given that reserves were all but nonexistent.

These units were unequally spread out along the coast, in an effort to mass the most forces in the areas the Germans thought most vulnerable to attack. As such, most of the divisions were concentrated in the sector of Army Group B, composed of the Seventh and Fifteenth Armies, which consisted of thirty-two divisions, including six tank divisions (or 468,000 men) spread out along 2,300 kilometers of coastline between the Loire and the Escaut Rivers. The Seventh Army, commanded by Gen. Friedrich Dollmann, head-quartered at Le Mans, was responsible for the defense of the coastal sector that extended 1,556 kilometers from the Loire to the Dives River (Brittany and Lower Normandy). At a strength of 161,000 men, it was divided into twelve divisions, each of which was divided

The ground crew of a Luftwaffe unit stationed at Carpiquet near Caen fabricates straw camouflage nets used to hide artillery pieces.

Dominique François

Organization of German Army in the West (June 1944)

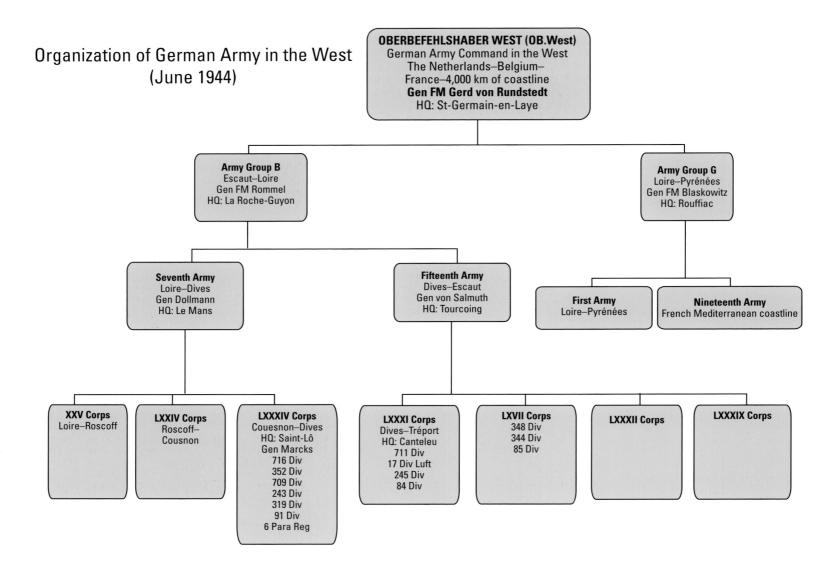

OBERBEFEHLSHABER WEST (OB.West)
German Army Command in the West
The Netherlands–Belgium–
France–4,000 km of coastline
Gen FM Gerd von Rundstedt
HQ: St-Germain-en-Laye

Army Group B
Escaut–Loire
Gen FM Rommel
HQ: La Roche-Guyon

Army Group G
Loire–Pyrénées
Gen FM Blaskowitz
HQ: Rouffiac

Seventh Army
Loire–Dives
Gen Dollmann
HQ: Le Mans

Fifteenth Army
Dives–Escaut
Gen von Salmuth
HQ: Tourcoing

First Army
Loire–Pyrénées

Nineteenth Army
French Mediterranean coastline

XXV Corps
Loire–Roscoff

LXXIV Corps
Roscoff–
Cousnon

LXXXIV Corps
Couesnon–Dives
HQ: Saint-Lô
Gen Marcks
716 Div
352 Div
709 Div
243 Div
319 Div
91 Div
6 Para Reg

LXXXI Corps
Dives–Tréport
HQ: Canteleu
711 Div
17 Div Luft
245 Div
84 Div

LXVII Corps
348 Div
344 Div
85 Div

LXXXII Corps

LXXXIX Corps

into three army corps. The Fifteenth Army, commanded by Gen. Hans Eberhard Kurt von Salmuth, had eighty thousand more men than the Seventh Army, which was nevertheless responsible for defending a much wider territory. The disparity in the size of the territory the two armies were given to defend (a density of one division per thirty-nine kilometers for the Fifteenth Army, as compared to one division per 191 kilometers for the Seventh Army) resulted from the strong belief of the German high command that Allied landings would take place in Pas-de-Calais.

The divisions, all infantry, making up the Seventh and Fifteenth Armies were generally mediocre, given a few exceptions. In effect, most were fixed infantry divisions with no means of transport, consecrated first and foremost to defending the coastline. These divisions were created by the initiative of Gen. Karl Rudolf Gerd von Rundstedt, who had learned from the constant flux of soldiers on the eastern front that most men had no time to settle in and learn the particulars of the sector they were charged to defend. To remedy the problem, which diminished the quality of German defenses,

A Luftwaffe observer at the end of an airstrip runway studies the sky for Spitfires. He is armed with an MG-34 machine gun mounted on a tripod. *Dominique François*

von Rundstedt created permanent divisions "intended to guard the coasts, possessing a special organization adapted to their special needs." As their supreme commander declared, this system permitted soldiers to be very familiar with the sectors they were ordered to defend and guaranteed the most economical use of the scarce equipment at the disposal of Western troops.

The system nevertheless had its weaknesses, for increasingly younger contingents of Army Group B (who were sent to the eastern front) were replaced by lesser-trained reservists or by men who were older or ill. These divisions, made up of two infantry regiments with two field batteries of twenty-four guns and an average-sized battery of twelve guns, were equipped with assorted weapons. The cannons, which came from nine different countries, were all but immobile, for they depended on animals to pull them. The light arms came from France, Poland, and even Yugoslavia, and as a result, inevitably posed problems when it came to supplying ammunition.

Also present in Normandy was a large contingent of volunteers from the East (Osttruppen), often Russians who had formerly been German prisoners of war. They began arriving at the western front after 1943 to replace German troops who were sent to other theaters of operation. The Seventh Army included twenty-five thousand of these "volunteers" but placed very little faith in them, since their degree of loyalty to the German cause remained an unknown quantity.

Supplementing the fixed divisions, normal infantry divisions were given preference in the distribution of men and matériel. Many were placed toward the rear as reserves, to be used

In this highly symbolic photograph of the German occupation of France, a Luftwaffe soldier has taken over the desk at the mayor's office in Saint-André-sur-Orne. On the mantelpiece, Hitler's photograph hangs under a bust of Marianne, the traditional symbol of France, whose use will soon be forbidden under the Pétain government. *Dominique François*

The ambulance section of a Luftwaffe unit in 1941 or 1942. At the time, Luftwaffe forces on the western front consisted of no fewer than three hundred thousand men under the orders of Field Marshal Hugo Sperrle, headquartered in Paris. *Dominique François*

Two Luftwaffe soldiers practice firing the FM24/29 (fusil-mitrailleur modèle 1924 M29), the standard light machine gun of the French army in World War II. German weapons often came from conquered countries, which sometimes posed problems for replenishing ammunition. *Dominique François*

Throughout Normandy, the Germans requisitioned châteaux. This particular château near Caen served as the headquarters of a Luftwaffe unit. The contribution of the Luftwaffe to German defenses on D-Day was mediocre, although not entirely negligible. Field Marshal Sperrle was able to muster only sixty planes, in stark contrast to the Allied air forces, which employed over eleven thousand. He was obliged to become more aggressive in the future. *Dominique François*

in the event of future counterattacks. These divisions were more mobile than others, although their means of transportation, consisting of horses, bicycles, and a few trucks, still remained rudimentary. One of the best among them was the 352nd Infantry Division, which reached the coast of the English Channel in the Arromanche sector, later known as Omaha Beach, in possession of its full fighting potential and later inflicted heavy losses on the invading Americans.

Finally, it should be emphasized that most of the infantry divisions on the western front were under strength. During an inspection in Normandy in January 1944, Gen. Alfred Jodl noted that the 319th Infantry Division was at only 30 percent of its initial strength. To cite only two other examples, on the eve of the Allied landings, the 716th Infantry Division (in the Caen region) had 7,771 men instead of their normal 17,000,[6] and the 91st Infantry Division was down to only 10,555 men.

[6] They would be reinforced by Russian battalions.

The nine tank divisions of Army Group B (and an attached panzergrenadier division) were considered the spearhead of German defenses in the West. They could field a total of about 1,500 tanks. Six of them, the 21st Panzer Division, the Panzer Lehr Division, the 12th SS Panzer Division (the Hitlerjungend Division), the 116th Panzer Division, the 2nd Panzer Division, and the 1st Panzer Division, were stationed to the north of the Loire River and formed the I SS Tank Corps. The others, consisting of the 17th SS Panzergrenadier Division, the 11th Panzer Division, the 2nd SS Panzer Division, and the 9th Panzer Division, were stationed south of the Loire. Together, they formed the LXIII Rommel Panzerkorps within Army Group B, which had the following three divisions directly under its command: the 21st Panzer Division, stationed in the region from Caen to Saint-Pierre-sur-Dives; the 116th Panzer Division, stationed in the Seine estuary; and the 2nd Panzer Division, stationed near Amiens. Situated as strategic reserves in the Paris region were the Panzer Lehr Division, in the Chartres-Orléans-Le Mans region, and the 12th SS Panzer Division, in the zone between Evreux and Elbeuf.

Most of these were good, battle-ready divisions. However, despite the intensive training they received, they were never again even a third as good as they had been in 1940. Generally speaking, troop morale fluctuated according to division. Fighting spirit and political motivation had fallen considerably since the beginning of the war, with the exception of elite units like the SS and Luftwaffe paratroopers, who remained highly politicized. Most regular soldiers, as well as noncommissioned officers and officers from the early years of 1939–40, had been taken prisoner or killed, or were fighting on the

A Luftwaffe NCO inspects his men before they are dismissed to go on pass. Compared to the eastern front, a posting in Normandy was paradise for a German soldier. The situation changed shortly. *Dominique François*

Chow's on! Two stoves steaming with hot food are transported to Wehrmacht troops. The photograph was secretly taken by a French civilian. *Dominique François*

Soldiers with a horse-drawn cannon march to their barracks, led by two NCOs. *Dominique François*

eastern front. Except in certain units like the paratroopers or the 12th SS Panzer Division, the German soldier, on average, was more than ten years older than his Allied counterpart, a fact that also contributed to the general decline in morale.

THE NAVY

By 1944, the German navy was only a shadow of its former self. The fleet that once had ruled the high seas had either been destroyed or remained immobilized in Norway or the Baltic Sea. At this point, German sea power mainly consisted of submarines.

On the eve of the Allied landings, the forces under the command of Adm. Theodor Krancke were greatly reduced. On April 1, 1944, the only offensive surface naval force at the Germans' disposal was thirty-one torpedo boats, grouped in five flotillas. Forty of the 130 submarines commanded by Admiral Dönitz were ordered to leave bases in the Atlantic to confront the invading Allied fleet but actually played no defensive role: only sixteen among them took to the high seas. Of the fleet of destroyers under the direct orders of Admiral Krancke, only two were operational the day of the Allied landings.

THE AIR FORCE

Even more than the German navy, the Luftwaffe had lost much of its offensive character by 1944. Air activity was limited to the bare minimum on the western front before the

The soldiers stop en route in the village of Glacerie, overlooking Cherbourg. Hitler declared Cherbourg as a *festung*—a fortress city, crucial to German defenses. Under no conditions could it be allowed to fall. *Dominique François*

Wehrmacht soldiers stand at ease in the central square of Montebourg, at the heart of the Cotentin Peninsula. Like many of the villages and cities of the region, Montebourg was destroyed, partially by Allied artillery attack and partially by the Germans, who set the town on fire when they left. *Dominique François*

Two officers of a horse-drawn convoy cross a field where their horses are pastured. The Wehrmacht massively relied on horses to pull artillery pieces and provisions. During the Battle of Normandy, thousands of horses were slaughtered by Allied air attack. *Dominique François*

A German observer on a beach in Normandy. On the eve of the Allied invasion, there were 161,000 solders in the Seventh Army, whose divisions were largely stationed in static positions. For the most part, these units, which consisted mainly of German reservists, had little means of transport and were intended for defensive measures. They were thought to be of lesser quality than other German troops. *Dominique François*

German observer studies the mouth of the Cherbourg harbor. Behind him, a swiveling searchlight serves to illuminate both the port and the sky in case of Allied attack. *Dominique François*

Allied landings. This would remain true even after the invasion got under way. On the day of the landings, only nine planes would take to the air.

General Field Marshal Hugo Sperrle, commander of the Third Air Fleet, had five hundred airplanes at his disposal: these included 150 reconnaissance planes but only ninety bombers and seventy operational fighter planes. Although he commanded the Luftwaffe in the West, General Sperrle did not, in fact, exercise command over his entire fleet. This is because, given the general shortages, his superior, Herman Wilhelm Göring, had employed a portion of the fighters to protect German air space against Anglo-American bombardments, rather than leaving the Luftwaffe fighters sitting idle in wait of an eventual Allied invasion.

Despite shortages, ground support for the Luftwaffe was enormous, consisting of approximately three hundred thousand men, a ratio of one hundred men on the ground to every pilot!

AIRBORNE FORCES

Field Marshal Rommel stationed two reserve groups of airborne forces in the interior of the Cotentin Peninsula: the 91st Infantry-Air Landing Division and the 6th

On the western front, the Kriegsmarine (the official name of the German navy from 1935 to 1945) was under the authority of Adm. Theodor Krancke, the commander of Marinegruppe West. He directly reported to Adm. Karl Dönitz, head of all seaborne war operations. *Dominique François*

Fallschirmjäger Regiment. The 91st was a unit of the Luftwaffe, stationed in the region of La Haye-du-Puits and Saint-Sauveur-le-Vicomte and commanded by Lt. Gen. Wilhelm Falley, whose general headquarters were located at the Château de Bernaville at Picauville. On the eve of the invasion it numbered 10,555 men.

Like the 91st, the elite 6th Fallschirmjäger Regiment arrived on the Cotentin Peninsula at the beginning of May 1944, occupying the region around Lessay and Carentan. Commanded by Lt. Col. Friedrich August Freiherr von der Heydte, the regiment consisted of 3,500 young paratroopers, whose average age was seventeen and a half. All were volunteers and jump qualified.

In April 1944, gunboats based at Cherbourg, like the *Schnellboot* in this photograph, inflicted important damage during Operation Tiger, as the Allies rehearsed the upcoming invasion of Normandy in southern England. *Dominique François*

Cherbourg Harbor was full of floating mines like this one. Every night between June 10 and August 15, Luftwaffe support troops sent floating mines into the port, where Allied transports were anchored. Their explosions caused significant damage to ships and loading docks. *Dominique François*

The harbor train station at Cherbourg, the end of the line for incredible quantities of troops and matériel arriving from Paris before the Allied invasion. Except for Le Havre, Cherbourg possessed the only deep-water port in northern France, and the Germans would thus defend it at any price. *Dominique François*

On the Normandy coast, an artillery unit with a 75mm PaK37 readies for action at the mouth of an estuary. The Seventh Army defended 1,556 kilometers of coast stretching from the Loire to the Dives, including Brittany and Normandy. General Dollman took command of the unit in September 1939, with headquarters in Le Mans. *Dominique François*

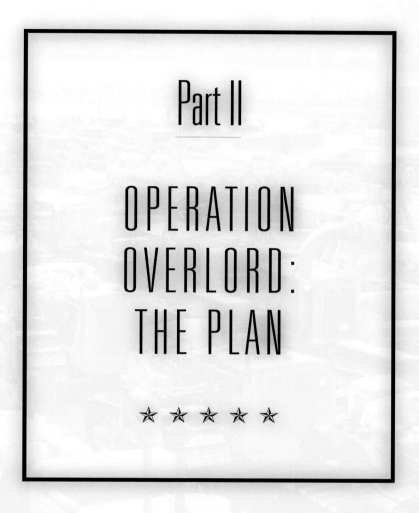

Part II

OPERATION OVERLORD: THE PLAN

★ ★ ★ ★ ★

I have nothing to offer but blood, toil, tears and sweat. We have before us
an ordeal of the most grievous kind. We have before us many, many long months
of struggle and of suffering. You ask, what is our policy? I can say: It is to
wage war, by sea, land, and air, with all our might and with all the strength
that God can give us; to wage war against a monstrous tyranny, never surpassed
in the dark, lamentable catalogue of human crime. That is our policy.
You ask, what is our aim? I can answer in one word: It is victory.

—WINSTON CHURCHILL, first speech as prime minister
to the House of Commons, May 13, 1940

In spring 1944, the entire south of England was transformed into a gigantic parking lot. Soldiers were fascinated by the number of tanks and vehicles of all sorts parked in the fields. *NARA*

5

STRATEGIC PREPARATIONS

★ ★ ★ ★ ★

GENERAL EISENHOWER ARRIVED IN ENGLAND just before Christmas 1943 to assume his new post as supreme commander of the Supreme Headquarters Allied Expeditionary Force (SHAEF). His documents at the time contained a directive from the Combined Allied General Staff outlining an invasion plan having as its objective the landing in Europe. The second paragraph of this directive summarized his mission:

> You will enter the continent of Europe and, in conjunction with the other United Nations, undertake operations aimed at the heart of Germany and the destruction of her armed forces. The date for entering the Continent is the month of May 1944. After adequate channel ports have been secured, exploitation will be directed towards securing an area that will facilitate both ground and air operations against the enemy.

At this stage, the preparatory phase of the original plan as designed by the Allied general command in 1943 seemed relatively simple, but it would prove to be a great deal more difficult to put into operation. The first outline of the Allied attack plan consisted of amphibious landings in Normandy, foreseen for the beginning of May 1944. The landings would take place between two separate beaches, situated between Caen and the base of the Cotentin Peninsula. In support of this amphibious assault, a jump by airborne American and British troops of company or battalion size was foreseen to neutralize German batteries along the coast where the landings would take place. The final plan was still being studied when Gen. George C. Marshall wrote a personal letter to Eisenhower suggesting that paratroopers of the three Allied airborne divisions be dropped near Paris to coincide with the amphibious assault in Normandy.

Ever the diplomat, Eisenhower argued in response to Marshall that it was preferable to use airborne troops on the coast of Normandy, where they could hit German rear

It took a formidable amount of organization to ship the thousands of tons of war material required for Overlord and to coordinate supplies to ever-evolving needs on the ground. Never in the history of warfare had soldiers required so much equipment and matériel. *NARA*

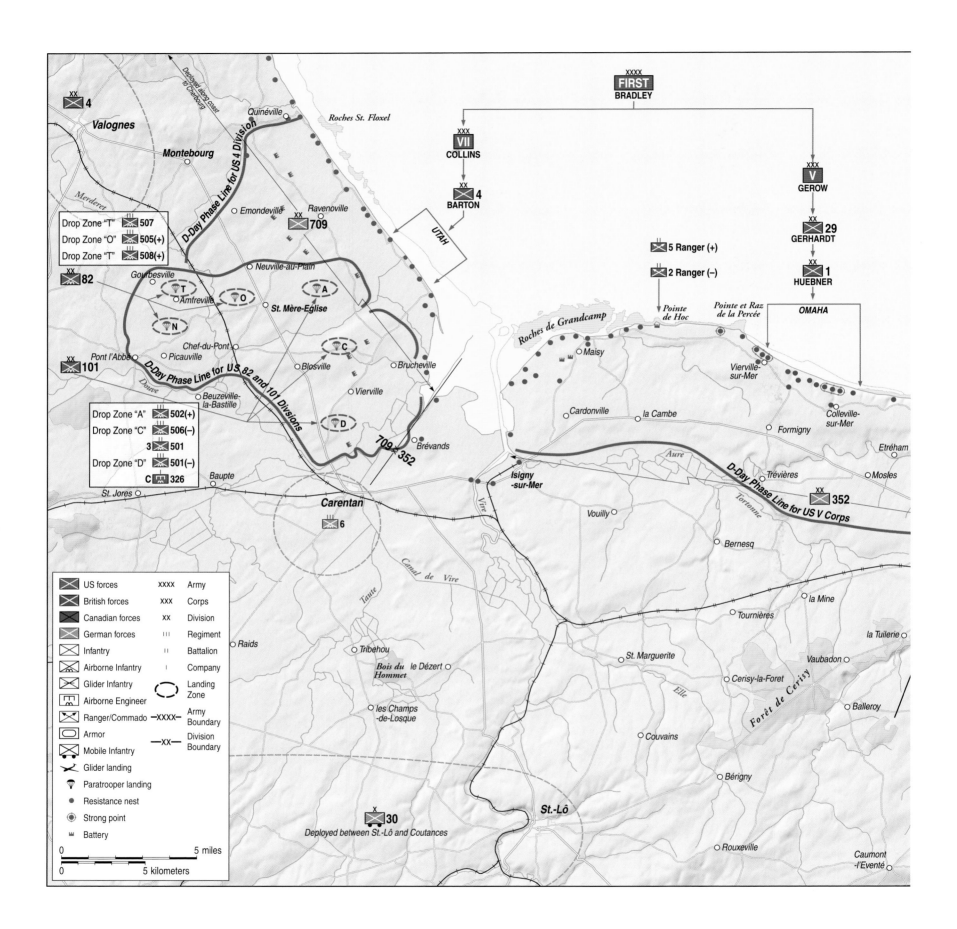

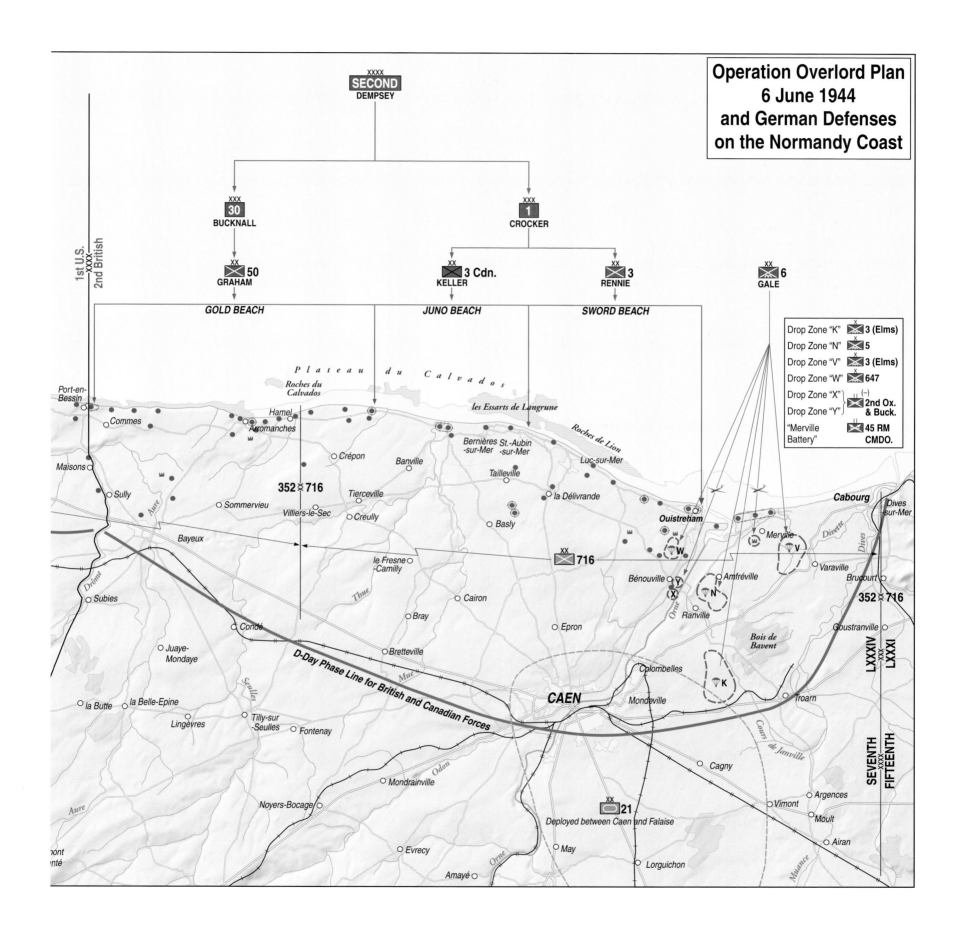

**Operation Overlord Plan
6 June 1944
and German Defenses
on the Normandy Coast**

XXXX
SECOND
DEMPSEY

XXX
30
BUCKNALL

XXX
1
CROCKER

XX
50
GRAHAM

XX
3 Cdn.
KELLER

XX
3
RENNIE

XX
6
GALE

GOLD BEACH

JUNO BEACH

SWORD BEACH

1st U.S.
XXXX
2nd British

Drop Zone "K"   3 (Elms)
Drop Zone "N"   5
Drop Zone "V"   3 (Elms)
Drop Zone "W"   647
Drop Zone "X"   (–)
Drop Zone "Y"   2nd Ox. & Buck.
"Merville Battery"   45 RM CMDO.

Plateau du Calvados

Port-en-Bessin

Commes

Maisons

Sully

Sommervieu

Aure

Bayeux

Roches du Calvados

Hamel

Arromanches

Crépon

Banville

Tierceville

Creully

Villiers-le-Sec

352 ⋈ 716

le Fresne-Camilly

Thue

Drôme

Subies

les Essarts de Langrune

Bernières-sur-Mer

St.-Aubin-sur-Mer

Tailleville

Basly

Cairon

Roches de Lion

Luc-sur-Mer

la Délivrande

XX
716

Ouistreham

Bénouville
Y
X

N

Ranville

Amfréville

Merville
E

Cabourg

Dives-sur-Mer

Divette

Dives

Varaville

Brucourt

352 ⋈ 716

Goustranville

W

Juaye-Mondaye

Condé

Bretteville

Mue

Bray

Epron

Odon

Mondrainville

Noyers-Bocage

Seulles

la Butte

la Belle-Epine

Lingèvres

Tilly-sur-Seulles

Fontenay

D-Day Phase Line for British and Canadian Forces

CAEN

Colombelles

Mondeville

Bois de Bavent

K

Troarn

Cours de Janville

Cagny

Orne

Evrecy

May

Amayé

Lorguichon

XX
21
Deployed between Caen and Falaise

Vimont

Moult

Argences

Airan

Muance

LXXXIV
XXX
LXXXI

SEVENTH
XXXX
FIFTEENTH

Aure

GENERAL DWIGHT D. EISENHOWER (1890–1969)

A TEXAN STEMMING from Germanic origins, Dwight David Eisenhower was fifty-four years old in 1944. Steadily rising through the ranks throughout his military career, he graduated from West Point in the middle of his class and was posted to a number of general headquarters, including service under Gen. Douglas MacArthur and Gen. George C. Marshall, head of the U.S. Army General Staff in 1942.

Although Eisenhower had not yet exercised a major command, General Marshall recognized his exceptional organizational abilities and conferred on him the daunting task of organizing the invasion of Europe from England. Praised by de Gaulle as "a good and grand Allied commander," Eisenhower was neither a warmonger nor a lover of strategy, in the classical sense of the term. Modest, jovial, and easily approached, he exercised excellent judgment and showed great initiative when it came to preparing and organizing large plans of action. As an administrator who also knew how to charm, he maintained privileged relationships with Churchill and Roosevelt, and felt at ease with British leaders like Montgomery, who had a reputation for high-handedness. His assignment on assuming command was enormous: dismissing initial plans for Overlord as far too modest in their means and objectives, he entirely re-envisioned the Allied invasion, greatly enlarging the scale of operations. His most difficult task was to assemble many widely disparate units into a single, homogeneous, efficient, and battle-ready force, and combine all branches from land, air, and sea for a coordinated attack on the Atlantic Wall. *Image credit: NARA*

These bulldozers will soon be used to open up landing beaches and dig runways for Allied airstrips once the bridgeheads are secured. *NARA*

In the moat of an old Victorian mansion, American soldiers training for D-Day practice climbing from their "ship" into landing craft. *NARA*

On March 24, 1944, British Prime Minister Winston Churchill examines a bazooka during a visit to an American training camp. A veteran of the Boer War, he was experienced in the use of arms. *NARA*

Troops trained throughout all of England. On June 6, 1.85 million soldiers would depart for Normandy. *NARA*

FIELD MARSHAL BERNARD LAW MONTGOMERY (1887–1976)

MONTGOMERY IS PROBABLY the most controversial English general of World War II. Widely considered a leader of men, he was nevertheless often faulted for his absence of feeling toward his front-line troops.

After the North African campaign, Montgomery returned to Great Britain to retake command of the 21st Army Group, which consisted of all Allied ground forces taking part in Operation Overlord. Victorious over General Rommel and his Afrika Korps in North Africa, Montgomery would face his old adversary again in Normandy.

During the intensive Battle of Normandy, combat was prolonged for two and a half months. Montgomery, unable to follow his original plans, nevertheless devised and carried out a series of improvised offensives that ultimately led to one of the largest German defeats on the Western European front. The occupation of the Cotentin Peninsula and other offensives to the east allowed him to capture Caen and confine German tanks to the region.

The concepts behind Operation Market-Garden (September 17–25, 1944) were mainly those of Montgomery. This operation, designed to end the war before Christmas, ended instead in a bloody Allied defeat.

Image credit: NARA

A German high-speed torpedo boat stationed at Cherbourg. During Operation Tiger in April 1944, nine such boats, alerted by intense radio traffic, emerged from the fog to cause numerous Allied losses in the coastal waters of England. The torpedo attack cost the lives of 198 sailors and 550 infantrymen.

Dominique François

GENERAL GEORGE CATLETT MARSHALL (1880—1959)

A BRILLIANT CAVALRY OFFICER, Marshall fought in World War I, where he proved himself as a leader of men. During World War II he was promoted to general. The creation of the Marshall Plan, which he designed to feed a starving Europe after the war, rendered him famous and won him the Nobel Peace Prize in 1953. *Image credit: NARA*

GENERAL LEWIS BRERETON (1890—1967)

AN AVIATION STRATEGIST, General Brereton was appointed commander of the U.S. Middle East Air Forces in 1942, a unit which eventually became the U.S. Ninth Air Force. In August 1944, he became the commander of the First Allied Airborne Army, a unit composed of Allied airborne divisions, and remained in this post until the end of hostilities in Europe. *Image credit: NARA*

troops and destroy enemy reserve units in direct support of the amphibious assault. Moreover, if the Germans decided to contain the landings within Normandy, Allied airborne troops far away in Paris would be cut off from reinforcements and supplies, and would probably be annihilated before support from the beaches could reach them. Luckily, after reading Eisenhower's response, Marshall decided to let his proposition die a quiet death.

Eisenhower was surrounded by many first-rate officers who aided him to conceive and carry out the truly Herculean mission of breaking Hitler's iron defenses in Europe. Field Marshal Bernard Montgomery, responsible for defeating Rommel in the deserts of North Africa, took command of the Allied ground forces destined to land in Normandy. Serving under him, Gen. Omar N. Bradley commanded the Americans, and Gen. Sir Miles C. Dempsey commanded the Anglo-Canadians.

Overlord was to unfold in two phases. During the first phase, Montgomery's ground troops were to get a foothold on the continent, then broaden their positions to secure a number of ports for the debarkation of further troops and matériel. The largest and most vital of these was Cherbourg. Once Montgomery's positions on the French coast were strong enough, he could

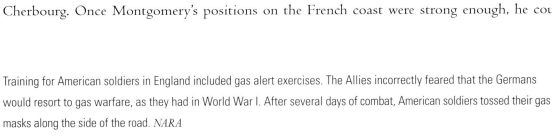

Training for American soldiers in England included gas alert exercises. The Allies incorrectly feared that the Germans would resort to gas warfare, as they had in World War I. After several days of combat, American soldiers tossed their gas masks along the side of the road. *NARA*

GENERAL OMAR NELSON BRADLEY (1993–1981)

AFTER COMMANDING THE U.S. Military Academy at West Point, Bradley took command of the 82nd Infantry Division at Fort Benning before the division became airborne. He later served under General Eisenhower and was given command of II Corps. He next took command of the U.S. First Army during preparations for Normandy. He was one of the principal planners of Operation Cobra.

Image credit: NARA

unleash the second phase, breaking out from the beaches to launch a full-scale ground offensive aimed at the heart of Germany itself.

The airborne troops had an essential role to play in phase one of this plan. Their task was to drop behind established beachheads and take control of key sectors, breaking German defenses. Because of enemy coastal defenses and antiaircraft installations, and the absolute necessity to maintain the element of surprise, the airborne assault would have to take place in the deep of night, at approximately 1:00 a.m. on the morning of D-Day, about five hours before the seaborne troops hit the beaches.

Meanwhile, on 27 April, three hundred vessels and thirty thousand soldiers participated in major maneuvers codenamed Exercise Tiger. The first wave of the assault landed on the beach at Slapton Sands, defended by five hundred "enemy" who greeted the "invaders" with live ammunition. An error in timing resulted in 750 deaths, cutting men to shreds in a hail of bullets.

GENERAL GEORGE SMITH PATTON (1885–1945)

A CAVALRY OFFICER out of West Point, Patton was one of the most brilliant American generals of World War II. He was, nevertheless, disgraced in the public eye and temporarily relieved of command of the U.S. Seventh Army after a highly publicized incident, when he slapped a weeping soldier at a military hospital in Sicily. Patton was later given the command of the U.S. Third Army, destined to join the Battle of Normandy at the beginning of August 1944. He conceived and victoriously implemented the decisive Allied breakthrough at Avranches in an aggressive offensive that spelled an end to slow and costly fighting in the hedgerows. *Image credit: NARA*

The Dakota C-47 was used to transport U.S. airborne troops in World War II. Each plane could carry a "stick" of sixteen to twenty paratroopers, or tow one (and sometimes two) Waco gliders. *NARA*

6

AIRBORNE OPERATIONS

PLANNING FOR THE AIRBORNE PHASE of Operation Overlord was a source of considerable controversy among the officers in charge of conceptualizing the airborne assault. To better understand the final version of the operation, it is necessary to look at how the plan evolved.

On March 12, 1943, Lt. Gen. Sir Frederick Morgan became chief of staff to the supreme Allied commander (COSSAC) in charge of cross-Channel operations from 1943 to 1944, with an inter-Allied general staff composed of English and Americans. It was incumbent upon the COSSAC staff to prepare detailed plans for a second front and form a skeletal structure for SHAEF. Planning of the aerial phase of the operation fell to Air Marshal Sir Trafford Leigh-Mallory.

In April 1943, Leigh-Mallory's American counterpart, Brig. Gen. Robert Candee, commander of the 8th Ground Air Support Command (GASC) in England, assumed his functions as officer in charge of the U.S. Army Air Forces (USAAF) within COSSAC. He quickly recommended that the Allies muster no less than twenty-three troop-carrier groups for the invasion, or 1,196 planes, a number that exceeded the total troop carriers at the disposition of the USAAF. In May, the general combined command informed COSSAC it could only count on the participation of the American 8th GASC and seven British squadrons, for a total of 634 planes.

As early as June 1943, COSSAC chose Normandy as the landing site. The coastal defenses were weak, beaches suitable for the landing were within the range of fighter planes stationed in England, and coastal geography easily permitted the building of airstrips. The COSSAC invasion plan envisioned landing two British divisions and one American division on the beaches between the Orne and Vire rivers. Two British paratrooper brigades would drop near Caen to cover the eastern flanks of the landing troops. Finally, seven battalions of American paratroopers would attack coastal batteries and take control of

The Parachute School was established at Fort Benning, Georgia, to train the future paratroopers who would jump into combat in all theaters of operations. *NARA*

GENERAL JAMES GAVIN (1907–1990)

A GRADUATE OF THE U.S. Military Academy at West Point in 1929, Gavin served in several units, including the 25th Infantry Regiment, where he remained for three years. In July 1941, he enrolled in the Airborne School at Fort Benning and received his wings in August. He then served in one of the earliest airborne units, the newly formed 503rd Parachute Infantry Battalion, where he commanded Company C.

In October 1941, he was promoted to the rank of major. In August 1942

he was given command of the 505th Parachute Infantry Regiment and was shortly promoted to the rank of colonel. In April 1943, Gavin and his regiment left for North Africa, where they embarked for Sicily and then for Italy. One of the most famous officers of the United States Army, Gavin was appointed assistant commander of the 82nd Airborne Division and later fought at the head of that division in Normandy and Holland. He also fought in the Battle of the Bulge in Belgium, and in Germany. *Image credit: NARA*

Paratrooper candidates were all volunteers. To obtain their wings, they had to pass a specific training course that lasted for several weeks. They soon became the spearhead of the U.S. Army. *NARA*

access to the beaches in support of the amphibious assault. To accomplish this mission, the airborne troops would need eight hundred transport carriers, which led COSSAC to call on the USAAF to supply five more troop-carrier groups.

Lieutenant General Ira Eaker, commander of the Eighth Air Force in England, strongly supported the plan, which Roosevelt and Churchill approved at the Quebec Conference of August 1943. Four of the supplementary troop-carrier groups needed were to be pulled out of the Mediterranean theater. In December, the leaders of the general command brought the number of troop carrier planes for Operation Overlord up to 880, amounting to thirteen and a half American troop-carrier groups.

The opponents of COSSAC reacted quickly. From September onward, their ranks included Brig. Gen. James Gavin, who had returned from Sicily. Gavin was extremely concerned about the wide dispersion of airborne troops on the ground after witnessing for himself the isolation of the general staff, which was separated far from the troops in Sicily, and the lack of coordinated planning. Allied forces in Sicily had furthermore suffered heavily from confusing air corridors and nervous antiaircraft defenses on Allied ships. Glider pilots and the infantrymen they transported had experienced all the difficulties of a night landing, and the deficiencies inherent to aerial navigation had required the creation and training of pathfinders, a group of specially trained airborne volunteers who used new navigational aids to help guide airborne units to the drop zone.[7] For all of these

---

[7] Notable is the use of a radar transponder system consisting of a ground emitter (Eureka) and an airborne component (Rebecca).

Learning to land and quickly get out of the chute was critical. Combat situations often forced paratroopers to jump at very low altitudes and under enemy fire. The reception on the ground could be ferocious, as was the case in Normandy. *NARA*

reasons, General Gavin firmly opposed COSSAC's idea of sending parachute battalions on individual missions and insisted instead on the necessity of staging a narrowly concentrated and closely timed drop of airborne troops.

The core of the landing plan was beginning to take shape. In October 1943, the Ninth Air Force included all tactical aerial units, including the 9th Troop Carrier Command of Lt. Gen. Lewis Brereton. In November, Air Marshal Leigh-Mallory was named commander in chief of the Allied Expeditionary Air Forces. At the head of the planning committee, he drew up the air plan for Normandy, combining the 38 Group and 46 Group of the Royal Air Force with the American 9th Troop Carrier Command. Major General Matthew Ridgway headed the American airborne troops, while his British counterpart, Sir Frederick Browning, recently promoted to major general, led the British airborne.

At the end of April 1944, sufficient planes and crew became available to render possible a simultaneous drop by two American airborne divisions and two-thirds of the British 6th Airborne at dawn on D-Day.

However, new problems now arose. Also in late April, Leigh-Mallory expressed serious doubts about the viability of dropping two American divisions in the Cherbourg region because of the heavy losses the operation would entail. Combat in Crete and Sicily had convinced him that airborne troops should avoid heavily defended areas in favor of drop zones well beyond principal enemy defenses so that paratroopers could regroup

Training at Fort Benning was very tough, and candidates were required to do everything on the double. The young volunteers were trained step by step and learned each stage of the jump before they went up in a plane. *NARA*

The moment of joy that followed a successful first qualifying jump validated the rigors of training and erased lingering feelings of fear and self-doubt. Some candidates wore charms or carried other good-luck objects. *NARA*

and organize before facing a strong enemy engagement. In the end, he reticently approved the plan, on condition that American glider landings would not take place before dawn on D-Day.

New intelligence also contributed to changes in plan. At the end of May, incoming reports indicated that the German 91st Air Landing Division, a unit of regular motorized reserves, were stationed on the west coast of the Cotentin Peninsula, right in the middle of the sector the 82nd Airborne had chosen as its drop zone. The attendant risks were deemed unacceptable. The target zone for the division was moved further east, closer to the drop zones of the 101st Airborne. The 82nd Airborne was originally slated to jump near Saint-Sauveur-le-Vicomte, to the west of the peninsula, to interdict enemy troops moving up from the south. The adopted modifications were meant to give better control over bridges on the Merderet River,

Paratroopers were trained to use specific weapons and equipment, starting with their principal T5 parachute and reserve chute. They jumped into combat with all personal weapons and equipment strapped to their persons. Crew-served weapons and ammunition as well as other heavier items would be dropped in equipment bundles and collected on the ground. *NARA*

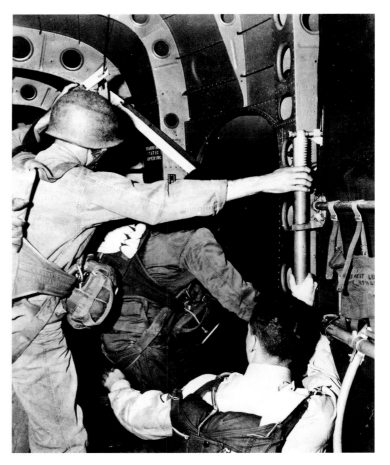

A jumpmaster gives the sign to go during a training jump. For combat jumps, the pilot switched a red light to green, signaling the time to jump. *NARA*

Airborne troops continued their training in England. Although the location of the upcoming operation was a closely guarded secret, something was clearly afoot. *NARA*

and hence facilitate the advance of VII Corps and the capture of the important crossroad at Sainte-Mère-Église.

The two American divisions, the 82nd and the 101st, were set to jump between 1:15 a.m. and 1:30 a.m. on D-Day. Pathfinders would go in an hour earlier in order to prepare the drop zones.

The plans for Operation Overlord were ready. Although it was still necessary to fill in numerous details, the bigger picture was well defined: the night before D-Day, the British 6th Airborne Division would jump between the Orne and Dives Rivers, northeast of Caen, while the Americans would drop on the Cotentin Peninsula. Just after dawn, the naval forces would debark to form two beachheads by D-Day night. The main beach was to be at the confluence of the Vire and Dives Rivers, including Isigny, Bayeux, and Caen; the second would be on the east coast of the peninsula. Because German defenses were so strong at Carentan, planners did not foresee that the Allies would take the city and therefore unify the two beachheads before D-plus-1, at the earliest.

The two American divisions thus would drop six regiments of paratroopers on the Cotentin Peninsula. They would also be supported by gliders, a new

GENERAL MATTHEW RIDGWAY (1895–1993)

A 1917 GRADUATE of West Point, Ridgway served in several posts in the American army. During World War II, he commanded the 82nd Airborne Division in Sicily, in Italy (1943), and during the Allied invasion of Normandy.

Image credit: NARA

Members of a parachute field artillery battalion wheel a 57mm howitzer into position. The disassembled cannon could be dropped in seven different equipment bundles or brought in by glider fully assembled. *NARA*

On March 23, 1944, a full-fledged dress rehearsal for the upcoming jump in Normandy took place on the divisional level in England. Other than a few light injuries, the practice jump was a total success. *NARA*

Like their American counterparts, British paratroopers from the 6th Airborne Division, commanded by Gen. Sir Richard Gale, met with General Eisenhower a few days before D-Day. *NARA*

weapon that would deliver two infantry regiments as well as much-needed equipment and matériel on D-Day.

The introduction of the glider at the beginning of the war still remains one of the least known remarkable feats of the industrial war effort in the United States. It began in February 1941, when Gen. Henry Harley "Hap" Arnold, the commander of the Army Air Corps (the predecessor of the United States Air Force), ordered a study on the feasibility of creating a glider for wartime use. By the end of 1946, when production came to a halt, over sixteen thousand gliders had been produced. The government contracted with the Waco Aircraft Company to build the Waco CG-4, a glider that could transport fifteen infantrymen or a jeep and its crew. Capable of carrying a load heavier than its own weight, the Waco was very light, consisting of a tubular metallic and wooden frame, encased in tightly woven canvas. There were two points of access: through the nose of the craft, which opened from the top to permit loading and unloading heavy equipment, and a side door for personnel.

Aside from the danger of flak, the worst problems in Normandy for the Waco and its British counterpart, the Horsa, were obstacles the gliders encountered on their landing zones. These included Rommel's asparagus, as well as natural obstacles like hedgerows, streams, and houses. In addition to these problems, the majority of pilots had had very little training. This was particularly true for copilots, who rarely had any flight experience at all before they came into Normandy. Military planners predicted D-Day losses at 70 percent for glidermen, as compared to 50 percent for paratroopers.

MISSIONS

On the British side, the 6th Airborne was to cover the left flank of I Corps of the British Second Army. Their mission was to seize highways and junctions between the Orne and Dives Rivers, thereby preventing enemy movement between Caen and Ouistreham toward the bridgehead. The main objective was to capture two bridges, if possible intact: one over the Caen Canal at Bénouville (codenamed Euston I) and the other over the Orne River at Ranville (Euston II), and to establish a solid bridgehead in the surrounding area. This part of the mission was turned over to the 5th Parachute Brigade, led by Brig. Gen. Sir Nigel Poett. The 3rd Parachute Brigade, led by Brig. Gen. James Hill, was to destroy or neutralize the bridges over the Dives River and the artillery battery at Merville.

As for the Americans, the 101st Airborne Division, commanded by Gen. Maxwell D. Taylor, was given the mission (codenamed Albany) to secure the four exits from Utah Beach leading into the interior, which passed through the area flooded by the Germans. The mission fell to two regiments: the 502nd Parachute Infantry Regiment (PIR), supported by the 377th Field Artillery; and the 506th PIR, whose mission was to capture the two southernmost outlets at Houdienville and Pouppeville. The 501st PIR was assigned to seize control of the canal locks

GENERAL MAXWELL DAVENPORT TAYLOR (1901–1987)

AFTER GRADUATING AS an officer from the U.S. Military Academy at West Point, Maxwell Taylor decided to join the airborne at the beginning of World War II. First assigned to the 82nd Airborne Division, he later assumed command of the 101st Airborne Division and jumped at the head of the "Screaming Eagles" on June 6, 1944. *Image credit: NARA*

April 1944: A group of British paratroopers have just unloaded a jeep and its trailer from a Horsa glider. Like the Waco used by American glider infantry regiments, British Horsas participated in D-Day, delivering men and equipment to the sector of the Orne River. *IWM*

Paratroopers assembling a Welbike dropped in an equipment bundle. Weighing thirty-two kilos, the Welbike was a British single-seat motorcycle designed for the British Special Operations Executive ("Special Operations Executive" SOE) but more frequently issued to parachute regiments. It is easy to imagine the instability of the tiny bike under the weight of a heavily equipped paratrooper. *IWM*

Waco gliders are lined up, ready to take off on a mission. By the end of 1946, when construction ceased, over sixteen thousand gliders had been produced. *NARA*

Gliders were shipped disassembled in kits consisting of over seventy thousand pieces and were put together in assembly centers in England. *Dominique François*

On June 5, 1944, members of the 508th Parachute Infantry Regiment receive their copies of General Eisenhower's stirring words of encouragement, distributed to all U.S. troops about to assault "Fortress Europe." *NARA*

Regrouped in a temporary camp, airborne soldiers prepare their weapons and heavy equipment bundles, which will be dropped separately when they jump. Paratroopers received no reinforcements or provisions until several days after June 6. *NARA*

Colonel Robert Sink, commander of the 101st Airborne Division, engages in discussion with Col. Charles Young of the U.S. Army Air Forces (USAAF). Close cooperation between the army airborne units and the air force was crucial to the success of Operation Overlord. *NARA*

at La Barquette near Carentan, which the Allies feared could be used to flood a portion of the southeast peninsula, and thereby isolate the forces on Utah Beach, cutting them off from the interior.

The mission (codenamed Boston) of the 82nd Airborne Division was to seize and hold the bridges over the Merderet River to the west of Sainte-Mère-Église at La Fière and Chef-du-Pont and to capture the crucial crossroads at Sainte-Mère-Église. The division was divided into three forces. Force A, given the Boston Mission and commanded by Brig. Gen. James M. Gavin, would parachute into Normandy. It consisted of pathfinder units and three airborne regiments: the 505th, 507th, and 508th PIRs, supported by airborne artillery and engineers. Force B, commanded by Brig. Gen. Matthew B. Ridgway, would go in by glider. Participating airborne infantry and artillery units included the 325th Glider Infantry Regiment (GIR), the 319th Glider Field Artillery Battalion (GFAB), and the 307th Airborne Engineer Battalion (AEB). More than four hundred gliders would be needed to transport men and matériel on missions codenamed Detroit, Elmira, Galveston, and Hackensack. Force C, commanded by Brig. Gen. George P. Howell, was to arrive by sea and debark at Utah Beach between D-plus-2 and D-plus-7, bringing in field artillery units and various service units, such as military police, and tank and medical units.

On May 29, Leigh-Mallory confessed to Eisenhower his anxiety concerning the dangerous operation in which he estimated that no more than thirty percent of the troops would engage the enemy.

Parachutes have been distributed, and troopers fit up for the jump. Overloaded with equipment, buddies had to help each other buckle up their harnesses. *NARA*

Two 506th Parachute Infantry Regiment (PIR) troopers with Mohawk haircuts, Clarence Ware and Charles Plaudo, apply war paint in anticipation of the assault. Ware would soon be wounded at Saint-Côme-du-Mont. *NARA*

The pathfinder team of the 3rd Battalion, 508th PIR, commanded by Lt. Gene Williams. Every battalion had its own pathfinder team, which was dropped an hour in advance of the various regiments in order to clear and secure the drop zones. Their mission was extremely dangerous but crucial to ensure the success of the operation. *Dominique François*

FINAL PREPARATIONS: EXERCISES TIGER AND EAGLE

As winter gradually gave way to spring, thousands of soldiers and matériel of all sorts were amassing in southern England. In preparation for D-Day, the Allies conducted a series of exercises, including a landing on the southern English coast in the region of Torquay in Devonshire, whose beaches uncannily resembled those in Normandy. Slapton Sands, fifteen kilometers from Torquay, perfectly corresponded to a sector of Utah Beach. Several weeks before D-Day, the army evacuated some 3,500 civilians from the farms and villages of the area and began detailed exercises in rehearsal for Normandy.

On April 28, toward 2:00 a.m., a long convoy slowly made its way toward the coast to deliver heavy matériel. The single-file procession, over five miles long, consisted of eight tank landing ships (LSTs) loaded with gasoline, tanks, cannons, munitions, vehicles, and soldiers; and two antiquated escort ships. Suddenly, nine German torpedo boats emerged from the darkness. Based at Cherbourg and alerted by unusual intensity in radio traffic, they struck the convoy with disastrous effect, sinking two of the LSTs in a matter of minutes and seriously damaging a third.

Lieutenant Gene Williams, 508th PIR, 82nd Airborne Division, volunteered as a pathfinder. He here is loaded up with arms and equipment, ready to join his jump stick. *NARA*

Men from the 82nd Airborne Division are ready for combat outside British Horsa gliders. The wings and fuselages of gliders and planes both were painted with distinctive markings to identify them as Allied carriers. No other planes would be permitted in Allied airspace during Operation Neptune, the naval part of D-Day operations. *NARA*

Lieutenant Colonel Robert Wolverton, 506th PIR, 101st Airborne Division, prepares to get into his chute on June 5, 1944. *NARA*

On June 5, 1944, Gen. Dwight Eisenhower inspects 101st Airborne Division troops, one of the divisions that will spearhead Operation Overlord. Planners projected casualties of 50 percent during the initial hours of the airborne mission. *NARA*

Fully loaded 101st Airborne Division troopers read General Eisenhower's inspiring message. In four hours, they will jump behind enemy lines in Normandy. *NARA*

Screaming Eagle troopers wait to hear the engines of their C-47 rev up, the sign that their great adventure is about to begin. Their inexpressive faces reflect the fact that elite troops used periods of inaction to rest and save their energy—an opportunity these men will not have the luxury to enjoy for several days to come. *NARA*

Troops wait for the jolt of takeoff seated in the rounded fuselage of a Horsa glider. While casualties for paratroopers were projected at 50 percent, the figure rose to 70 percent for glidermen. *NARA*

Having failed to receive the warning sent by the escort ships, for the simple reason that they did not share the same radio frequencies, the LST commanders initially mistook the German attack for a simulation exercise. As German torpedoes ravaged vessels loaded with explosives, one LST mistakenly machine-gunned the deck of another amidst the panic. In all, 198 sailors and 550 infantrymen were cut to pieces by explosions or thrown into the sea, where they perished, paralyzed by cold.

The Tiger exercises resulted in a total of 946 dead and 500 wounded, three times more than the losses that would be suffered on Utah Beach six weeks later on June 6, 1944. A thousand families received letters stating that their sons were "missing in action," with no further detail. The dead were buried in utmost secrecy in common graves dug by bulldozer. The survivors were sworn to secrecy and subject to court-martial if they spoke about what had happened.

A last exercise on Slapton Sands, codenamed Eagle and planned for May 11 and 12, 1944, approximated as closely as possible the conditions the 101st Airborne Division would encounter on D-Day behind Utah Beach, when they would fight for control of the beach exits and the roads leading inland. Wooden bridges were constructed in a sector of Slapton Sands to simulate the route the 101st would take. Their first "jump"

The archetypal paratrooper: taken on June 5, 1944, this famous photograph depicts T/4 Joseph Gorenc, 506th PIR, laboriously climbing aboard his C-47, heavily loaded with all his gear. He is headed for Drop Zone D, located east of Saint-Côme-du-Mont. *NARA*

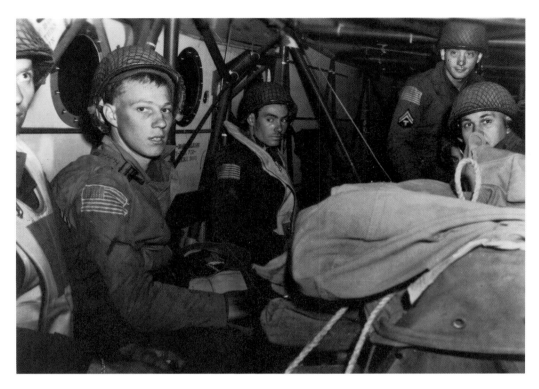

Airborne troops wait to take off in their fragile Waco glider for the largest military operation of all time. Many obstacles, both man-made and natural, await them in their landing zones (LZs). Many among them will perish in glider crashes. *NARA*

exercise consisted of exiting trucks, which dispersed them around the area at the back of Slapton Sands. The paratroopers transferred for exercises to the airfields whence they would depart for Normandy in a few weeks. All equipment was identically prepared.

Preceded by the pathfinders, the Screaming Eagles of the 101st took off around 11:00 a.m. As would be the case on D-Day, only the plane leading the formation was equipped with radar to receive the signals sent by the pathfinders, who were already at the drop zones. The lead plane also carried an Aldis (or signal) lamp that would flash and illuminate the Plexiglas windshield at the appropriate moment. Other pilots, seeing the signal, would then illuminate their green lights, giving the troopers the signal to jump.

The exercise took place without incident until a misunderstanding between a radio operator and the pilot of the lead plane, who was carrying a stick of troopers from H Company, 502nd PIR, sowed confusion. Still several kilometers from his drop zone, the pilot, speaking over the intercom, asked his radio operator to "check on" the Aldis lamp. The radio operator misunderstood, thinking he was to "turn on" the lamp. No sooner had he done so, than paratroopers began descending on the sleepy village of Ramsbury, fifteen kilometers from their drop zone. Plagued by poor visibility, twenty-eight planes in another formation, which also missed their drop zones, turned around and returned to base without dropping their sticks.

A Dakota C-47 towing a Waco glider: the "mule" of the USAAF, the C-47 was used to transport troops and vehicles and tow gliders in all theaters of operation. *NARA*

Men from B Force of Operation Neptune wait to board their gliders. *NARA*

Despite this error, all participating units had reassembled by 3:30 a.m. Just before daylight, gliders full of troops and heavy arms successfully landed in the sector. With the help of these reinforcements, parachute units began a series of attacks at dawn, capturing all objectives before noon. While Eagle was considered a total tactical success, no fewer than 436 parachutists were injured, many sustaining fractures or suffering broken bones.

Paratroopers from the 101st Airborne Division in a landing craft have just received their copies of General Eisenhower's order of the day for June 6, encouraging them as they "embark on the Great Crusade." They are headed for Utah Beach. *NARA*

AMPHIBIOUS AND NAVAL OPERATIONS

★ ★ ★ ★ ★

OPERATION FORTITUDE

Operation Overlord was made possible through an extended campaign of disinformation, whose complicated orchestration was without historical precedent. Its origins go back to the beginning of the war, when the British deceived the Germans into thinking they had sufficient troops to repulse an invasion. Again, in 1942, the Allies disguised their plans for Operation Torch, the landings in North Africa, through perpetrating misinformation, leading the Germans to believe the Allies were preparing to land in Norway (codename Solo I), the north of France (Overthrow), or in Dakar (Solo II). It was nevertheless only after the Casablanca Conference, where the Allies adopted the principle of inter-Allied planning, with a view toward a decisive landing in France, that they actively pursued systematic and far-reaching dissemination of misinformation.

Under the authority of the unified supreme command, the London Controlling Section (LCS), led by Col. John Henry Bevan, constructed a veritable maze of disinformation. Actively participating in 1944 were Military Intelligence, Section 5 (MI-5); the Secret Intelligence Service (SIS), or MI-6; the Government Code and Ciphering School (GC and CS); the Naval Intelligence Division (NID); the Special Operations Executive (SOE) of Air Intelligence; the Political Warfare Executive (PWE); the Foreign Office; and the Double-Cross (or XX) Committee; as well as the Committee of Special Means (CSM) from within SHAEF. The London Controlling Section used many means to keep the enemy guessing. Reports by German agents working for the Allied side, false messages easily decrypted by the enemy, the creation of fictitious armies, disinformation planted in newspapers, allusions in official conversations, false information given to real German agents, confidences discretely imparted to diplomats from neutral countries, messages to nonexistent Resistance groups, and diversionary raids on enemy-occupied beaches

Long lines of infantrymen wait to embark on landing craft, assault (LCAs); landing craft, vehicle, personnel (LCVPs); and landing craft, infantry (LCIs). *NARA*

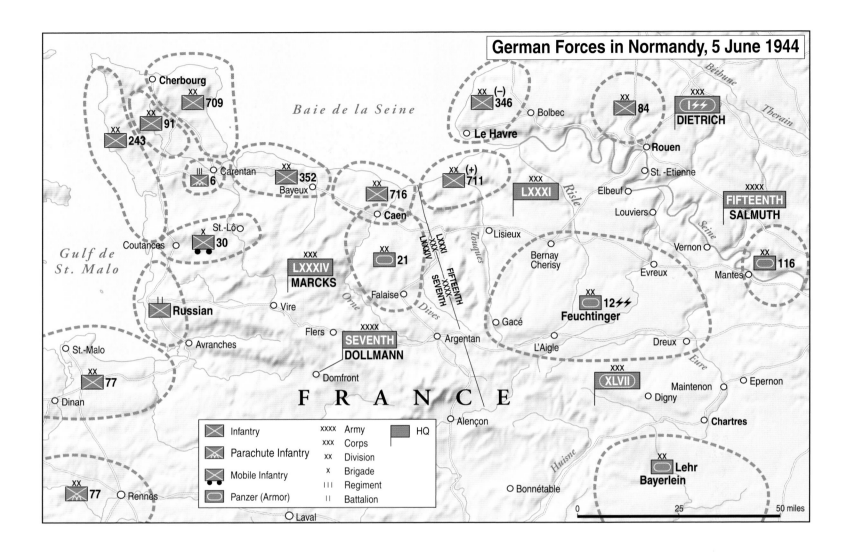

German Forces in Normandy, 5 June 1944

Infantry	XXXX Army	HQ
Parachute Infantry	XXX Corps	
Mobile Infantry	XX Division	
	X Brigade	
Panzer (Armor)	III Regiment	
	II Battalion	

all combined to surround the Allied strategy with an astonishing and highly effective wall of lies.

The Jael Plan, the first following the Casablanca Conference, consisted of two major components. The first, Operation Cockade, was an unsuccessful attempt to relieve the eastern front by deceiving the Germans into retaining as many forces as possible in western Europe. The other, the highly successful Zeppelin Plan, designed to make the Germans believe that landings were imminent in Greece, the Balkans, and Sardinia, served to camouflage the Allied invasion of Sicily, slated for July 10, 1943.

Following the Quebec Conference, which set the date for Overlord as May 1, 1944, the Allies set the Bodyguard Plan in motion. This was intended to conceal the impressive buildup of troops and arms in England and to trick the Germans into positioning their forces as far as possible from the chosen objective. And indeed, many of the sixty German divisions stationed in France, Belgium, and the Netherlands, as well as the sixteen divisions in Norway and Denmark and the forty-six divisions located between Italy and the Balkans, could quickly be rushed as reinforcements to France. In all these regions, Bodyguard worked to multiply threats to German forces, implementing approximately three dozen different plans, including the continuation of many activities previously proven to be highly successful.

The Zeppelin Plan aimed at keeping the Germans in the eastern Mediterranean. This is the framework of the notorious Cicero spy affair, wherein Elyesa Bazna, the valet of the British ambassador to Ankara, Sir Hughe Knatchbull-Hugessen, sold the Germans a clever mixture of false and authentic documents for monetary gain. Among other actions, these foresaw a unified Allied action in the Balkans in the spring of 1944. Taking the documents very seriously, Hitler gave the order to station twenty-five divisions, much needed elsewhere, in the region.

To protect the fleet from Luftwaffe attack, barrage balloons attached by metal cables were flown above the ships, presenting serious obstacles to enemy planes. *NARA*

Vehicles chained to the deck were parked in position to back out of an LCVP. Trucks, jeeps, and other vehicles were brought in as support on the second wave, after first-wave troops established the beachhead. *NARA*

Fortitude North, the worthy successor of Solo I, aimed to make the Germans believe in a planned British invasion of Norway aided by the Soviets. To make the story credible, the Allies created a fictitious Fourth British Army in Scotland, comprising seven divisions and complete with pasteboard billets, rubber tanks, and wooden cannons and planes. The operation, which proved enormously successful, included considerable radio traffic, constant movement of vehicles by land and sea, raids on the Norwegian coast, innumerable flyovers by the Royal Air Force, and increased activity on the part of the Norwegian Resistance. The Germans not only maintained their divisions in Norway; they reinforced them. In June 1944, almost half a million German soldiers were stationed in Norway. Better yet, they remained there until the fall of Berlin.

Fortitude South was without doubt the most elaborate Allied plan. As D-Day approached, it became increasingly difficult to hide the fact that the invasion of France was imminent. The Allies thus attempted to convince the Germans that the landings would occur at Pas-de-Calais. As if by magic, a new army appeared in Kent and Sussex, the First U. S. Army Group (FUSAG), commanded by the famous Gen. George S. Patton, Jr. Initially composed of thirteen divisions, it could rapidly be expanded to fifty divisions at the time of the landing, projected to take place somewhere in the area between Calais and Dunkirk.

The measures thus taken remained in place after D-Day, with a view to making the latter appear a diversionary operation before the principal action unfolded at Pas-de-Calais. Operation Fortitude had every chance of succeeding, since the Germans themselves were persuaded that a realistic assessment would force the Allies to strike Fortress Europe as near as possible to the Reich itself, or in other areas where invasion forces would not have to cover long distances.

Effecting this plan and maintaining the deception to the end required considerable extra effort on the part of the Allies. Thus, for every aerial reconnaissance mission conducted over Normandy, two similar missions were flown north of the Somme. The Allies bombed targets in the latter area twice as heavily as those in the sector they actually intended to invade. In England, the main naval forces were concentrated to the south, but it was important to throw the enemy off the track. Artificial vessels, supposedly ready for launching, were therefore "anchored" at quays in ports on the eastern and south-eastern seaboards, creating the impression that these ports harbored just as many ships as ports in the south. The forces deployed northeast of London made no effort to hide their preparations. Numerous ships, ultimately destined to resupply troops in Normandy, remained concentrated in Scottish ports. A false general headquarters was set up at Dover. Artificial gliders as well as fictitious airborne units were placed in plain sight in airfields in Kent.

Infantry soldiers climb into an LCVP in an English port. *NARA*

Stormy weather caused General Eisenhower to rescind his original departure orders, delaying D-Day until June 6. Meanwhile, thousands of troops remained in wait on heavily loaded ships and other craft. *NARA*

Considerable means thus were used to deceive the Germans, and as of February 1944, the Americans also became involved in misleading German information services. Fictitious inflatable ground-transport vehicles, such as tanks and trucks, fabricated by the Dunlop Tire Company, were judiciously stationed, and other artificial vehicles, including LCTs, Spitfires, Mustangs, and others, were also deployed. In Scotland and Belfast, the Allies organized a fictitious headquarters and set about transmitting much misinformation designed to persuade the Germans that an assault on Norway was under preparation.

The plan was to convince the Germans that Pas-de-Calais would be the main site of the invasion and that six divisions would launch the assault, two to the east of Cap Gris-Nez and four to the south. According to the deception, these were to be followed by six others, so that fifteen days after the invasion, the landing forces would supposedly total fifty divisions. As for action along the coast of Calvados, the Allies aimed to keep the Germans in uncertainty by maintaining two divisions and their means of transport in reserve at the mouth of the Thames and in ports along the southern and eastern English coasts.

ARTIFICIAL PORTS

While waiting to seize a large operational port, the Allies constructed artificial harbors to ensure the supply and reinforcement of landing troops. Churchill won Roosevelt over to the concept at the Quebec Conference in 1943, and the decision was made to construct two harbors for upcoming operations in Normandy, each comparable in size to that at Dover. To keep the project secret, the constructions were codenamed Mulberries. Mulberry A, meant to serve American troops, was installed in the inlet of Vierville-Saint-Laurent, on Omaha Beach, to the west of the landing zone. Mulberry B, to be used by British and Canadian troops, was constructed facing Arromanches, further to the east on Sword Beach.

To protect the loading docks from waves and storms, a protective semicircle facing the shoreline was placed around each harbor. These consisted of a giant system of derelict ships, or blockships, called Gooseberries, used to extend the harbor and form a breakwater, and Phoenixes, huge, hollow, floating blocks made of reinforced concrete, attached together and laid end to end to serve for unloading cargo. The Phoenixes came complete with antiaircraft gun emplacements to protect the ports from aerial attack, and sea valves that permitted the interiors to be flooded, and thus stabilized, once they were in place. These artificial seawalls had openings at only three points: in the center and at the east and west extremities, designed to give access to liberty ships and coasters.

Once they reached the shelter of the seawall, ships discharged their cargo onto floating structures called whales. Designed to be functional at all hours, they followed the movement of the tide through the use of pylons at all four corners. Once unloaded, vehicles and matériel were driven to firm ground along five floating iron roadways. An underwater pipeline, codenamed Pluto and stretching from the Isle of Wight, completed the system.

While the Americans took charge of the liberty ships, the English constructed the Phoenixes. British shipyards, working overtime, were so overwhelmed with the task of construction that it became necessary to erect temporary work sites along rivers, located at times far upstream, as the site at Reading exemplifies. It took fifteen thousand workers eight months to construct 213 Phoenixes, each of which was sixty meters long and eighteen meters high, the height of a five-story building. Before they captured Cherbourg, the Allies hence relied on the Mulberries to unload troops and equipment dispatched to Normandy.

THE BUILDUP TO H-HOUR

As soon as preparations were complete, the first-wave troops and their equipment were moved into areas of concentration. Sent on from there to holding zones, they transferred to their points of departure only at the very last moment. The three British naval assault forces were located respectively at Felix-Stowe and Tilbury, Shoreham and Newhaven, and Portsmouth and Southampton. American troops were to leave from Weymouth, Portland, Torquay, Brixham, Dartmouth, and Plymouth.

Lightweight transport vehicles lined up on an LCT are ready to debark at Utah or Omaha Beach. The motor of every vehicle was rendered watertight before the invasion.
NARA

Equipment for first-phase troops was packed in the days immediately preceding the invasion. All equipment and vehicles susceptible to contact with water were waterproofed. Then came the vast task of separating first-wave troops from units that would follow on, and moving those who would participate in the later phases to areas that would permit them to join up easily with participants of the initial assault.

The definitive plan for the amphibious arm of the invasion, Operation Neptune, constituted the initial phase of Overlord, including the delivery of Allied troops. Responsibilities among the various commands were distributed as follows:

The U.S. First Army would land northwest and east of the estuary of the Vire River:

> On the right wing, at Utah Beach, VII Corps, commanded by Gen. Joseph Lawton Collins:
> ★ The 4th Infantry Division in the first wave, followed by the 9th Infantry Division, the 79th Infantry Division, and the 90th Infantry Division.
>
> On the left wing, at Omaha Beach, V Corps, commanded by Gen. Leonard Gerow:
> ★ The 1st Infantry Division, with elements of the 29th Infantry Division in the first wave, followed by the rest of the 29th Infantry Division and the 2nd Infantry Division.

The Second British Army would land between Caen and Bayeux and capture the regions to the south and southeast of Caen:

> On the right wing, on Gold Beach at Asnelles, British XXX Corps, commanded by Gen. G. C. Bucknall:
> ★ The 50th (Northumbrian) Division and the 8th Armoured Brigade in the first wave, followed by the 7th Armoured Division and the 49th (West Riding) Division.
>
> On the left wing, at Juno Beach and Sword Beach, British I Corps, commanded by Gen. J. T. Crocker:
> ★ On Juno Beach at Courseulles, the 3rd Canadian Division of the 2nd Canadian Armoured Brigade in the first wave, followed by commandos of the 4th Special Service Brigade.
> ★ On Sword Beach at Ouistreham, the 3rd British Division and the 27th Armoured Brigade in the first wave, followed by Commandos of the 1st Special Service Brigade of the 51st (Highland) Division and the 4th Armoured Brigade.

Among the Americans, General Gerow's V Corps was assigned the task of taking a beachfront six and a half kilometers long at Saint-Laurent-sur-Mer on Omaha Beach. VII Corps was to secure its side of Cherbourg by D-plus-8, and V Corps, moving south, would take Saint-Lô on D-plus-9. Once the Allies had seized control of the entire peninsula by D-plus-20, VII Corps was to swing south to establish a front with

V Corps running from Avranches to Domfront. The landing of General Patton's Third Army would complete the capture of Brittany by D-plus-30, freeing up the First Army, commanded by General Bradley, to advance along the Loire River and deploy on a front from Angers to Le Mans by D-plus-40.

By D-plus-20, British troops were to have taken Caen and advanced inland to establish a line between Vire and Falaise. The second phase of their mission consisted of enlarging the area under their control all the way to the Seine, where they would meet up and cross the river with American forces deployed to their right. Finally, on D-plus-90, with Brittany entirely under Allied control, the new front line was foreseen as stretching from Fontainebleau to Paris and up to Le Havre.

Such was the plan on the eve of D-Day. Although it may have seemed realistic to Allied strategists, it could not yet, however, take into account such factors as the German response, or whether or not the enemy knew where the Allied invasion would actually take place.

On Saturday, June 3, 1944, tension was mounting among the high command as the troops gradually began to load onto landing crafts. The decision to launch had to be made that night, at latest, if the fleet was to arrive on the French coast according to plan at dawn on June 5. However, although the month of May had been beautiful, the weather had now taken a turn for the worse, with wind gusting from the west and a gathering layer of low-lying clouds.

At 9:30 p.m., a tense meeting took place in the library of the maritime prefecture at Southwick House, the headquarters of Adm. Sir Bertram Ramsay. Reporting to Eisenhower and the top commanders assembled about him, the meteorologist was certain of inclement weather: the coming four days would be marked by strong winds, low clouds, and fog. Despite this discouraging information, Eisenhower gave the order for Allied Task Forces U and O, stationed farthest to the west along the coast at Devonshire and Portland, to launch.

On Sunday, June 4, at 4:15 a.m., two hours before the preponderance of the fleet was scheduled to weigh anchor, Eisenhower convened the high command. With no improvement in the weather, the supreme commander, despite the disagreement of Montgomery, decided to wait for twenty-four hours. The entirety of Allied Task Force U, commanded by Rear Adm. Alan Goodrich Kirk, and part of Task Force O, who were already on their way, received the order to turn around and head back.

At 9:00 p.m. of the same day, Eisenhower convened another meeting at Southwick House, attended by Montgomery, Air Chief Marshal Arthur William Tedder (Eisenhower's deputy in the Mediterranean and Northwest Europe), Leigh-Mallory, Ramsay, Gen. Walter Bedell Smith (Eisenhower's chief of staff during his tenure at SHAEF), and others. If the order to go was not given before June 5 at dawn, the entire mission would have to be postponed for fifteen days, entailing serious consequences.

The chief meteorologist reported, however, that there would soon be a break in the storm, predicting decreasing winds and clearing skies for June 5 and the night of June 5–6. Eisenhower asked for the opinions of those in the room. Leigh-Mallory and Tedder remarked that clear skies were an absolute necessity for the success of preliminary bombings. Bedell Smith said that to postpone the operation again carried the real risk of

Full of soldiers from B-Force (Backup Force), LCVPs set off from a troop carrier. *NARA*

Sea-borne elements of the 327th Glider Infantry Regiment, 101st Airborne Division embark for Utah Beach. Part of General Howell's C Force, they were slated to arrive on D-plus-2. *NARA*

calling the entire operation into question, while Ramsay insisted on the urgency of making a decision in order to give the navy sufficient time. Eisenhower then questioned Montgomery, who again categorically opposed any postponement.

The immense responsibility of the final decision weighed squarely on Eisenhower's shoulders. After weighing the pros and cons, he gave the order after a long silence: "OK. Let's go!"

Even before the first bombers took off from England to attack the Normandy coast, the German high command knew the invasion had begun. Through their usual means of spying and treason, the German military espionage agency, the Abwehr, had succeeded in surreptitiously infiltrating the Allied network: Overlord was no longer a secret. No one— not an officer of the German general staff, not a commander in the field, not a single soldier—was surprised on June 6 by the invasion.

Nevertheless, the invasion came to pass. The Allied high command had succeeded in establishing a vast organization of spies and saboteurs in France. Capable leaders were in charge of operations for the principal sections, including the impeccably functioning *Alliance des Animaux* (Animal Alliance), so called because its members knew each other only by call names taken from the animal kingdom. Extending throughout all of France, it consisted of thousands of members, led by district chiefs or commandos. The alliance sent information to the Allies by radio or carrier pigeon, and spied and organized acts of sabotage on a grand scale.

The organization had two missions: to sabotage and destroy the preparation of German defenses and, even more importantly, to prepare for mass action at the decisive moment of invasion. It was largely unknown, for example, that a mere ten grams of sugar, tossed opportunely into a cement mixer, sufficed to render a hundred kilos of cement devoid of strength. A single Resistance member in the Obligatory Work Service, posted handily close to the cement mixer, could thus easily wreak havoc on elements of the German fortifications by introducing relatively tiny portions of sugar into either the dry mixture or the water used to make the cement.

A British organization, the Special Operations Executive (SOE) headquartered in London, which directed and coordinated Resistance sabotage, drew up a plan to be executed on D-Day. According to *le Plan Vert*, or the Green Plan, 571 French train stations and switching stations were to be simultaneously destroyed and thirty principal roadways rendered impassable several hours before the invasion began. Another plan, *Tortue*, or Tortoise, aimed to interrupt all communications and blow up a number of important crossroads, bridges, and viaducts.

The order to execute these plans was to be given by code over the radio. Resistance leaders in charge of sabotage were told to listen carefully to the BBC on the first, second, fifteenth, and sixteenth day of each month. The first verse of "Nevermore," by the French poet Paul Verlaine, contained a coded message signaling that the invasion was about to occur. From that point forward, they were to listen to the BBC continuously. The last three verses of the poem would signify that the landing would take place within forty-eight hours, and the leaders of participating networks should put le Plan Vert and le Plan Tortue into effect.

For all its cleverness, the system did not escape the Germans, and agents at the Abwehr managed to decode it. Too many people were in on the secret, one of whom delivered the key to the use of Verlaine's poem to Adm. Wilhelm Franz Canaris. From that day on, German radiomen lay in wait for the broadcast of the final verses.

Most important to this operation were agents of the Abwehr with the Fifteenth Army, commanded by Gen. Hans von Salmuth, headquartered at Tourcoing. Refusing to be fooled by countless red herrings, they knew the text exactly, word for word. Their patience did not go unrewarded. The last verses of the poem were broadcast on June 5 at 10:15 p.m. General Field Marshal Gerd von Rundstedt, head of the navy in Paris, and Rommel's Army Group B now were informed the invasion had begun.

And yet, they did not react! As incredible as it seems, by a strange aberration the German high command literally gave the Allies the gift of victory. General Salmuth put the Fifteenth Army on alert, but their sector would not be involved in the coming events.

Otherwise, nothing happened. Army Group B did not alert its Seventh Army, thus leaving it, in the hours immediately following, the unsuspecting prey of the largest attack in all of history. Neither the commander of the navy, Rear Adm. Walter Hennecke, who disposed of powerful fixed batteries, nor German radar stations were warned of the invasion about to descend on them. Rommel was not recalled from Herrlingen, where he

Troops about to embark from a port in southern England attend a religious service. Here, a Catholic chaplain officiating on a quay under a construction crane blesses the men about to participate in the "Great Crusade" against Nazism. *NARA*

had gone to spend time with his family. For fourteen decisive hours, his army group was deprived of its commander.

The Germans simply could not believe the story was true. "All the same," the attitude ran, "General Eisenhower would hardly announce the Allied invasion over the BBC!"

By the afternoon of June 5, the 9th Troop Carrier Command had regrouped its C-47s and Waco and Horsa gliders on fourteen airfields between Lincolnshire and Devon, and their crews were ready to take off for the big adventure. Delivered by truck the preceding evening, hundreds of buckets of paint sat near the planes. Black and white identification stripes would now be painted over and under their wings and around their fuselages. The orders were clear: during Operation Neptune, any plane without these distinctive markings was to be considered an enemy and shot out of the sky. Mechanics, ground crews, and seagoing personnel were all put to work to paint the planes before they left for their missions. They even used brooms as paintbrushes in order to speed up the process.

On June 5 at 9:30 p.m., the planes of the 9th Troop Carrier Command Pathfinder Group were the first of the immense armada to take off from their base at North Witham, near Grantham. The planes took off at eleven-second intervals. The first airplanes of the 53rd and 50th Troop Carrier Wings carried paratroopers from the 101st Airborne, followed by those of the 52nd Troop Carrier Wing, transporting paratroopers from the 82nd Airborne.

Lieutenant Colonel Joel Crouch piloted the lead plane, containing Capt. Frank Lillyman, the head of the 101st pathfinders. His plane was thus the first to participate in the invasion. Rising sharply, the plane quit the English coast at Portland Bill, leading the immense crusade. The pathfinders of the 101st would be the first to land on Norman soil.

At 10:30 p.m., the nine aircraft transporting the pathfinders of the 82nd Airborne Division were ready to depart. Their mission was to mark the drop zones for the paratroopers soon to follow. At 10:48 p.m., the first C-47 took off from Greenham Common Airbase, piloted by Col. John M. Donaldson, commanding officer (CO) of the 438th Troop Carrier Group.

Meanwhile, six thousand British paratroopers took off in the direction of the Orne River. Beneath them, seven thousand ships carrying 150,000 seasick soldiers were heading in a continuous line over the stormy waves toward the beaches of Normandy. The paratroopers with cork-blackened faces sitting in the planes fully realized that they were about to take part in the largest military confrontation of all time.

Rangers tasked with the mission of assaulting the rocky cliffs of Pointe du Hoc are ready to take to the sea in an LCVP. Their helmets bear the distinctive insignia of the 2nd Ranger Battalion, the number 2 in a red diamond. *NARA*

Part III

D-DAY: THE INVASION

★ ★ ★ ★ ★

SUPREME HEADQUARTERS
ALLIED EXPEDITIONARY FORCE

Soldiers, Sailors and Airmen of the Allied Expeditionary Force!

You are about to embark upon the Great Crusade, toward which we have striven these many months. The eyes of the world are upon you. The hopes and prayers of liberty-loving people everywhere march with you. In company with our brave Allies and brothers-in-arms on other Fronts, you will bring about the destruction of the German war machine, the elimination of Nazi tyranny over the oppressed peoples of Europe, and security for ourselves in a free world.

Your task will not be an easy one. Your enemy is well trained, well equipped and battle-hardened. He will fight savagely.

But this is the year 1944! Much has happened since the Nazi triumphs of 1941. The United Nations have inflicted upon the Germans great defeat, in open battle, man-to-man. Our air offensive has seriously reduced their strength in the air and their capacity to wage war on the ground. Our home Fronts have given us an overwhelming superiority in weapons and munitions of war, and placed at our disposal great reserves of trained fighting men. The tide has turned! The free men of the world are marching together to Victory!

I have full confidence in your courage, devotion to duty and skill in battle. We will accept nothing less than full Victory! Good Luck! And let us all beseech the blessing of Almighty God upon this great and noble undertaking.

—Dwight Eisenhower, official statement
issued to Allied troops on the eve of D-Day, June 6, 1944

C-47s towing Waco gliders toward their landing zones fly over positions held by paratroopers. They are bringing in vital reinforcements and equipment. *NARA*

8
AIRBORNE
MISSIONS

★ ★ ★ ★ ★

THE ASSEMBLED FORCES HAD JUST begun the great crusade against Nazism. Sailors, infantrymen, pilots, and paratroopers attentively read General Eisenhower's message of encouragement and blessing of their "great and noble undertaking." In the black of night before the historic day, they felt proud to be part of the magnificent operation.

As Admiral Ramsay later commented, the Allied crossing of the English Channel had an air of unreality. The convoys stretched in a seemingly infinite line, riding the gray, agitated sea under darkening skies filled with airplanes. Lines of ships forged through the waters from one horizon to the other, while barrage balloons sailed overhead. The formidable armada converged on a raging sea in a vast assembly zone that was so congested that the English baptized it "Piccadilly." Channels previously swept of mines provided access to the five landing beaches where the forces converged amidst stormy waves that rose two meters tall.

In the air, planes were flying toward the continent without the guidance of radio signals. The night that enveloped the formation and then the fog above the shoreline of the Cotentin Peninsula seemed, at first, to offer protection to the men who were about to jump into the void.

Gliders landed as best they could but often crashed, given the thick Norman hedgerows and many obstructions the Germans planted on potential landing zones. *NARA*

THE 82ND AND THE 101ST AIRBORNE DIVISIONS

Thirteen thousand paratroopers from the "All American" 82nd Airborne Division and the "Screaming Eagles" of the 101st Airborne Division packed into Dakotas and Waco and Horsa gliders. Their craft took off by the hundreds from airfields in southern England. The mission they had waited for, and for which they had so long prepared, was finally upon them!

Paratroopers of the 101st Airborne Division encounter their first local inhabitants at dawn on June 6 in Sainte-Marie-du-Mont. *NARA*

Paratroopers from the 502nd and 506th PIRs display a captured Nazi flag. The trophy belongs to James W. Flanagan of C Company, 502nd PIR. *NARA*

Infantrymen who landed at Utah Beach, three kilometers from Sainte-Marie-du-Mont, cross the village square. Paratroopers from the 101st Airborne Division are already on the scene. *NARA*

The spearhead of this amazing crusade, the pathfinders, were the first to reach the soil of Normandy. They had trained for many months to be able to find their way in complete darkness, to locate the drop zones, and to prepare them with the aid of special equipment. After waiting outside their planes since early afternoon on June 5, the pathfinders left the English coast an hour before the main body of the troops. Their formation flew southwest for about a hundred kilometers to a stationary marker boat, where they veered to the north, toward the Channel islands of Jersey and Guernsey, approaching the French coast from the west. They then cut over the Cotentin Peninsula, flying from west to east toward their drop zones.

It was midnight when the copilot of the lead plane carrying Capt. Frank Lillyman, head of the 101st Airborne pathfinders, recognized the village of Saint-Germain-de-Varreville near Drop Zone A, their objective. Lieutenant Colonel Joel Crouch, the pilot, switched on the green light, giving the men at the back of the plane the signal to jump. Lillyman immediately leapt into the void, followed by his stick.

It was exactly 12:15 a.m. The paratroopers of the 502nd PIR were at least two kilometers north of Drop Zone A. As soon as they hit the ground, the pathfinders installed their radar beacons and lamps without the slightest enemy interference.

They were followed by ten other teams from the 101st, who were to prepare drop zones C (at Hiesville for the 506th PIR) and D (at Angoville for the 501st PIR), as well as the landing zone for the gliders, Landing Zone E. They got the timing right but not the location. At Drop Zone C, the beacon and a single lamp were set up about four hundred meters to the southeast of the target location. At Drop Zone D, which came under heavy enemy fire, the beacon was installed a full 1,500 meters to the west of their target.

To the north and west of Sainte-Mère-Église, the pathfinders of the 82nd Airborne Division encountered the same problems as their comrades of the 101st. The teams of the 505th PIR landed on Drop Zone O near Sainte-Mère-Église and quickly lit up their drop zone. The pathfinders of the 507th PIR landed west of the Merderet River at Amfreville near Drop Zone T and had to fight a German patrol before they could set up their equipment. But the sticks were dispersed and the lamps were lost. Only one Eureka beacon could be put into operation. The pathfinders of the 508th PIR came to earth about two and a half kilometers to the southeast of Drop Zone N, near Pont-l'Abbé. They were able to install only one beacon and two Holophane lamps.

As a whole, conditions on the ground rendered it impossible for the pathfinders to accomplish their missions. Despite their valiant efforts, their inability to successfully prepare the drop zones and landing zones had negative repercussions on the mass drops of both of the American airborne divisions that followed just an hour on their heels.

An hour after the pathfinders took off, they were followed by 882 planes transporting thirteen thousand paratroopers from the 82nd and 101st Airborne Divisions to their drop zones. Arriving at the coast of the peninsula, the formations of C-47s encountered heavy fog that greatly reduced visibility, making it difficult for the young pilots to maintain formation. They then encountered intense German antiaircraft fire, which succeeded in completely dispersing the planes, as pilots attempted to escape a

The first gliders pass over the beaches before they land in the hedgerows. Many would be damaged in landing. *NARA*

LIEUTENANT MALCOLM BRANNEN

AN OFFICER IN Headquarters Company, 3rd Battalion, 508th Parachute Infantry Regiment, Brannen landed in a field near the headquarters of Lt. Gen. Wilhelm Falley, commander of the German 91st Air Landing Division stationed at Picauville. Brannen assembled a dozen soldiers from his regiment and attempted to locate his position with the help of a Norman family awakened from their beds. Over bread and cider, the men consulted a map spread out on the table, as the farmer pointed out their position and warned the troopers that a German headquarters was located just a few hundred meters from the farmhouse.

When a car was heard approaching the house, Brannen rapidly stepped outside and ordered his men to take cover along the narrow road. Stationing himself in the middle of the road, Brannen signaled the car to halt, but the vehicle, a German staff car, accelerated instead. Brannen fired a spray from his Thompson submachine gun, ordering his men to open up. The car swerved, riddled with bullets, then crashed into the wall of the stone farmhouse.

One of the occupants, thrown from the car, crawled toward his Luger, which had been tossed to the ground in the impact from the crash. Brannen ordered him to raise his hands, but the officer continued to crawl toward his weapon. Shouting at him to stop, Brannen knew he could not allow the officer to reach his gun. He pulled the trigger and shot the man in the forehead.

On examining the body, Brannen discovered he had just killed a general. A search of the car revealed a cap marked with the name "Falley" and the body of a German, Oberstleutnant Joachim Bartuzat, slumped on the front seat. Brannen's men took the driver prisoner and conducted him to a command post. *Image credit: Dominique François*

living hell by accelerating or breaking formation. The presence of the pathfinders had touched off an explosive enemy reaction, and now the Germans were ready and waiting. On board the planes, troopers impatiently waited the command to jump. Better to leap out into the black of night than remain at the mercy of German flak!

The 101st Airborne Division, on Mission Albany, jumped north of Carentan. The 2nd Battalion of the 502nd PIR was dropped on the left flank of Drop Zone C instead of on Drop Zone A, as initially intended. A maze of hedgerows made it very difficult for the troopers to get oriented and reassemble. The 3rd Battalion of the 502nd PIR was extremely dispersed to the east of Sainte-Mère-Église. Seventy-five troopers managed to assemble and reach the German battery at Saint-Martin-de-Varreville, which the Germans had deserted after removing the guns from their emplacements.

At Utah Beach, exits three and four were quickly secured, permitting a linkup with the 4th Infantry Division around 1:00 p.m.

The 1st Battalion of the 502nd PIR landed near Saint-Germain-de-Varreville and saw fighting around Mesières. The battalion took part in cleanup operations at the northern access to Utah Beach.

Some of the first paratroopers enter Sainte-Mère-Église mounted on horses seized from the Germans. *NARA*

The drop of the 506th PIR went more according to plan, landing close to Drop Zone C in spite of flak that knocked out several C-47s. Successive skirmishes with the Germans made it impossible to secure Exit 1 at Pouppeville and Exit 2 at Houdienville, behind Utah Beach, which were taken later in the morning by the 4th Infantry Division as they came up off the beaches. The 377th Parachute Field Artillery Battalion was the most scattered of all and could only set one of its howitzers in place. The 3rd Battalion of the 501st PIR was tasked with the mission of securing Landing Zone E near Hiesville.

The All Americans were given Mission Boston, employing drop zones O, N, and T and landing zones O and W to deliver General Ridgway's 82nd Airborne Division west of Sainte-Mère-Église. Their mission was to organize a line of defense west of the Merderet River, take Sainte-Mère-Église, and capture the bridges at La Fière and Chef-du-Pont.

The drops of the 82nd Airborne varied in their precision in hitting their intended drop zones, and many of their missions necessarily changed on the ground. One regiment, the 180 paratroopers from the 3rd Battalion led by Lieutenant Colonel Krause, captured Sainte-Mère-Église at dawn on June 6. They did so with the help of Lt. Col. Benjamin H. Vandervoort's 2nd Battalion, 505th PIR, who had the best drop of all units on D-Day. The 2nd Battalion had been redirected mid-route to their original objective, Neuville-au-Plain, when the Germans heavily counterattacked Sainte-Mère-Église from the south. Around 10:00 a.m., the 795th Battalion (Georgian) and the Germans of the 91st

The crossroads at Sainte-Mère-Église was a crucial objective for the 82nd Airborne Division. To the east, the road led to Utah Beach; to the south, to Carentan; to the west lay the Merderet and its all-important bridges; and to the north, the deep-water port of Cherbourg. *NARA*

A smiling 505th PIR trooper transports a heavy suitcase, happy to help local civilians regain their homes at Sainte-Mère-Église. *NARA*

Luftlande Division attacked with several tanks. They were repulsed by the 3rd Battalion, which laid waste to a retreating German convoy with grenades.

The mission of the 1st Battalion, 505th PIR, was to capture the bridge over the Merderet River at La Fière. After German soldiers took up positions around the Manoir de La Fière, the 1st Battalion wrested away control of the bridge and held it until the entire sector, including the village of Cauquigny, was secured June 9.

The 507th PIR and 508th PIR, the two regiments that had landed on the west bank of the Merderet, remained very scattered. The presence of Germans had prohibited their pathfinders from correctly marking the drop zones, and a large portion of paratroopers and their equipment came down in the flooded portions of the marshes. The only high ground in the marshland area was the Cherbourg–Caen railroad line, which the troopers used as a landmark and assembly point. Some men landed several dozen kilometers away from their drop zones, like the 180 members of the 507th PIR who ended up south of Carentan in the marshes of Graignes, or those who became isolated in the Val de Saire near Quettehou, or at Negreville, east of Valognes. The unluckiest came down into the ocean and drowned. There was, however, also an advantage for the Allies in these widely scattered drops, for the Germans found it extremely difficult to organize an effective counteroffensive against so many small bands of paratroopers, who were seemingly cropping up everywhere at once.

LIEUTENANT GENERAL WILHELM FALLEY

COMMANDER OF THE 91st Air Landing Division, based in La-Haye-du-Puis and Saint-Sauveur-le-Vicomte, Falley set up his headquarters at the Château de Bernaville in Picauville, where he was visited by Rommel during his inspection of defensive fortifications on the Cotentin Peninsula. Having left for Rennes the evening of June 5, Falley became concerned by the number of air raids in the area and decided to return to headquarters in the middle of the night. He met with catastrophe several hundred meters outside of Bernaville, when he encountered Brannen's group and was killed. He is buried alongside his chief of staff, Oberstleutnant Joachim Bartuzat, at the German Cemetery at Orglandes, France.

The death of Falley, the first German general killed in Normandy, was followed by many others: Gen. Erich Marcks, head of the 84th Armoured Flak Battalion, based at Saint-Lô, was killed by bomb in his command post at Venoix, in Caen, on June 14. General Heinz Hellmich, commander of the 243rd Infantry Division on the Cotentin Peninsula, was killed on June 17 between Bricquebec and Portbail. General Rudolph Stegmann, commander of the 77th Infantry Division, a replacement unit that arrived on June 10, was killed in an air attack near Bricquebec on June 18.

On August 2, Gen. Dietrich Kraiss, commander of the 352nd Infantry Division, was mortally wounded south of Saint-Lô. Finally, Gen. Viktor Draebich-Waechter, commander of the 306th Infantry Division, was sent to Normandy in July and killed shortly after in an artillery attack on August 2 in the region of Caumont and L'Eventé.

Image credit: Bunderarchiv: German National Archives (BA)

THE FORGOTTEN PARATROOPERS

For several days, one group of paratroopers lived among the townspeople of the little village of Graignes. The parentheses of this short peace were brutally closed on June 11, when the Germans attacked the village.

Graignes is located on the road to Saint-Lô, a dozen kilometers south of Carentan. No Germans were garrisoned in the village, which the occupiers judged to be without strategic importance. But on the night of June 5–6, as the 507th PIR dropped in the sector of Amfreville, nearly 180 members of the regiment mistakenly jumped into the marshland surrounding Graignes.

The troopers were completely lost when they touched the ground—or rather the water—in the flooded fields and marshes. Small groups of Americans quickly began to gather at farms along the border of the marshland. They then assembled in the center of the village, where they were met with approximately twenty other troopers who had come from the neighboring village of Tribehou. Following a few tense hours, the atmosphere rapidly warmed when the mayor of the community, Alphonse Voydie, and members of his administration offered to help the troopers, who were under the command of Major

Johnson. The heights of Graignes provided an ideal surveillance point, easily defended atop a hill overlooking surrounding marshes. Here, the Americans established their command post (CP) near the grocery store–café run by Madame Boursier, where meat contributed by the inhabitants of the village was prepared. Milk and bread, bought in large quantities in Montmartin-en-Graignes, provided the sustenance to defend against a siege.

The Americans set up defenses around the town and mined the road to Carentan. As amazing as it may seem, the presence of 180 paratroopers in such a small town nevertheless went unnoticed! It may be that the Germans, who already had their hands full elsewhere, chose to ignore this particular band of soldiers.

Awaiting an enemy who did not appear, the Americans became friendly with the villagers, who all had rallied to their cause. The troopers kept the children well supplied with chewing gum and chocolate, and shared photos of their families with the townsfolk. Some of them were even invited into French homes to share a family meal. There was singing, laughing, and attempts to communicate with hand gestures—moments of grace suspended in time. The war seemed far away.

Nevertheless, it was very close, for the Americans were itching for a fight. On June 8, the first skirmish took place at the Graignes bridge, when the troopers attacked a German horse-drawn convoy. The next day, a new attack was attempted when Johnson learned that two hundred enemy soldiers were bivouacked in fields at Montmartin, where he dispatched seven men with the order to take no prisoners. Luckily, the seven troopers arrived too late: the Germans had already packed up and left. The same day, at a road crossing marked by a Catholic cross, a landmark locally known as "au Calvaire," Germans traveling in a sidecar were shot and killed. The same day, a team under the instructions of Lt. Frank Naughton

A paratrooper talks with two small children at Saint-Marcouf. *NARA*

Paratroopers pass along the walls of the Saint-Marcouf cemetery. German snipers presented a real threat. *NARA*

A 508th PIR captain questions a local inhabitant for information. *NARA*

Paratroopers and members of the 4th Infantry Division who landed on Utah Beach meet up at approximately 1:00 p.m. on June 6. *NARA*

Norman cows graze peacefully in the shadow of a Horsa glider. Its large, open side door most likely was used to deliver a jeep and trailer. *NARA*

blew up the bridge at Graignes, and two Mongolian soldiers captured at Saint-Jean-de-Daye were led back to the village. Finally, on June 10, in a new blood-soaked skirmish, the Americans attacked a German truck, leaving four dead enemy soldiers.

Finally, the inevitable took place. The next day, a Sunday morning, while the population of Graignes and a few of the troopers were attending mass, a villager suddenly burst through the church door with a loud cry: "The Germans are coming!" The Americans immediately took up their positions, telling the villagers to stay under cover. As the sounds of battle raged all around them, the civilians of Graignes remained in the church, holed up for the entire day.

Initially, the Americans took the situation in hand and were able to push back the Germans. By approximately 5:00 p.m., they had won the first phase of the battle. Taking advantage of a calm in the fighting, the civilians hurried to their homes from the church. On the way, some of the villagers chanced upon an impressive number of German reinforcements, some of whom wore the insignia of the Waffen-SS. Some two thousand soldiers of the deadly 17th SS Panzergrenadier Division were preparing to assault. The Americans' situation now became more complicated: the Germans fired on the village with cannons, hitting the school and the church. Despite the losses inflicted by the Americans, the Germans relentlessly pressed forward. Vastly outnumbered, the paratroopers finally gave ground and slipped away into the night.

Made furious by heavy losses estimated at five hundred, and highly dissatisfied by the welcome the villagers had given the Americans, the Germans unleashed their rage. First they pillaged and burned the presbytery and several houses, and then they killed wounded paratroopers, unable to walk, who had remained behind in the church with the 3rd Battalion surgeon, Capt. Abraham Sophian. Still burning with anger, they put the two priests, who had also stayed in the church, up against a wall and shot them. Several days later they burned their bodies. The walking wounded and Captain Sophian were thrown into a truck and summarily executed in a field in a nearby village, Mesnil-Angot. Other civilians were executed in the hours that followed.

With the help of courageous local inhabitants, the Americans succeeded in crossing the swamps in boats and were able to rejoin their lines at Carentan. Graignes was finally liberated on July 12, but the village was no more.

THE BATTLE FOR SAINTE-MÈRE-ÉGLISE

To the north, Sainte-Mère-Église had been liberated, but the town was quickly threatened by a counterattack. An initial salvo from artillery in Fauville, where the Germans were entrenched, exploded in the center of Sainte-Mère-Église, killing several victims and putting an end to the jubilation of its newly liberated inhabitants. The city was shelled until June 8, bringing the civilian death toll to forty and killing several paratroopers as well. Further north at Neuville-au-Plain, after a serious battle on June 6, the Americans made two more attempts before the village was definitively liberated on June 8. It was to the west, however, in the marshlands, that Americans endured the most precarious circumstances.

These men suffered the terrible fate of many troops delivered by glider. Their Horsa seems to have crashed on its back. *NARA*

A Horsa glider opened from the rear in order to unload a vehicle. *NARA*

CAPTAIN ROY CREEK

THE COMMANDER OF Company E, 507th Parachute Infantry Regiment, Captain Creek was charged with taking the bridge at Chef-du-Pont, which, like that at La Fière, was strategically important to establish a bridgehead on the Cotentin Peninsula.

Image credit: Roy Creek

A Waco glider crashed in a hedgerow. One of its occupants remains entangled in the wreckage.
NARA

At Chef-du-Pont, the troopers were forced to reduce their defenses in order to send reinforcements to La Fière, leaving only thirty or so men commanded by Captain Roy Creek of the 507th PIR to hold the bridge.

THE GLIDERS

The glider mission, Mission Chicago, was confided to 155 men of the 101st Airborne. They arrived in Normandy aboard fifty-two Waco gliders, which also delivered 57mm antitank guns, jeeps and trailers, a light bulldozer, and tons of ammunition and equipment. The landing zone, three kilometers south of Sainte-Mère-Église, was located next to Sebbeville, in the hamlet known as Les Forges. At 4:54 a.m., a glider carrying General Pratt crashed at Hiesville. Still going at full speed, it hit a tree, instantly killing the general and breaking both legs of the pilot, Mike Murphy.

On Mission Detroit, another set of fifty-two gliders delivered 220 troopers of the 82nd Airborne, including divisional headquarters, divisional artillery support, and their matériel, to the sector at Sainte-Mère-Église between 4:00 a.m. and 4:10 a.m. Following were troops on Mission Elmira, which brought in service units, and the Galveston and Hackensack missions, which transported the 325th GIR.

A 101st Airborne trooper takes a moment's break, holding a young child coiffed with an airborne cap. *NARA*

PRIVATE ED JEZIORSKI

ONE OF THE most dramatic assaults of the Normandy campaign was the capture of the bridge at La Fière on June 9. Stretching for nearly a kilometer, the bridge and its causeway offered no cover, nor was there any possibility of crossing elsewhere. Several hundred paratroopers were assembled on the east bank of the Merderet River, awaiting the assault. The 325th Glider Infantry Regiment was given the mission of leading the attack but bogged down in the face of a highly armed enemy. Finally, a single company of the 507th Parachute Infantry Regiment managed to push the enemy back far beyond the other side of the causeway. One of their members was Ed Jeziorski. *Image credit: Dominique François*

Lieutenant Gene Williams, leader of the 3rd Battalion, 508th PIR pathfinders, is seated amidst the hedgerows in front of a fence in Normandy. He was killed shortly after in an attack on the village of Prétot on June 20. *Jack Williams*

Only seventeen of the gliders taking part in Mission Detroit were able to land on or near their landing zones. Fourteen pilots and soldiers lost their lives in the landings, principally due to poor visibility, which prevented the pilots from seeing trees and hedgerows.

Codenamed Keokuk, the second mission carried in reinforcements for the 101st Airborne on the evening of June 6. Thirty-two heavily loaded Horsa gliders headed for the landing zone situated at Hiesville, carrying 160 men consisting of signal, medical, and staff personnel; forty vehicles; six artillery pieces; nineteen tons of ammunition; and soldiers from the 327th GIR. Two gliders landed in the German lines. The division had fourteen killed in action and thirty wounded.

At midnight on June 6, 4,500 of the 13,350 paratroopers and glider men who participated in the Normandy invasion had joined their divisions. Only 10 percent of them had landed on the drop zones and landing zones to which they had been assigned.

THE 6TH BRITISH AIRBORNE DIVISION

Contrary to their American counterparts, the British Red Berets flew directly to their objectives from the south of England, passing over the Isle of Wight. Seated in planes and gliders, men with blackened faces, dressed in the distinctive camouflage vests worn by British paratroopers, reflected in quiet before the great assault. These were the men who would spearhead the eastern flank of Operation Overlord.

A prewar photograph of the bridge across the Merderet River at La Fière, west of Sainte-Mère-Église. The bridge was the focus of deadly combat between June 6 and 9, 1944. *Dominique François*

Three tanks destroyed on the La Fière Causeway on June 6 by the heroic bazooka attack of Marcus Heim, 505th PIR. *NARA*

The 6th Airborne, given the illustrious mission of jumping in Normandy, had been preparing for its various tasks for several months in the south of England and now was fully battle ready. Led by Gen. Sir Richard Gale and composed of approximately six thousand men, the division was charged with the mission of seizing the rolling-bascule bridge at Bénouville and the bridge extending over the Caen Canal. Its mission also included destroying the Merville Battery on the coast (which could fire on Sword Beach) and five bridges on the river Dives. Once these missions were accomplished, they were to hold the area between the Orne and the Dives until the rest of the division, commanded by General Lovat, arrived. The division also needed to defend against any eventual counter-attacks by General Feuchtinger's 21st Panzer Division.

THE BRIDGE AT BÉNOUVILLE

Just before 11:00 p.m. on June 5, six Albemarle planes took off from Harwell Airfield, each towing a Horsa glider. The mission of the paratroopers they carried, led by Major Howard, was to capture the Bénouville and Ranville bridges over the river Orne and its canal. They landed at 12:20 a.m. Meanwhile, two pathfinder teams jumped to mark the drop zones for the other units scheduled to follow a half hour later.

Three gliders landed near the bridge over the Orne and the other three close to the Caen Canal. No sooner had the gliders crashed to earth than their occupants leapt into

Colonel Harry Lewis of the 325th GIR (left) and his headquarters staff in the field. *NARA*

MAJOR JOHN HOWARD

MAJOR HOWARD WAS the com-
mander of the British commando unit
that launched the glider assault on the
bridge at Bénouville on June 6.

Image credit: Dominique François

action. Distracted by the bombing inland behind him, the German sentinel posted
at the bridge had no time to realize his immediate danger before he was killed by
a well-lobbed grenade. Benefiting from the element of surprise, Major Howard's
men immediately launched a furious assault against the German position and
rapidly cleaned it out. Three hundred meters away, the occupants of the three
other gliders encountered very little resistance. In a matter of minutes, the
paratroopers had perfectly accomplished the first of their missions.

The pathfinders were not so lucky. An imprecise drop and insufficient time
left them unable to properly mark the drop zones. The drops of the 7th, 12th,
and 13th Battalions of the 5th Brigade, led by General Poett, were terribly
scattered and forced to assemble under difficult conditions.

While the engineers worked to construct a landing zone for gliders soon to
arrive, the 3rd Brigade set out to capture the Merville Battery. Meanwhile, the 8th
Battalion and the Canadians were to destroy the five bridges over the Dives River.
Both units had bad drops, as a number of their pilots confused the Orne and the
Dives. Many misdropped troopers died when they became bogged down in
the marshes or hung up on trees in the Bavent woods. It took a great deal of

The liberation of Saint-Marcouf. Soldiers off the beaches march through the town to the delight of Jean Tissier, an eighteen-year-old citizen. *NARA*

"It only hurts when I laugh, doc!" Lieutenant Beaudin, a 508th PIR medic, sports a German cap, while his buddy, a fellow medic with a head wound, takes a swig of wine. *NARA*

Corporal William Judd, 325th Glider Infantry Regiment (GIR), informs his superiors of the situation at Etienville, near Picauville. *NARA*

These 325th GIR troops have set up a water-cooled machine gun in the bank of a hedgerow. *NARA*

An 82nd Airborne medic bandages a German prisoner, who will be treated and then evacuated to a POW camp in England. *NARA*

South of Carentan, paratroopers from the 82nd and 101st engaged in battle at Graignes. When the paratroopers were forced to withdraw, the Germans executed the wounded they left in the church, along with the two parish priests. *Dominique François*

PRIVATE MARCUS HEIM

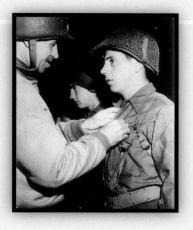

A BAZOOKA MAN in Company A, 505th Parachute Infantry Regiment, Private Heim was posted beside the bridge at La Fière on June 6. For holding their position and knocking out three tanks, Marcus Heim and Leonard Peterson received the Distinguished Service Cross in a ceremony presided over by General Bradley. Those who witnessed their heroic actions later stated that they should have received the Congressional Medal of Honor. *Image credit: Dominique François*

Nurses of the 325th GIR at Etienville use enemy vehicles to evacuate the wounded after rapid treatment at an aid station set up in a barn. *NARA*

Lieutenant Colonel Maloney, 507th PIR. He and his men played a crucial role in the battle for La Fière Causeway. *Dominique François*

LIEUTENANT FRANCIS "FRANK" NAUGHTON

ALONG WITH APPROXIMATELY 180 other paratroopers, Lieutenant Naughton of the 507th Parachute Infantry Regiment was misdropped near Graignes, twenty miles from his drop zone. With the help of local inhabitants, he and his unit held the village for nearly six days before a German division finally overran them. *Image credit: Col. Francis Naughton*

The entrance to Sainte-Mère-Église, which would serve as the temporary capital of Normandy. Broken walls testify to violent combat in the area. *NARA*

Sergeants Robert D. Henderson and Harvill W. Lazenby of the 505th PIR were dropped very far from their drop zone. It took them thirty-seven days to rejoin their unit. *NARA*

Troops of the 325th GIR are in a "liberated" Kettenkrad, a vehicle much appreciated by airborne forces. *NARA*

At Ravenoville, paratroopers from the 502nd PIR, 101st Airborne Division, use a French tracked vehicle captured from the Germans, who had earlier appropriated it from the French Army. The vehicle was manufactured by Renault. *NARA*

courage and solid survival skills for men to rejoin their respective units and orient themselves in an unknown landscape, far from their assigned objectives. Assembling approximately sixty men and a supply of explosives, Major Roseveare led his troops for ten kilometers to blow up the bridge between Troarn and Saint-Samson, on Route Nationale 815. Only after numerous difficulties and adventures were they able to rejoin their division.

THE MERVILLE BATTERY

The 3rd Brigade's objective was to seize the battery at Merville, a formidable base of operations where intelligence had identified four powerful guns capable of shelling the beaches at Ouistreham. The solidly defended position was surrounded by a network of barbed wire, antitank ditches, and mine fields. Heading the mission to destroy the menace was Lieutenant Colonel Otway, who received his orders in April. Working for several weeks with a contingent of seven hundred men, he methodically prepared the assault in the English countryside, where the site at Merville had been re-created in order to provide the best possible training. His men were divided into thirteen units, and each was assigned a precise mission: the plan even foresaw landing three gliders with a total of sixty men inside the enemy position.

A paratrooper rests for a moment, his back against a hedgerow. Normandy was won field by field through determined combat. *Dominique François*

CAPTAIN ROBERT RAE

CAPTAIN RAE WAS an officer in Service Company, 507th Parachute Infantry Regiment. For his heroic action at La Fière, he was awarded the Distinguished Service Cross by General Bradley.
Image credit: Albert Parker

A small artillery piece set up near Carentan on RN-13. The German tank in the background was knocked out just a few hours previously. *NARA*

General Gale, the British airborne commander during Operation Overlord. *IWM*

A railroad bridge in the Carentan sector blown up by German troops. Von der Heydte's paratroopers effectuated their withdrawal by train. *NARA*

British paratroopers proceed through a wheat field in Normandy after exiting their Horsa gliders. With landing zones in the open plain, English glider troops were luckier than their American counterparts, who often suffered from forced crash landings in hedgerow country. *IWM*

Major Howard's troops came in by glider to capture the Bénouville Bridge. They seized the bridge intact and held it until the arrival of Lord Lovat's commandos. *Dominique François*

Major Howard's men are seen on the bridge as soldiers sent to relieve them arrive from the British sector of the beachhead. *IWM*

British infantry soldiers cross the Bénouville Bridge, which their airborne troops have captured. The bridge was a vital objective on the march to Caen. *IWM*

General Gale engages in discussion with Lt. W. G. Rothschild at his CP in Ranville. *IWM*

"He who laughs last . . ." Private Watkins of the 12th Battalion, 6th Airborne Division, smiles a wide smile on rejoining his unit after four days alone behind enemy lines. *IWM*

In actuality, nothing happened as planned. Preliminary bombardment of the position missed the battery and destroyed the neighboring village, narrowly missing the pathfinders as they worked to clear the drop zones. Hit by flak, the glider carrying Lieutenant Colonel Otway crashed into the CP of a German battalion, causing the hastiest of deployments in chaotic conditions. Only 150 men managed to assemble. The only option was to act with the means at hand, for some men had landed as far as fifty kilometers from their objectives, and many others had drowned in the flooded marshes.

Such were the conditions when the paratroopers attacked, assaulting the battery without a mortar and with only one machine gun. Launched at 4:30 a.m., the assault, involving bloody, hand-to-hand combat, lasted barely a quarter of an hour. The troopers emerged victorious from this quick but violent confrontation, only to discover that the formidable cannons they had been sent to neutralize were nothing, in fact, but 75mm guns—much too small a caliber to be able to threaten the beaches!

Arriving with seventy-two gliders at 3:30 a.m., General Gale had every reason to be satisfied with his men, for the division had attained every one of its objectives.

A makeshift hospital is set up on Omaha Beach to care for the wounded before evacuation to England. *NARA*

9

THE BEACHES

OMAHA BEACH

One of the beaches destined for American landings, codenamed Omaha Beach, stretches east from the Baie des Veys over a band of coast extending from Vierville-sur-Mer to Colleville-sur-Mer. The distance measures six kilometers and is divided into eight sectors. The 1st Infantry Division, or "Big Red One," already famous at the time, conducted the first wave of the assault, accompanied by elements of the 29th Infantry Division.

Occupying the positions the Americans were tasked to take were elements of two enemy divisions of the *Heer* (army), the 352nd and 716th Infantry Divisions. Well protected by mines and barbed wire, German defenses relied on fortified bases of operation meant to stop an assault dead on the beaches.

Omaha is surmounted by a grassy plateau forty meters high, embedded among the cliffs. There are only five exits inland off the beaches. German fortifications were thus constructed with a view to several kinds of defense. The bunkers were equipped with 50mm and 75mm guns of French manufacture, 88mm guns, mortars, automatic flamethrowers, and tank turrets mounted in concrete. About one hundred machine guns, including Tobruk positions, or concrete gun emplacements, were also in place.

Other means, such as antitank walls and ditches designed to impede troop movement inland, rounded out the German defenses. On the beaches themselves, a variety of obstacles were placed to obstruct the progress of assailants, including tree trunks rigged with antitank mines and tetrahedra made from railroad rails.

It was vital for the Americans to seize the five exit draws and valleys leading into the interior so they could rapidly quit the beaches and find cover. Once they had taken the beaches, the troops were to head inland to establish a line running from Isigny, to the south of Tour-en-Bessin and Trevieres, to the northern line of demarcation at the Aure marshlands.

On the whole, the U.S. general command were well acquainted with German forces facing the American assault and had correctly identified the caliber of the heavy

Infantry soldiers wearing assault jackets transfer to a landing craft off the shore of Omaha Beach. *NARA*

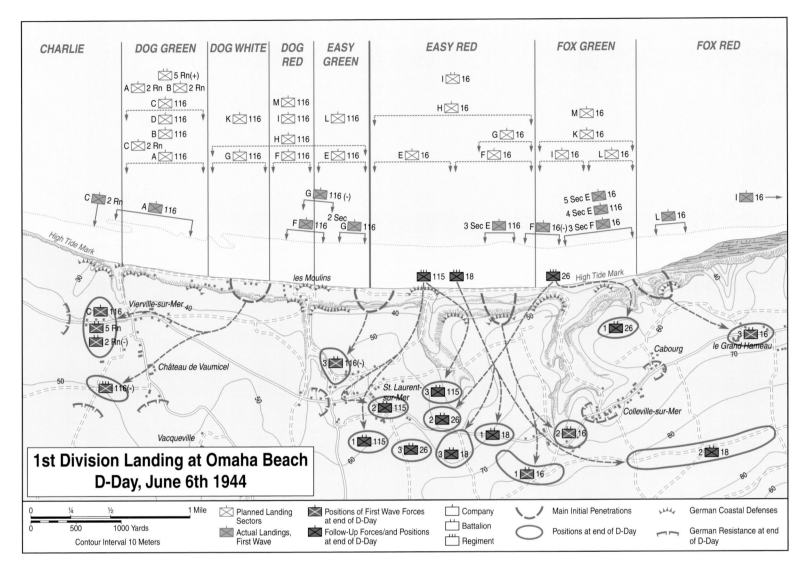

1st Division Landing at Omaha Beach
D-Day, June 6th 1944

CHARLIE   DOG GREEN   DOG WHITE   DOG RED   EASY GREEN   EASY RED   FOX GREEN   FOX RED

Legend:

Planned Landing Sectors	Positions of First Wave Forces at end of D-Day
Actual Landings, First Wave	Follow-Up Forces/and Positions at end of D-Day

Company	Main Initial Penetrations
Battalion	Positions at end of D-Day
Regiment	

German Coastal Defenses

German Resistance at end of D-Day

0 ¼ ½ 1 Mile
0 500 1000 Yards
Contour Interval 10 Meters

batteries in the sectors of assault, the presence of the German 716th Infantry Division, the location of major points of defense along the coast, and the various CPs in the sector. The American plan nevertheless presented a serious deficiency. The forces about to debark in Normandy were unaware that elements of the 352nd Infantry Division were positioned along the coast: the batteries of that division's 1st and 4th Artillery Groups were not to be found on any map of Normandy. Moreover, without consulting the German high command (OKW), Rommel had lined up an entire flak regiment consisting of approximately forty 88mm guns, whose presence the Allies totally ignored, behind Route Nationale 13 (RN-13). The Allied advance was considerably slowed by the 88s, which created many road blocks for the GIs. The Americans thus would face not only the 716th Infantry Division waiting on the beaches, but also an entire regiment of the 352nd Infantry Division supported by two artillery groups and a flak regiment!

At 5:55 a.m. on June 6, the Eighth Air Force began to soften up the areas behind Omaha Beach, dropping bombs in the Vierville sector. The countryside around Formigny,

Smoke screens were laid down along the shore in the effort to conceal debarking troops from enemy fire. *NARA*

At 6:30 a.m., first-wave troops from the 29th Infantry Division and the 1st Infantry Division debarked at Saint-Laurent. *NARA*

Surrain, and Louvières was particularly affected. To the west, other planes flew over Pointe du Hoc, dropping hundreds of tons of bombs at approximately 5:00 a.m.

Heavy bombing of target areas on the beaches began at 5:50 a.m. and continued until 6:30 a.m. Bombs fell on the beach exits, and destroyers took aim on the major points of defense. Unfortunately, it was impossible to actually observe the results of the attack, for if they had been known, it may well have changed the course of the battle. Most of the navy's firepower missed its objectives. When the first GIs hit the beach, German defenses largely remained intact.

The mission of the 1st Infantry Division was to wage a frontal assault with two reinforced infantry regiments on the western side of Omaha Beach. The 16th Regimental Combat Team (RCT) landed in the eastern subsectors (Easy Red and Fox Green) of the front, an area three thousand meters wide, with two battalions leading the charge and a battalion of reinforcements assigned to the three subsectors. The Provisional Ranger Force, composed of the 2nd Ranger Battalion and the 5th Ranger Battalion, was attached to the 116th Infantry Regiment and assigned to the right flank. Three companies of the 2nd Ranger Battalion attacked Pointe du Hoc, while one company of the battalion was engaged on Charlie (codename for Omaha Beach's western sector).

Five minutes before H-Hour, duplex-drive (DD) tanks from B and C Companies of the 743rd Tank Battalion were planned to land on Dog Green and Dog White. Equipped with propellers and flotation skirts, the amphibious tanks could be launched into the waves six kilometers from shore and, once ashore, engage the enemy to cover the assault of first-wave troops.

Such was the plan envisioned by the Allied high command. The men who landed on the beaches quickly discovered a different reality.

While the initial assault was subjected to heavy enemy fire, by the afternoon the beachhead was largely obstructed by vehicles as troops made their way forward.

Both images: NARA

With the rising tide behind them, first-wave soldiers were blocked on the beach, facing furious fire from German fortifications. *NARA*

Zie Kommen!

On the German side, troops watched tranquilly over the beach at Omaha. Although there was no doubt that the Allies would soon land and open another front, the assault was expected at Pas-de-Calais, and hence on the beach at Vierville. And so, the troops at Omaha dreamed serenely on.

The first to spy the invasion fleet was Maj. Werner Pluskat, the officer in charge of four coastal batteries attached to the 352nd Infantry Division, including twenty cannons covering the entire length of the shoreline where the debarkation would take place. In response to Allied bombing of his sector, Major Pluskat was ordered to his forward CP at Sainte-Honorine. Scrutinizing the horizon with his powerful binoculars from the vantage of his cliff-top bunker overlooking the beach, he at first saw nothing to arouse suspicion. Then, at daybreak, as he was preparing to leave his post, a swarm of phantasmagoric shapes suddenly appeared: hundreds and hundreds of ships, of all shapes and sizes!

Major Pluskat leapt to the telephone, alerting 325th Infantry Division Headquarters. "If you don't believe me, just come over here and see for yourself! It's incredible! It's unbelievable!" he shouted to the skeptical officer on the other end of the line. Asked which direction the armada was heading, the major, beside himself, cried out, "Straight at me!"

H-Hour: The First Wave:

Packed into LCAs and LCVPs, American infantrymen forged through the waves toward the beaches with ready arms and an unbearable sense of apprehension. The officers aboard knew that only one out of two soldiers would survive the frontal assault.

Eight American companies approached the coast veiled by the smoke from smoke bombs: facing them, between six hundred and eight hundred Germans from the 716th

Infantry Division and the 352nd Infantry Division lay in wait, well protected by casemates and trenches.

In the sector of the 16th RCT, the landing plan was analogous to that of the 116th Infantry Regiment. Company B of the 741st Tank Battalion would land on Easy Red and C Company on Fox Green. Companies from the 16th Infantry Regiment would then debark; E and F Companies were to take Easy Red, and I and L Companies were assigned Fox Green.

At H-Hour, 6:30 a.m., A Company, 166th Infantry Regiment, landed under extraordinarily intense fire on Dog Beach, facing Vierville. Caught in the heavy fusillade of enfilading machine gun fire, men fell dead right and left, or were paralyzed by terror. Some took shelter behind the tetrahedra or other obstacles on the beach. Shouting encouragement, their officers urged them on, but the troops could not advance into the hell raining down on them. Off the coast, the troop transports were also under heavy enemy fire, and an LCA was sunk, taking solders from A Company down with it. The company paid a very heavy price in the very first moments of the assault on Omaha Beach.

Further east, G Company disembarked on a sector of beach protected by smoke from the earlier bombardment. Ten minutes later, they were assembled and ready for action. Consulting among themselves, their officers realized they had landed in the wrong sector and debated what to do. On Easy Beach, the other boatloads of G Company men also came under machine gun fire and shelling.

The first of the many wounded hug the wall of the cliff, taking cover from enemy fire. The first dramatic hours of battle on "Bloody Omaha" cost many American lives. *NARA*

On Fox Red, soldiers who have just crossed through hell shelter themselves briefly behind a rock shelf, the look of terror still in their eyes. *NARA*

Working in sand and water, medics administer first aid to wounded men who have fallen to enemy machine gun fire. *Both images: NARA*

Soldiers from the 3rd Battalion, 16th Infantry Regiment on Fox Red, loaded down with heavy weapons and equipment, advance along the base of a cliff before assaulting WN-60, a *widerstandneste*, or German strongpoint. *NARA*

A soldier still under the shock of violent combat rests for a moment covered with a blanket. *NARA*

In turn, F Company arrived on Dog Red. A third of the men were decimated at the shoreline, while others, like those of G Company, were able to gain some concealment from smoke billowing down from the cliffs. A single word sums up the situation: panic. As for E Company, 116th, assigned to the Easy Green sector, landings were scattered widely from Easy Red to Fox Green, in the middle of the zone assigned to the 1st Infantry Division.

The assault of the 29th Infantry Division threatened to turn into a blood-soaked failure. Its survivors were prostrate, incapable of advancing. Nearly all of their officers and NCOs had been killed, and their supporting tanks had gone up in flames one after another.

The Special Engineer Task Force, made up of engineers and sappers, was planned to land with two companies from the 299th Engineers just a few minutes before H-Hour but in fact arrived only in the Easy Red sector. Their mission was to clear the obstacles from the beaches in order to permit the debarkation of troops who would later arrive at high tide. Conditions made it impossible for them to carry out their mission. Infantry-men everywhere sheltered behind the obstacles, thus preventing their destruction, and only five of the sixteen teams of engineers landed in their assigned sectors. The last of these teams arrived on Omaha at 7:30 a.m.

Tanks from the 741st and 743rd Tank Battalions were planned to support the first-wave assault. The forty or so Shermans, some of which were amphibious DD tanks, were immediately taken under antitank fire, and an LCT was sunk off the coast at Vierville. By 6:35, only about thirty tanks were left to support the 29th Infantry Division. The decision was made to employ DD tanks in the sector assigned to the 16th RCT. Only three

Seriously wounded men on litters at Fox Red await urgent medical evacuation to England. *NARA*

of the thirty-some tanks that took to the water managed to make it ashore. A Company, supported by standard Shermans rather than the modified DD tanks, succeeded in landing approximately fifteen tanks, which immediately engaged the enemy. About thirty other tanks arrived over the morning to the aid of the 16th RCT.

The first wave of the assault on Omaha had been partly decimated. Others remained flattened on the beach, unable to move.

A medic with a facial wound comes to the aid of soldiers beneath a sheltering cliff. A number of the men have been wounded in the head. *NARA*

Pointe du Hoc

Pointe du Hoc, one of the few rocky outcrops on the Normandy coast, is situated between Omaha Beach and Utah Beach. The Germans had installed artillery and infantry positions at its summit, unassailable by sea. The Allied high command had received conflicting information from the French Resistance indicating that the battery contained large-caliber guns that would endanger the landings at Omaha. It was thus decided to eliminate the position, a task assigned to Lieutenant Colonel Rudder's rangers.

The two hundred men of the 2nd Ranger Battalion had the mission of assaulting Pointe du Hoc by sea and scaling the cliff. At 7:40 a.m., twenty minutes behind schedule, the first rangers reached the shingle at the foot of the cliff and were taken under lateral machine gun fire. The rangers threw grapnels and rope ladders up onto the cliffs in a battle scenario recalling the vertical assaults of castle walls in the Middle Ages. Amidst a hail of bullets, rangers began their ascent, while others fell victim to the fire of hidden German

A soldier who has just come out of the water gazes on the bodies of those unluckier than him, who drowned in the effort to reach the beach after their landing craft exploded. *NARA*

riflemen firing from above. Less than five minutes after the assault began, a group of rangers had reached the top and took off in three different directions.

The men advanced through a rocky terrain resembling a lunar landscape. Everything had been plowed from the ground, and the entire position was riddled with bomb craters. The bullets flew at them from every seeming direction.

Arriving at the top, Rudder took command and ordered the rangers to proceed. Teams arriving at the summit next cautiously approached the gun emplacements. To their grand consternation, the 155mm guns that so concerned the high command were nowhere to be seen! Heading toward the interior, the rangers reached the coastal road later in the morning, suffering new losses on the way by falling victim to snipers or artillery fire. Rangers from Company F later discovered the five artillery guns hidden in a little lane and finally destroyed them.

But the Germans had managed to recover themselves. Soon, the rangers would be pitted against elements of the II/914 and the 9/726, supported by artillery from the 352nd Infantry Division and antiaircraft guns from the Flak Abteilung 32. At the site of the battery itself, the Germans managed to sneak up on the rangers' positions. Rudder's men were scattered, and they endured a hard battle at close quarters amidst much confusion.

During the afternoon, thirty more men and supplies arrived by LCVP. Pushed back by German counterattacks, all the rangers withdrew to Pointe du Hoc. By the end of the battle on June 8, seventy-seven members of the 2nd Ranger Battalion had been killed. Of the entire battalion, only 120 men remained standing.

A sailor still in shock flattens himself against the foot of the cliff. His landing craft was probably sunk on the way into shore. *NARA*

The second wave of American troops arrives on Omaha before the beach is cleared and while the Germans still hold the high ground. *NARA*

Infantry soldiers in a lifeboat have managed to escape drowning. As was often the case, they will arrive on shore exhausted, without their weapons and unable to fight. *NARA*

In a makeshift medical ward, a nurse gives a wounded soldier an infusion. Beneath his head, his life preserver serves as a pillow. *NARA*

Beach battalions take care of men who arrive on shore exhausted by their struggle in the water before they have even begun to fight the enemy. *NARA*

Second-wave soldiers debark on Fox Red under protective cliff banks. *NARA*

As they advance from the beach, troops must immediately attack enemy fortifications blocking their advance. Here, two infantry engineers use a flamethrower to take out an artillery position. *NARA*

Debarkation of the Second Wave

At 7:00 a.m. in the 29th Infantry Division's sector, the remaining companies debarked, following the disaster of first-wave troops partially annihilated in the first hour of combat. Along the shore and further out to sea, sinking landing craft forced the troops into the waves, leaving them no solution but to wade or attempt to swim to shore as best they could, loaded down with heavy equipment. Many of the soldiers who made it to shore had lost their weapons and were unable to fight. The survivors took two hours to reach the beaches: almost all of their heavy equipment had been lost or rendered unfit for use.

One company was scattered from Charlie to Dog Red, and three landing craft hit the shore opposite the D1 Exit. Another company landed at 7:10 near Hamel-au-Prêtre. Here, sheltered by the seawall, almost all equipment was intact, and squads began to organize within the Dog White sector. Meanwhile, a company of first-wave troops moved laterally toward the Dog White sector to which it had been assigned, attaining the area around 8:30 a.m.

Major Bingham, landing with forward headquarters behind the remnants of F Company, 116th, launched an attack against enemy positions on the facing bluffs. Their rifles jammed up on them, forcing the fifty GIs in the mission to take cover against a

This German soldier was buried alive when a shell exploded in a trench outside his bunker. *NARA*

Infantry soldiers come to the rescue of men still fighting the waves. Many soldiers drowned before they even touched the soil of Normandy. *NARA*

An 88mm gun captured at Vierville-sur-Mer. *NARA*

After its capture, the bunker at strong point WN-65, seen from behind, became the American command post for organizing the beaches. *NARA*

A barrage balloon lies on the roof of an 88mm gun emplacement at Vierville-sur-Mer. *NARA*

Once the beachhead is secured, vehicles and tanks arrive en masse on Omaha Beach, ready to head inland. By nightfall on June 6, thirty-four thousand troops had landed at Omaha. *NARA*

Numerous landing craft were destroyed or sunk at Omaha. The lack of sufficient landing craft, in turn, set back the Allied invasion of southern France until August 1944. *NARA*

Access inland has been secured, and troops and vehicles head for the heartland of Normandy. The next objective is to link Omaha and Utah Beaches. *NARA*

This rapidly constructed artificial port served Allied needs before the capture of the deep-water port at Cherbourg. *NARA*

An aerial reconnaissance photo of the coast of Normandy before the Allied invasion. *NARA*

A German prisoner receives first aid before his evacuation to England. *NARA*

house on the beach at about 7:30 a.m. All attempts at radio contact with other elements of the division failed because of malfunctioning equipment.

The 121st Engineer Battalion began to debark toward 7:10 a.m. in the sector assigned to the 29th Infantry Division, losing a large portion of their equipment on the beach at Vierville. On the beaches assigned to the 16th RCT, the last company finally debarked at the end of the beach. Losses here were also heavy, including their company commander, who was killed in the landing. Company G managed to join up with the first-wave survivors from E Company, 16th RCT, and E Company, 116th Infantry Regiment. Fifteen minutes later, they were engaging the enemy with machine guns and mortar fire.

H Company, 16th RCT, ended up at a strong point at the E3 Exit, where few had landed before them, and were completely blocked by the enemy for several hours. Meanwhile, K Company, 16th RCT, would lose fifty-some solders and four officers on D-Day, most of them killed on the beach. The company landed in two distinctly separate groups, which only contributed to the confusion. The 37th and 1st Engineer Battalions landed in scattered fashion all along the 1st Division beaches. Debarking later, Gen. Norman Cota and General Canham were able to organize an assault on the

As the engineers clear the beaches, thousands of obstacles planted by the Germans are piled up along the shore. Those pictured here, tetrahedra, or element-C obstacles, were popularly known as hedgehogs. The metal rods were flattened at the ends so they would not sink into the sand. Later, American engineers ingeniously adapted them into huge forks and attached them to the front of Sherman tanks, thus permitting them to plow through the Norman hedgerows. *NARA*

A recently captured bunker shows the scars of violent combat. *NARA*

Another view of WN-65, captured by the 1st Infantry Division and used as a triage center on the evening of June 6. *NARA*

Thousands of ships daily delivered the men, vehicles, and weapons necessary for Operation Overlord to succeed. *NARA*

The American flag flies proudly over one of the principal fortifications on Omaha Beach after a hard-won victory. The casualty list for D-Day on Omaha Beach alone numbered 3,881 dead, wounded, and missing. *NARA*

Soldiers from the 29th Infantry Division who have just made it off the beach question a local inhabitant about the location of enemy positions. *NARA*

bluffs from the Dog White sector, where the forward headquarters of the 116th Infantry Regiment was posted. The generals immediately set to reorganize the troops and remotivate the exhausted soldiers.

The afternoon of June 6, assaults on Saint-Laurent were carried out by the 116th Infantry Regiment, soon to be supported from the 115th approaching from the northeast. The solders succeeded in capturing part of the village and reorganized their artillery that evening.

Widerstandneste 62 (WN-62), the major nest of resistance in the sector, finally fell at 2:30 p.m., giving the Americans access to the Colleville exit. Many furious battles took place in this wooded region, where German reinforcements had already arrived. Blocked at the E3 Exit, the engineers constructed a route parallel to the shore running to the F1 Exit, and by evening, twenty Shermans from the 746th Tank Battalion were rolling down the road. The D3 Exit at Moulins was still under fire from the German strong point to its east, but American engineers nevertheless managed to fill in the anti-tank ditches by 8:00 p.m.

In the area around Vierville, the D1 Exit was finally opened to traffic late in the evening, although troops were able to advance only a few kilometers. Around 9:00 p.m., the 26th Infantry Regiment landed opposite the E3 Exit and positioned two battalions east of Saint-Laurent and one north of Colleville to protect the left flank of the 16th RCT.

As night fell on June 6, Allied leaders reviewing strategy were faced with a terrible reality. At every level, the assault had been a disaster. Colleville and Saint-Laurent had only been captured at nightfall. Vierville, occupied since noon, had held, despite a counterattack by German paratroopers.

The 2nd Ranger Battalion on the cliffs of Pointe du Hoc exchange fire with a solidly entrenched enemy protected by bunkers and trenches. *NARA*

By battle's end, Lieutenant Colonel Rudder's rangers had lost seventy-seven men in the effort to seize control of cannons that were not in their expected positions. *NARA*

The situation at Omaha Beach remained precarious. Thirty-four thousand men had waged the assault, but the beachhead was still only one to two kilometers wide and seven kilometers long. Only one of the four exit draws leading to the interior could accommodate vehicles. The majority of Allied artillery, tanks, transmission equipment, matériel, and supplies lay at the bottom of the ocean. Finally, nearly three thousand dead and wounded testified to the heavy human cost of the longest day on this sector of the beach, henceforth and forever known as "Bloody Omaha."

UTAH BEACH

The southeastern coast of the Cotentin Peninsula and the countryside behind it was chosen as the second American landing beach. Success in this delicate sector depended on the combined efforts of the 101st Airborne Division, commanded by General Taylor, and the 4th Infantry Division, under the orders of General Barton. This was also a vital sector, meant to provide a base for forces departing for Cherbourg, which the Allies needed to capture as quickly as possible. Finally, if all else failed, this area, codenamed Utah, would act as a fallback, providing an entry of last resort onto the Continen Peninsula. The success of Utah Beach was thus essential.

Located north of the Baie des Veys, the delineated sector extended along the coast between the dunes at Varreville and Beau-Guillot and stretching along either side of the road from Audouville-la-Hubert to the sea, opposite the village of Sainte-Marie-du-Mont. The objective of the landing was a gray sand beach leading to a band of low dunes about four meters high, which covered approximately six meters of terrain. Beyond the dunes, the Germans had flooded a low-lying area. About three kilometers past the flooded zone, the terrain rose up to an altitude of thirty meters near villages overlooking the coast at the edge of hedgerow country.

The importance of the exits at Utah Beach was strikingly clear: if the Germans managed to hold them, a monstrous traffic jam would ensue, cutting the paratroopers off from seaborne forces. Two beaches comprised the sector planned for the landings: Tare Green and Uncle Red, to the south. These two beaches stretched from Exit 3 to Exit 4, located just before an important German stronghold.

Ships from the American fleet's Task Force 125 opposite Utah Beach are protected from enemy air attack by barrage balloons. *NARA*

As at Omaha, the Germans planted a variety of beach obstacles at Utah Beach on the orders of Field Marshal Rommel. *NARA*

Although the Germans resisted at Utah Beach, American losses were less heavy than those they suffered at Omaha. *NARA*

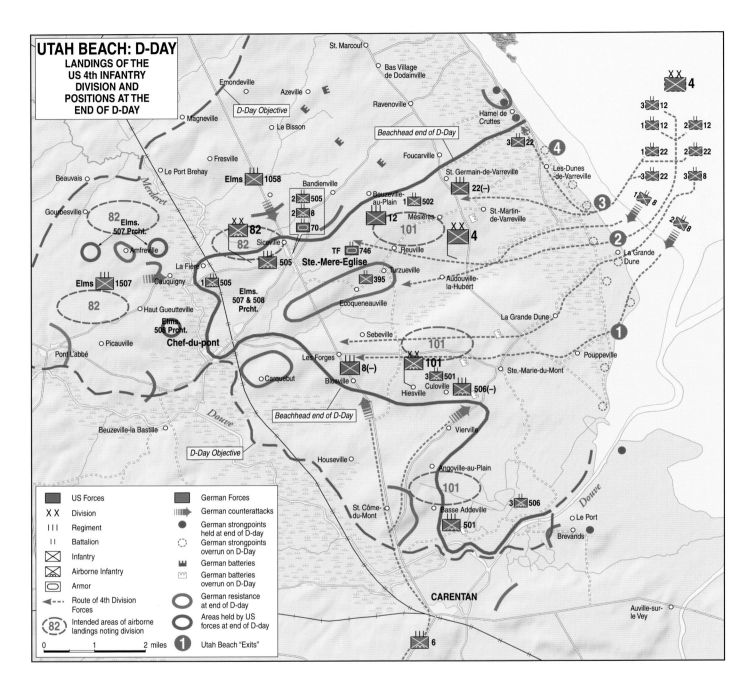

UTAH BEACH: D-DAY
LANDINGS OF THE
US 4th INFANTRY
DIVISION AND
POSITIONS AT THE
END OF D-DAY

Legend:

	US Forces		German Forces
X X	Division	⫸	German counterattacks
I I I	Regiment	●	German strongpoints held at end of D-day
I I	Battalion	○	German strongpoints overrun on D-day
⊠	Infantry		German batteries
⊠	Airborne Infantry		German batteries overrun on D-day
▭	Armor		
◄---	Route of 4th Division Forces	◯	German resistance at end of D-day
(82)	Intended areas of airborne landings noting division	◯	Areas held by US forces at end of D-day
	0 1 2 miles	➊	Utah Beach "Exits"

The honor of the first-wave assault devolved to the 4th Infantry Division, to be followed by the 90th Infantry Division. Sailing in separate convoys, 865 ships made for Utah Beach, after a detachment had secured Isle Saint-Marcouf, located off the shore of the peninsula, at 4:30. The 4th Infantry Division and the 90th Infantry Division were to create a beachhead, then race for Cherbourg, while the 9th Infantry Division would debark on D-plus-4 and capture the northwestern zone of the peninsula. The 70th Infantry Division, planned to land on D-plus-8, was held as VII Corps reserve.

German defenses built along an antitank wall contained a number of strong points, including small-caliber cannons and machine gun nests. Early on the morning of June 6,

Along the dunes at La Madeleine, the 4th Infantry Division assaults German fortifications defending the beach. *NARA*

a commando group with blackened faces set foot on the Isle of Saint-Marcouf, opposite Utah Beach, with the mission of destroying any cannons on the island. Other than minefields, which wounded several men, the island was deserted and devoid of artillery.

At 6:00 a.m., ships from Task Force 123, crossing opposite the shore, opened fire on the coastal batteries and beach defenses. The battleship USS *Nevada* bombarded the battery at Azeville, containing four 105mm guns. *Erebus*, a British ship, attacked artillery positions at Pernelle, north of Quettehou, where 170mm guns, camouflaged among the hills, menaced Utah Beach until June 18. The warships USS *Tuscaloosa* and USS *Quincy* hit Mont-Coquerel and the Crisbecq Battery at Saint-Marcouf, which boasted three 210mm cannons capable of a range of twenty-seven kilometers.

At 6:40 a.m., Companies E and F of the 8th RCT hit the beach at the Tare Green sector of Utah, opposite a German nest of resistance, W5. The rest of the first wave—Companies B and C, accompanied by DD tanks from Companies A and B of the 70th Tank Battalion—arrived ten minutes later. The Americans quickly realized they had landed outside their assigned zone, 1,800 meters farther south than initially planned. A rapid decision was imperative.

Brigadier General Theodore Roosevelt, President Roosevelt's cousin and second in command of the 4th Infantry Division, had landed with the first wave. He immediately sent a reconnaissance patrol into the interior, while the rest of his men attacked German

By nightfall on June 6, twenty thousand men have debarked on Omaha Beach, and almost seventeen vehicles of all sorts are headed west into the Norman countryside. *NARA*

Soldiers arriving on Utah Beach battled to link up with paratroopers from the 82nd and 101st Airborne Divisions. Contact took place at midday in the area of Pouppeville. *NARA*

A dead German infantry soldier, killed at the entrance to his bunker at La Madeleine. *NARA*

The 12th Infantry Division debarks at Utah Beach and heads for the beach exits secured by first-wave troops. *Both images: NARA*

Passing through Exit 1, Pouppeville and Sainte-Marie-du-Mont, the 2nd Battalion of the 8th Infantry reaches Les Forges on the main highway, RN-13. It will be reinforced by elements of the 70th Tank Battalion. *NARA*

defenses on the beach. A few minutes later, he decided to continue to debark in the same sector, which was less hostile and obstructed with fewer beach obstacles. Engineers immediately set to work clearing the beach of the few obstacles it contained and opening a passage in the antitank wall. One hour later, the beach had been cleared. By 8:00 a.m., the Americans had extended their authority over six hundred meters of shoreline. At approximately 9:30, the entire beach was under their control.

So it was that Colonel Van Fleet's 8th Infantry was completely assembled. It was joined at 7:45 a.m. by the 3rd Battalion, 22nd Infantry Regiment, which entirely debarked by 10:00.

The 1st Battalion, 8th Infantry advanced on the right, heading for La Madeleine and the German strong point W7. It proved necessary to use the Exit 3 roadway leading to Audouville-la-Hubert. One company sufficed to quiet the nest of enemy resistance, while the other two battalions headed in other directions. While 3rd Battalion moved toward Exit 2 and Vierville, the 2nd Battalion reached Exit 1 in the direction of Pouppeville by noon.

While advance elements were approaching the exits, men and equipment were flowing onto the beaches under sporadic fire from the batteries at Azeville and Saint-Marcouf. At 10:00 a.m., the 8th Infantry Division advanced toward the interior. At noon, the 12th Infantry Regiment, part of the 4th Infantry Division, began to debark.

continued on page 160

A view of Utah Beach after American troops had established a solid hold over the sector. The objective in upcoming days was to consolidate the beachhead by linking up to troops on Omaha. *NARA*

Troops take off toward the Norman countryside to reinforce the beachhead. To the right side of the horizon is the Maison Rouge, the famous Red House that served as a landmark for the landings on Utah Beach. *NARA*

The formidable Crisbecq Battery at Saint-Marcouf, whose deadly 210mm cannons, capable of a range of twenty-seven kilometers, sunk ships off the coast of Utah and steadily shelled the beach. American infantry soldiers were finally able to destroy the cannons. *NARA*

The beach exit at La Madeleine. The presence of British soldiers in the photo most likely date it to several days after D-Day, after the beaches were consolidated. *NARA*

The command post on Utah Beach for thousands of troops in the 4th Infantry Division under the command of General Barton. *NARA*

continued from page 157

At noon, German artillery east of the Baie des Veys entered the scene, opening fire on Utah Beach. In spite of this interdicting fire, the Americans inexorably continued to advance inland.

Passing through Exit 1, Pouppeville, and Saint-Marie-du-Mont, the 2nd Battalion, 8th Infantry, reached Les Forges on RN-13. It was reinforced by elements of the 70th Tank Battalion. Both battalions were thus in position at this crucial crossroads, which led north to Sainte-Mère-Église, west to Chef-du-Pont, south to Carentan, and east to

One of the German cannons that took soldiers of the 4th Infantry Division under direct fire, rendered silent after the first day of battle. The photo shows one of the many soldiers who assisted the immense armada to debark, seated on the front of the cannon, looking out to sea. *NARA*

The battle over, an engineer measures the depth of impact of American weapons fire on the metal shield to an enemy machine gun. *NARA*

Now that all is quiet on the beach at La Madeleine, the immense American armada engaged in the "Great Crusade" is free to pursue its course. *NARA*

Convoys are organized after the beach has been secured. *NARA*

The second wave debarks on Utah Beach. On the horizon, slightly left of center and partially obscured, is the Maison Rouge, the single dwelling on the beach. *NARA*

Engineers lay grids over the sand opposite the exit draws to help get vehicles moving off the beach. *NARA*

Viewed from the interior of a fortification on Utah Beach, landing craft approach the shore at La Madeleine. *NARA*

Sainte-Marie-du-Mont. The first tie-in with paratroopers, the 3rd Battalion, 501st PIR, took place at Pouppeville toward 1:00 p.m.

Toward nightfall, the amphibious arm of the 82nd Airborne Division, Task Force C, landed to reinforce the paratroopers. Company C of the 746th Tank Battalion and ninety men from the 325th GIR, commanded by Col. Edson Raff, were sent to Sainte-Mère-Église to reinforce the embattled 505th PIR.

At the end of the first day of combat, the 8th and 22nd Infantry Regiments had suffered 118 losses, of which only twelve were KIA. The total losses for the 4th Infantry Division numbered 197 men.

A forward observer (FO) radios artillery coordinates to a ship off the beach, allowing navy artillery to adjust its line of fire on enemy positions. *NARA*

DUKWs go back and forth between ships and delivery points on the beach, ferrying in matériel. Pronounced "ducks," the name of this amphibious vehicle derived from military shorthand: D (year of design, 1942), U (amphibious utility vehicle), K (all-wheel drive), W (two powered rear axles). *NARA*

Although all the objectives of D-Day were not attained—in particular, the linkup with the 82nd Airborne, which remained isolated at Sainte-Mère-Église and along the banks of the Merderet River—over twenty thousand men, seventeen thousand vehicles, and 1,700 tanks had landed on Utah Beach and were ready for offensive action on D-plus-1.

GOLD BEACH

The westernmost of the three invasion beaches assigned to units of the English Commonwealth was divided into four sectors, running east to west: How, Item, Jig, and King. How signified Longues; Item was Arromanches; Jig was the code for Asnelles; and King was the hamlet of La Rivière. Together they made up the seventeen kilometers of shoreline known as Gold Beach.

The invasion of Gold Beach fell to the 50th Infantry Division of the British Second Army, whose mission was to establish a bridgehead from Arromanches to Ver-sur-Mer and then head in the direction of RN-13, the highway linking Caen to Bayeux. The division was slated to meet up with the landing forces from Omaha Beach at Port-en-Bressin. On

At Lion-sur-Mer, the German 761st Infantry Division installed beach defenses, like this "Stalin's Organ," mounted on a French tracked vehicle. *BA*

British troops from the 2nd Infantry Division debark at Colleville-sur-Orne on Sword Beach, with the mission to capture Caen. *Imperial War Museum IWM*

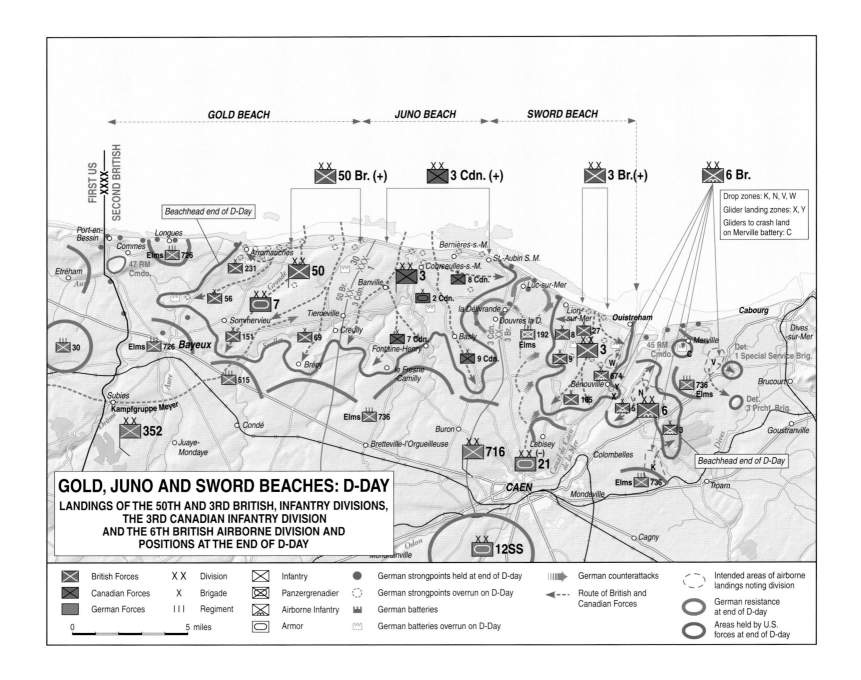

GOLD, JUNO AND SWORD BEACHES: D-DAY

LANDINGS OF THE 50TH AND 3RD BRITISH, INFANTRY DIVISIONS,
THE 3RD CANADIAN INFANTRY DIVISION
AND THE 6TH BRITISH AIRBORNE DIVISION AND
POSITIONS AT THE END OF D-DAY

⊠ British Forces	X X Division	⊠ Infantry	● German strongpoints held at end of D-day	⤳ Intended areas of airborne landings noting division
⊠ Canadian Forces	X Brigade	⊠ Panzergrenadier	⌣ German strongpoints overrun on D-Day	
▬ German Forces	‖‖ Regiment	⊠ Airborne Infantry	⌷ German batteries	◯ German resistance at end of D-day
0 5 miles		⊟ Armor	⌷ German batteries overrun on D-Day	◯ Areas held by U.S. forces at end of D-day

German counterattacks ⫸

Route of British and Canadian Forces ◄---

its left, the Canadian 3rd Infantry Division was also to advance toward RN-13 and capture Carpiquet, the airfield at Caen. After the initial assault by the 69th and 231st Infantry
Brigades, the 56th and 151st Infantry Brigades, held in reserve, were to advance southwest,
supported by the 8th Armoured Brigade. H-Hour in the sector was 7:25 a.m.

Facing them to the east, German troops in the village of Ver-sur-Mer consisted of the
4/441 Ost.Abt (a battalion of Eastern European troops) and the 7/736 Infantry Regiment,
716th Infantry Division. Strong points in this part of the British sector principally consisted
of 50mm guns in concrete emplacements, 75mm guns installed in pillboxes, and two 88s,
one at each extremity of the 50th Infantry Division's zone of assault.

On Queen Red, British Hussar tanks are quickly on the scene attacking enemy fortifications. *IWM*

To the west of the sector, opposite Asnelles, the 1/916 of the 325th Infantry Division was spread out in *widerstandnesten* bordering the beach. In the center, the cordon of dunes behind the marshes was held by Osttruppen, or Eastern troops (the 3/341), positioned to guard a lane leading from the beach into the marshes. Behind these positions were several artillery batteries covering the beaches. In the area south of Creuilly, the Germans could, moreover, call on eight 88s from Panzerjager-Abteilung 200 of the 21st Panzer Division, which was well positioned to stop any tanks from advancing on RN-13.

In preparation for the invasion, the Allies began to soften up the sector at 11:00 p.m. on June 5. Over a thousand heavy bombers from the RAF dropped six thousand tons of bombs on German batteries along the Normandy coast. In turn, five warships from K Force went into action, shelling artillery batteries and enemy positions along the beach.

The 1st Suffolk reorganizes on Queen White at approximately 8:40 on D-Day morning. *IWM*

On Queen Red, the second wave of the 1st Suffolk debarks in turn. *IWM*

All along the beach, British soldiers discovered remote-control devices called Goliaths. In actuality, they played little role in German beach defenses. *NARA*

On the Queen Red sector of Sword Beach, East Yorkshire soldiers move munitions to safety out of the path of vehicles. *IWM*

The British dug trenches at Hermanville-sur-Mer before heading on their mission inland. *IWM*

At 6:40 a.m. on June 6, the German battery at Longues again turned its guns against Allied ships off the beach. Toward 7:00 a.m., RAF fighter-bombers attacked nests of resistance on Gold Beach with missiles and bombs.

The first wave of the British assault took off a few minutes later. As they approached the coast, LSTs loaded with troops shot thousands of rockets onto the beach in a final artillery attack before the men hit the shore.

At 7:35 a.m., two companies of the 1st Hampshire Regiment debarked with slight casualties near the area known as "Les Roquettes," seized the enemy strong point, then bore toward Hamel. The casemates and fortifications at Hamel were still intact, although they had been targeted by aerial and naval bombardment and undergone Typhoon rocket attack just before H-Hour. The officer leading the battalion and his artillery observers were all hit, his radio equipment was destroyed, and the attack had bogged down. An assault was launched after the arrival of C and D Companies, but it lacked artillery support, and progress was slow and costly in terms of human lives.

Removing German beach obstacles, engineers on Sword Beach begin to clear a path for vehicles clogging the shore. *IWM*

Soldiers take a break at the shoreline of Sword Beach before taking up the march. By nightfall on June 6, thirty thousand men had landed in this section. *IWM*

Marching to the tune of bagpipes, the 7th Seaford Highlanders of the 15th Scottish Infantry Division cross an orchard shortly after dawn. *IWM*

Trucks and artillery pieces are unloaded on a section of Sword Beach that has just been cleared of obstacles. *IWM*

On D-Day afternoon, the 2nd Middlesex Regiment, the reserve for the British 3rd Infantry Division, moves through Hermanville-la-Brèche on tracked carriers. *IWM*

Using special equipment, the 6th Assault Regiment and B Squad of the Westminster Dragoons, aided by engineers, cleared the beach of obstacles under enemy fire. Tanks were destroyed in the enfilading fire of the German 88s. Given the huge losses, the survivors of A and C Companies combined into one group. General Stanier, commanding the operation, reorganized the troops, sending B Company from Asnelles to attack the strong point from the west, while C Company, Devons, landed at 8:15 a.m. and engaged the enemy. Thanks to the support of tanks and self-propelled guns from the 147th Rank Field Artillery Regiment, Hamel finally fell and was mopped up by 4:00 p.m.

Following the coastal road, Company D, 1st Hampshires, headed for Arromanches. Troops reached the city at approximately 8:00, and invested it by 9:00. By the night of June 6, the 1st Hampshire Regiment had paid the heavy price of 180 dead and many wounded, most of whom fell during the furious combat for Hamel.

For its part, the 1st Dorset debarked at 7:30 a.m. near Les Roquettes; Companies A and B headed west along the coast to attack their objective. Company C, part of the second wave, seized Les Roquettes, cleared out the sector, and left for Hamel to add its force to the 1st Hampshire Regiment. Company B of the 1st Dorset established a defensive cordon around the conquered territory. Meanwhile, A and D Companies headed directly inland. Arriving at Meuvaines at 9:30 a.m., they then headed west. Companies C and D launched an assault on German positions held by elements of the 1/916 at

British commandos depart from the beach at Colleville-sur-Orne, well prepared to accomplish their missions.
IWM

French troops from 4 Commando, 1st Special Service Brigade, head out of Hermanville toward their objective. *IWM*

A British infantry soldier loading a PIAT (projector, infantry, antitank). *NARA*

The same soldier, now ready to fire. A platoon-level antitank weapon, the PIAT had a reputation for imprecision. *NARA*

Riflemen from the Welsh Guards run across a road, ready to take aim on German positions at Gagny. *IWM*

Petit-Fontaine and Puits d'Hérode, south of Arromanches. The assault was supported by tanks from the Nottingham Yeomanry and self-propelled guns from the 90th Field Artillery Regiment. At the end of D-Day, the battalion numbered 128 dead, including fourteen officers.

The 47 (Royal Marine) Commando (attached to the 231st Brigade) landed at 8:30 a.m. near Les Roquettes and suffered heavy losses in men and matériel. Several landing craft were sunk before they touched the shore, lost to the storm and fire from well-entrenched enemy troops at Hamel. Nevertheless, approximately three hundred commandos assembled back of the beach, with the objective of seizing Port-en-Bessin. To do so, they would have to cross twelve kilometers of enemy terrain.

At 8:50, Maj. Patrick M. Donnell, second in command of the 47 (Royal Marine) Commando, assembled Troops B and X and a number of soldiers from Q Company. Troop A had debarked farther to the east and had assembled on the beach, but the whereabouts of Troop Y were unknown. Most of the arms of the heavy-weapons troops lay at the bottom of the Channel.

In the absence of contact with his commander, Lt. Col. C. Farndale Phillips, Major Donnell set off for Asnelles, crossing in the midst of a veritable traffic jam caused by the presence of self-propelled guns. Arriving at the church, the designated assembly point, he awaited the arrival of the rest of his unit with a sapper from the engineers, watching

During Operation Jupiter, the 43rd Infantry Division was positioned along the road to Caen. *IWM*

On June 26 during Operation Epsom, elements of the 15th Infantry Division battled it out in the tangled hedgerows. The soldiers shown here were taking cover on the now-famous Hill 112. *IWM*

Soldiers of the 3rd Infantry Division (identified as Private Clarke and Private Leech) man a Bren gun in the ruins at Banneville-la-Champagne. The name of this light machine gun combines the first two letters of Brno and Enfield—respectively, the Czech city where the weapon was designed, and the city of its manufacture at the British Royal Small Arms factory. *IWM*

Two soldiers from the 43rd Infantry Division dug in nice and deep. *IWM*

Commando troops move into town at Douvre-la-Délivrande as citizens watch in the foreground. *IWM*

Like their German counterparts, forward troops in British units often used bicycles. *NARA*

the lines of soldiers passing by. Were they Dorsets or Hampshires? In any case, they were not his men. Moving to the crossroads south of Saint-Côme-de-Fresné, the major waited longer still for the appearance of his troops, which finally arrived after the passage of Dorset elements. It was 2:00 p.m., and Port-en-Bressin was a long way off. Once assembled, the men headed toward Rosière, where they engaged enemy troops and were able to recover arms and ammunition from the Germans. After reaching Hill 72, the unit settled in for the night.

The second wave, the 2nd Devon Battalion, reserve forces for the 231st Brigade, landed on the beach at Les Roquettes, heavily encumbered with men and vehicles of all sorts. By the end of D-Day, the battalion had lost eighty men and officers.

At 11:00 a.m., the 151st and 56th Brigades landed in the King sector, with the mission of capturing the area to the east, north of Bayeux. The end of the day saw the arrival of the 153rd Brigade, 51st Infantry Division, and elements of the 7th Armoured Division. The 2nd Hertfordshire cleaned out Ver-sur-Mer, and a heavy flow of reinforcements and equipment poured onto the beaches.

Overall, the 50th Infantry Division had accomplished its D-Day objectives. In all, twenty-five thousand men had landed to carry out the mission. Compared to the situation on other beaches at the end of June 6, the beacheads at Gold and Juno were the most solidly established of all the invasion sites.

Snipers from No. 3 Commando are assigned their posts. Facing them are opponents from the 6th Company, 857th Regiment, 346th Infantry Division. *IWM*

A pair of infantrymen assaults the ruins of a farm, one armed with a Webley revolver, the other with a Lee-Enfield rifle. *IWM*

The No. 3 Commandos march down a narrow street in Colleville, where they are warmly welcomed by the townspeople. *IWM*

JUNO BEACH

Two brigades from the 3rd Canadian Infantry Division, composed of fifteen thousand Canadians and nine thousand British, were assigned to take the next beach over from Gold. This was Juno Beach, which stretched from Graye-sur-Mer through Courseulles and Saint-Aubin-sur-Mer. The objective was to establish a beachhead eighteen kilometers deep and to seize the Carpiquet airfield and the village of Authie, located on a dominant plateau northwest of Caen.

The town of Courseulles, at the center of the area slated for assault, was the most heavily fortified position to come under Canadian attack. A dozen antitank guns, mortars, and machine guns bristled from concrete structures manned by infantrymen and artillerymen from the 736th Infantry Regiment, 716th Infantry Division, commanded by General Richter.

The first sector of the beach, codenamed Nan Green, containing twelve casemates defended by a company of the 736th Infantry Regiment, had not been affected by preliminary bombardment.

At 7:55 a.m., the Regina Rifles charged from their LCA, preceded by fourteen Sherman DD tanks from Squadron B, 6th Armoured Regiment. Unfortunately, thirteen other tanks had previously sunk in the turbulent waves along the shore. Although the raging waves had damaged the flotation skirts of his tank, Major Duncan managed to reach the shore. Hitting the beach, he set the tracks of his tank in gear. The DD tanks immediately opened fire on the German positions.

A moment of respite for Warwickshire soldiers (197th Brigade, 59th Infantry Division) dug into a defensive position at Saint-Contest. *IWM*

Company A of the Regina Rifles touched the beach east of the mouth of the Seulles River later than scheduled, and all the DD tanks planned as support had been sunk. The Churchill and Centaur tanks of the 1st Royal Marine Regiment, intended to supply additional support, still remained in the LCTs. However, the excellent training the men had received under their company commander, Major Grosh, and their precise knowledge of the area helped to compensate for the absence of tank support. Position I, which contained a bunker with a PaK40 75mm antitank gun supported by machine guns and trenches full of flamethrowers, was particularly difficult to overcome. It would take the Centaurs' 95mm howitzers and all the skills of the 26th Engineers to neutralize the German 75mm and surrounding defenses. When the battle came to an end at 9:45 a.m., losses were unfortunately very heavy.

Company B had an easier task. Its objectives had already been attacked by DD tanks as they reached the sand all along the beachfront. The platoons crossed the beach and cleaned the houses of enemy soldiers, while the engineers used armored vehicles to open breaches in the beach wall for the passage of tanks.

While Company A went to the left of Position I, reserves debarking in the Nan Green sector discovered the tide had risen considerably, greatly reducing the depth of the beach. Company C, the first to land, followed the path opened by Company A. Directly following them, Company D suffered disaster when two of its assault boats encountered mined beach obstacles, with the loss of sixty men. Only fifty survivors managed to make it to shore.

A private identified as E. MacLaren mans a Bren gun through an opening in the wall of a ruined house. *IWM*

Two British solders on a country road check the identity of one of the local inhabitants. Although the vast majority of Normans joyfully welcomed the Allies, a few nevertheless continued to offer intelligence to the Germans. *IWM*

Company C was quick to occupy Courseulles-sur-Mer and install its CP in the center of the village. Meanwhile, Company B advanced toward the church and the village exit to the south. Their next objective was Reviers. Company B continued to clean out the residential part of the village, killing several snipers holed up in the houses.

Farther to the west in the Mike sector, the Royal Winnipeg Rifles of Lieutenant Colonel Meldram leapt into the waves as a salvo of well-adjusted mortar rounds hit their LCAs. Company B lost twenty-some men before they even touched the sand. A considerable battle took place, with the "Black Devils" using grenades to take out enemy machine gun positions. Several Shermans attempted to make it to shore but were rapidly hit by 88s and 75s positioned at the far edges of the beach. Furious hand-to-hand combat ensued with a determined enemy who refused to give up a single meter of terrain.

At 11:00 a.m., DD tanks from A Squadron finally landed, rolling out of their LCTs directly onto the beach. The 26th Armoured Engineers were already at work blowing up the remaining casemates. Leaving the dunes, Company B of the Winnipeg Rifles crossed the metal bridge over the river Seulles to mop up Valette. At 12:00 noon, Brig. Gen. Harry Foster, the commander of 7th Brigade, was able to cable his command ship, HMS *Hilary*, that the beaches at Mike and Nan Green had been cleared.

Soldiers enjoying a bit of fun play leapfog over hedgehogs on the beach after Sword, Juno, and Gold have been secured. The metal obstacles were later collected by the thousands and melted down to help relaunch the French economy. *IWM*

On Nan White in the Besnières sector, the assaulting battalion had the toughest time of any in the 3rd Canadian Division, largely because their supporting DD tanks were late in reaching the beach. At 8:05, the Queen's Own Rifles, commanded by Lieutenant Colonel Spragge, jumped into waist-high water and waded toward the beach. Companies A and B led the assault. Company B lost a third of its men in a section heavily defended by machine guns and two antitank guns. Major Oscar Dalton radioed the navy for assistance. Fifteen minutes later a ship appeared equipped with a six-hundred-meter-range 40mm Bofors gun, which rained down shells on the German bunkers. An assault of riflemen finally wiped out the strong point.

By 9:30, the sector was completely cleared. Company B had already occupied the village by the time the French Canadian unit from Quebec, the Regiment de La Chaudière, arrived, along with 105 self-propelled guns from the 14th Field Artillery Regiment. The village of Anguerny was reached by 5:30 p.m.

To the east, on the Nan Red sector, the 8th Brigade was assigned to capture Saint-Aubin-sur-Mer. The North Shore (New Brunswick) Regiment landed at 8:00 a.m. on the beaches west of Saint-Aubin, heavily defended by the Germans. The 48 (Royal Marine) Commando would then attack Langrune from positions secured by the North Shore. This latter would then march straight south toward Tailleville and the radar station at Basly-Douvres, the final D-Day objective. By the end of the day, the North Shore Regiment had succeeded in its mission to break through the Atlantic Wall at Saint-Aubin and capture the garrison at Tailleville, although Maj. Archie McNaughton and thirteen members of his regiment lost their lives in the battle for the garrison. Although the radar station was within rifle range, it was necessary for British I Corps to hold Basly under siege for eleven days before it could take control of the bastion.

On the night of June 6, the casualties at Juno Beach numbered 319 dead and 45 wounded or prisoners of war.

SWORD BEACH

At the east end of the landing zone, the third British sector was situated between Lion-sur-Mer and Riva-Bella. Codenamed Sword Beach, the sector was assigned to the British 3rd Division. Its mission was to liberate Caen after linking up with airborne troops on the east flank of Overlord.

Early in the morning, the navy heavily bombarded German battery positions with artillery fire at the mouth of the river Orne and the mouth of Ouistreham Harbor in preparation for the assault. There was little response from German artillery. On the other hand, the Kriegsmarine here made its only appearance on D-Day, when three torpedo boats attacked a Norwegian destroyer, sending it to the bottom of the Channel.

German forces in this sector consisted of the 736th Grenadier Regiment, commanded by Colonel Krug, and the 3rd Company of the 642nd Ost Battalion. The quality of these troops was mediocre, and although they possessed heavy weapons and strong defensive positions, they did not long resist the Allied assault. Behind them, several batteries of the 1716th Artillery Regiment were stationed to take the Baie de l'Orne under fire.

Members of the Second Tactical Air Force and a commando enjoy a card game; behind them is a RAF Mustang fighter plane. *IWM*

Payday! Two soldiers receive their wages from NCOs who have adapted a German Goliath into a pay table. *IWM*

At 7:30 a.m., twenty LCAs landed according to schedule: forward elements of the 2nd East Yorkshire came ashore between Hermanville and Riva, while the 1st South Lancashire landed between Hermanville and Lion. A quarter of the forty amphibious tanks following the infantry assault were lost to enemy fire. Effective air and naval assaults permitted the assailants to get a solid foothold on the beach. Nevertheless, the 1st South Lancashire was unable to take Lion-sur-Mer, where a Royal Marine commando unit had landed, not without difficulty, at 8:45. The battle for La Breche d'Hermanville was just as furious. The combat raged for three hours, inflicting heavy British losses. The fighting on the beach alone resulted in 630 dead and wounded.

Meanwhile, the 2nd East Yorkshire encountered less resistance and drove toward Ouistreham, reinforced by the 1st Special Service Brigade, a Franco-British commando unit that had landed at the base of Colleville-sur-Orne. Commander Kiefer's Green Berets proved themselves illustriously in the capture of the casino strong point at Riva-Bella, which was the high point of battle in the prelude to Ouistreham. The same commando, No. 4, linked-up with the paratroopers guarding the Bénouville (Pegasus) Bridge, under the command of General Lovat. The 1st Suffolk, which came ashore shortly later, captured Colleville-sur-Orne but was unable to advance on Caen.

After the 8th Brigade had landed, the 185th Brigade in turn hit the beach, arriving at late morning with the mission to push inland to Caen. The 185th similarly faced difficulties getting off the beach, due to the number of obstacles obstructing their progress and the large confluence of arriving troops. Beuville, then Biéville fell before them, costing the lives of 150 soldiers, but advance forces ran the risk of being cut off from the main body of troops. By nightfall, the brigade was no closer to Caen than Blainville.

Landing in the afternoon, the 9th Brigade was to cover the left flank of the division but found itself immediately engaged with the only vigorous German counterattack on D-Day. This was waged by the 21st Panzer Division—the sole unit in proximity to the beaches that was ordered to cross the Orne to attack the flanks of the troops on Sword Beach.

Caen had suffered bombing and was now in flames. Hindered in its attempts to cross the city, and constantly taken by surprise by fire from Allied planes, the first tanks of the 21st Panzer Division managed to arrive at Biéville at 4:00 p.m., and then arrived at Périers. Losing six and ten tanks, respectively, in these areas, the division was forced to withdraw into the woods at Lebisey.

The troops who took Sword Beach were unable to reach their ultimate objective of Caen, notably because they encountered the threat of the only panzer division engaged in the first day of combat. On the other hand, the action illustrated the limits of any German counterattack unaccompanied by air support.

Thirty thousand men had landed in Normandy; a solid beachhead had been established; and the river Orne, the canal, and a pocket of territory to the east remained in Allied hands, despite the enemy's efforts to reconquer the ground it had lost.

★ ★ ★ ★ ★

By the end of the day on June 6, it was clear that the Germans had mustered strong resistance to the Allied assault but had been totally taken by surprise by the landings. The lack of seriousness with which the highest echelons treated the debarkation on this most decisive of days speaks for itself. Rommel, alerted that morning at his home, hurried to his headquarters, unconvinced that this was the "real" invasion. On the battlefield, his armies met the worst imaginable fate. The Luftwaffe launched very few attacks, leaving the sky to the Allies. The tank divisions held in reserve, positioned far from the beaches on the orders of von Rundstedt and Hitler, were too distant to mount a decisive counterattack.

On the Allied side, 150,000 men and twenty thousand vehicles were now on Norman soil. The five beachheads were still fragile and needed to be enlarged and consolidated. The entire logistical infrastructure had yet to be created. German resistance promised to be fierce.

Not exactly high tea: British soldiers prepare their national brew in the courtyard of their makeshift command post. *IWM*

Omaha Beach, now serving as a temporary port for the thousands of men who will take part in the "Great Crusade." *NARA*

10

CONSOLIDATING THE BEACHHEADS

ONCE THEY HAD ACHIEVED A toehold on the beaches, the Allies quickly set about sending in follow-on troops, prohibiting the arrival of enemy reinforcements, consolidating and extending the various zones of assault, and cutting off the Cotentin Peninsula. These tasks were accomplished with the support of the French Resistance and the Allied air forces.

It was first necessary to join all five beaches and then extend the consolidated beachhead inland, while also ensuring control of the nearest ports, in order to permit the arrival of troops, supplies, and equipment. The success of this first phase was vital for the Allies, who remained subject to a strong German counteroffensive. The Germans aimed to thrust the Allies back into the sea by exploiting the separation of American and British responsibilities and the physical disjunction, or distance, between the various sectors of the beaches. Only on Sword Beach and Juno Beach were the British and Canadians, respectively, able to join up their sectors by the evening of June 6. Very fortunately for the Allies, the enemy did not call upon the Fifteenth Army, with divisions positioned north of the Seine, or the armored units that the OKW was holding in reserve in France, for the high command still suspected the Normandy landings to be a diversionary operation designed to distract them from the "real" Allied invasion they expected to take place at Pas-de-Calais.

Between June 7 and 13, the Allies concentrated on two major objectives with a view to guaranteeing the security of the landing beaches: these consisted of connecting the five beaches and enlarging the depth of the beachheads.

The first religious services on Omaha Beach. Three thousand Americans sacrificed their lives in the first hours of battle on "Bloody Omaha." *NARA*

Ambulances are brought in on the barges that originally served to deliver first-wave troops. *NARA*

After landing at Omaha Beach, vehicles of every type head in a long convoy to the village of Saint-Laurent. Between forty thousand and fifty thousand men arrived on the beaches every day. *NARA*

VALOGNES AND MONTEBOURG:
THE STORY OF TWO TOWNS ON "FREEDOM WAY"

The evening preceding the Allied invasion, the ancient streets of Valognes, locally known as "Normandy's Little Versailles," presented their usual calm. The patina of the town's stone facades, polished by the ages, its grand *hotels particuliers*, and its many timeworn yet solid dwellings presented a comforting architectural vision of bygone days. That night, however, its inhabitants were awakened by the muffled growl of Allied planes coming over the Cotentin Peninsula. In the wee hours of June 6, American paratroopers who had missed their drop zones invaded Valognes, landing near the train station. The epic battle of Normandy, so long anticipated, had finally begun.

Tuesday, June 6

What hope the inhabitants must have felt as news traveled quickly by word of mouth all morning long: Sainte-Mère-Église liberated by the Americans, and landings at Saint-Marie-du-Mont! More than a hope, the certainty of imminent freedom stirred the emotions of a populace that had undergone four years of privation and clandestine struggle against the occupier, confident in their belief that liberation would come.

The Germans were on alert as the historic night began. American paratroopers, scattered everywhere over the peninsula, and often far from their objectives, found themselves isolated at Tamerville, Montaignu-la-Brisette, Saint-Germain-de-Tournebut, Quettehou, Valognes, and elsewhere. At dawn, the Germans escorted their first prisoners, their faces blackened and their eyes defiant, though the streets of Valognes.

Other paratroopers landed at Fresville, near the Paris–Cherbourg railroad line, which was guarded by civilians. The Americans asked the small group of seven Frenchmen at the 328–500-kilometer post to lead them to the Germans in the area. They led the troopers to a farm not far from La Fière, where the enemy was stationed. The battle that took place that night killed three of the Frenchmen.

At 2:00 p.m., the streets of Valognes were thronged with people. The droning of engines made everyone stop and look up: bombers! Coming into view from the west, they first appeared to skirt the town but then headed back straight for Valognes. The flak let loose with a furious antiaircraft defense: a shell, exploding in the midst of the formation, blew one plane to smithereens and set another on fire, sending it crashing to earth. The sudden whistling of bombs and the sound of explosions tore through the air.

The first support vehicles landed directly on the beach. In a few days, an operational artificial port would allow arriving vehicles to exit ship directly on terra firma. *NARA*

The resupply of munitions was of crucial importance, for any delay could cause a defeat on the battlefield. *NARA*

Eisenhower's use of American logistics illustrated the power of the American economy. *NARA*

A GI checks out an abandoned German cannon that probably served in World War I. *NARA*

Artificial ports constructed at Omaha and Arromanches now permitted the rapid delivery of troops and vehicles. *NARA*

Local civilians help GIs unload munitions on the beach. *NARA*

Wednesday, June 7

As everyday life began to reestablish itself, the citizens of Valognes worked steadily to assist the victims of disaster. Planes continued to cut across the sky, all at high altitude or on missions to strafe enemy movement on the roads.

The rest of the day went by without incident, but at 8:45 p.m., the first wave of bombers appeared. Others were soon to follow. Even before fear set into the population, or the flak gunners had time to react, a rain of bombs tore through the sky and burst in a hail of hellish explosions.

This time, the opposite side of the city was in flames. Fires shot up near the train station, covering the entire area in an immense cloud of smoke. Severely affected was "Le Refuge," the Bon Pasteur (Good Pastor) religious establishment, where fire spread from the roof down into rooms inhabited by nuns and pensioners. The mayor of Valognes, Henri Cornat, who lived nearby, was one of the first to arrive at the scene of the blaze. Standing in the cratered street, he heard the heart-wrenching cries of distress coming from the building. All alone, he climbed the stairs and single-handedly evacuated the nuns and other inhabitants of the establishment. Several nuns were killed in the inferno as they tried to reach the stairs.

On the other side of Rue Thiers (known today as Rue Henri Cornat), the Saint-Lin quarter was in ruins. Other rescue teams were struggling to save victims buried in debris. As at Bon Pasteur, this, too, was the site of many tragic scenes.

The construction of certain bunkers, like this one above Omaha Beach, was not fully completed. Seen in the distance, the formidable Allied armada continues to deliver thousands of soldiers every day. *NARA*

Follow-on troops walk in single file as they land on now silent beaches. Overhead, a barrage balloon, no longer necessary, protects from an eventual enemy air attack. The Luftwaffe no longer has the means to mount a counterattack. *NARA*

The Crisbecq Battery at Saint-Marcouf, whose 210mm cannons fired against the Allies on D-Day and were finally disabled by the American infantry. The principal bunker was destroyed when a stock of ammunition accidentally exploded. *NARA*

At Carentan, fierce combat between the "Screaming Eagles" and the "Lions"—the 6th Fallschirmjäger Regiment—resulted in enormous losses among Colonel von der Heydte's men. *NARA*

Thursday, June 8

The hasty bombings on June 6 and 7 were nevertheless only the beginning of the suffering in Valognes. The city center remained untouched. The twin spires of the collegiate church of Saint-Malo still reached skyward in a symbolic sign of hope.

By the light of dawn on June 8, firefighters in Valognes had managed to master the devastating flames. Toward 9:00 a.m., the sky began to reverberate anew, as if a gigantic swarm of bees had descended on the town. The terrified inhabitants barely dared to look up. Suddenly, the earth opened with the sound of thunder, shooting flames from its entrails. Ancient architectural jewels and modern buildings alike caved in under the force of apocalyptic fire. The very center of "Normandy's Little Versailles" exploded.

The archpriest had just left the church of Saint-Malo after celebrating a final mass, when a bomb struck the church between the dome and the steeple, severing the two in a formidable explosion.

The planes again appeared, raining down death on the town. Many streets in the center of town—Place Vinq-d'Azur, Rue du Château, Rue Carnot, the entire heart of the city, in fact—were reduced to absolute ruins. Flames from caved-in roofs told of the terrible fate of those who were buried alive in the inferno. Entire families were engulfed in flames. Others, buried in cellars, cried for help from basement windows. In a single dwelling on Rue Carnot alone, seventeen people were killed. Even worse was the drama that took place nearby, behind Rue des Religieuses in Rue du Vieux-Châteaux. Fleeing in terror toward the shelter of the Benedictine convent down a street lined with high stone walls, forty citizens were literally pulverized in a terrible wave of fiery destruction.

Friday, June 9

During the night, shelling began on the suffering city, a sign of approaching battle. Early in the morning, large-caliber shells from destroyers off the coast exploded at Beaumont and around the sports stadium. Next, the light bombers flew over yet again, and once more explosions rocked the center of town. The collegiate church of Saint-Malo, already horribly mutilated, received the coup de grâce: its dome caved in, and its bell tower crumbled, sending its bells tumbling down to be buried in the heap of ruins, where they nevertheless remained intact.

Clandestine radios broadcast the news that Carentan had been liberated, and the Americans were advancing. The beachhead was growing to the south but also spreading

Lieutenant Colonel Benjamin Vandervoort, the battalion commander of the 2nd Battalion, 505th PIR, with some of his men at Saint-Sauveur-le-Vicomte. They have just liberated the medieval town in very heavy fighting. Vandervoort, injured in the D-Day jump, is seen in the foreground with a crutch. *NARA*

An aerial view of Carentan, the objective of the 101st Airborne Division. *NARA*

On June 12, the 502nd PIR entered Carentan after a violent battle with German paratroopers. *NARA*

A jeep from the 81st Airborne Antitank and Antiaircraft Battalion in the streets of Carentan, heading for Périers. The jeep and gun were delivered by glider. *NARA*

Recently liberated French civilians converse near an American soldier posted on the Place du Marché in Carentan. *NARA*

toward Montebourg, crushed under heavy shelling, which the Americans were now encircling in order to double back and capture German strongholds at the Atlantic Wall by taking them from behind.

Monday, June 12

5:00 p.m., Valognes was subjected to another bombing. This time the hospital, the last available refuge in the city, was shaken by explosions.

Thursday, June 15

Artillery barrages intensified, raining shells down on city hall. During the night, before their definitive departure, the last of the Germans set to pillaging and did not even bother to resist when the Allies overran their outposts at Valognes.

Sunday, June 18

After more than a week of bombing, shelling was still in progress, although the battle was finally starting to die down. The Germans all seemed to have disappeared. Only a few tanks remained, lying in wait near the train station at one of the entrances to town.

Monday, June 19

Threatened with encirclement, the enemy evacuated Montebourg, leaving it a victim to the flames. Their departure took the only route still left to them, in the direction of Huberville and Saint-Germain-de-Tournebut. The Americans had cut off the main route, RN-13, at Saint-Cyr-Bocage. That evening, the first of their tanks arrived at the spot known as "La Victoire," at the entrance to Valognes. After a rapid bout of combat, the Germans fled, escaping through the hospital complex.

The main entrance to Valognes was now free. Before entering, the Americans, in keeping with their original plan, completely surrounded the town, which they did not realize the Germans had deserted. The execution of this vast maneuver caused run-ins with the rear elements of the Wehrmacht's general retreat toward Cherbourg. The American left

June 20: a ceremony for the 101st Airborne Division on the Place de la République in Carentan. The ceremony was interrupted by incoming German artillery fire, which killed a young girl from the town. *NARA*

Between forty thousand and fifty thousand troops flowed into Normandy every day through artificial ports at Arromanches and Saint-Laurent. *NARA*

A dramatic photograph of a monument to the soldiers who lost their lives in World War I. The statue of the soldier stands erect and seems to contemplate the ruins of the city, although the base of the statue has been damaged during battle. *NARA*

Like their paratrooper comrades, these infantry soldiers are delighted to use a German Kettenkrad as a handy means of transport. *NARA*

flank advanced rapidly, with two motorized groups already reaching Flottemanville Bocage on June 18. These elements were part of the column that had fought at Amfreville and Gourbesville, then advanced and largely encircled enemy units in Montebourg before rapidly heading for Valognes. Elements from this column skirted the town, while to the west, others deployed much farther out, toward Bricquebec.

The advance on the left flank of Valognes continued on June 19. Fighting took place at Pont-Cochon, Flottemanville Bocage, La Madeleine, Lieusaint, and at Le Gibet on the road to Saint-Sauveur-le-Vicomte. American artillery adjusted its range, but shells still fell in Valognes, in the area around the hospital. The Allies continued to encircle the area, moving to the south and the west, toward Yvetot-Bocage (where much of the city's population had taken refuge), Morville, and the woods at Bricque and Brix.

The first American patrols entering Valognes on Tuesday, June 20, were stupefied to meet nothing but deathly silence and deserted ruins. "Normandy's Little Versailles" had ceased to exist.

Montebourg

A few kilometers to the south, Montebourg was continually pummeled from June 8 through 19 by shelling from Allied naval forces and ferocious resistance from the Germans, who refused to give up the town. In the midst of all this, the inhabitants, often caught between enemy lines of fire in very close combat, struggled to survive the deathly chaos. Some attempted to flee the inferno, while others remained in cellars until the sounds of battle fell silent. They emerged in great distress among smoking ruins and the reek of death to weep over the fate of their town.

Despite their inferior numbers and lack of equipment and matériel, the German units, far from dispersing, used the terrain to their best advantage. The hedgerows, embankments, and woods that crisscross the Norman countryside cut the land into a seemingly infinite number of small parcels. This terrain favored the defensive and created propitious ground for rearguard actions, where German snipers would excel.

CLAUDE DRENO, fifteen years old in 1944, lived in the center of Valognes near the train station and was caught in the terrible bombing of June 7 and 8.

"On June 7 at 8:30 p.m., we heard a dull sound that started approaching and getting louder. We then saw forty-five bombers flying in three formations of fifteen each, and little black dots began to drop out of the planes and fall through the sky. My mother and I instantly left the house to take shelter elsewhere. We knew it was a bad sign if we did not hear the whistle of the bombs, because it meant they were headed straight for us. And we heard nothing—not until they exploded!

"The noise was unbelievably frightening, like an earthquake. I don't know how long it lasted; probably it was only a few minutes, but in situations like that you totally lose the notion of time. You are so afraid, you don't understand anything that's happening. Once it's over, you feel dazed. The atmosphere seems very strange. After all the deafening noise, suddenly everything's gone silent and you don't hear a thing!

"Our house was destroyed. We had gone to my aunt's, who lived right in the center of town. The next day, the bombs started falling again. By some miracle, no one in our family was killed or hurt. This time we took refuge at Yvetot-Bocage, three kilometers from Valognes, where eighty people had already gathered. At moments like that, there are no social barriers, no questions of class. Everyone helps everyone else, and chips in. Some people slaughtered animals for food; others returned to Valognes to bring back whatever provisions they could scrounge up.

"When the Americans arrived, their reception was very reserved—not hostile, but reserved. People in Valognes didn't understand the reason for all the bombing. For that matter, neither did the American soldiers!" *Image credit: Claude Dreno*

The Germans were unable to launch any true counteroffensives of considerable power, notably because of the superiority of Allied air support, which interdicted the mass movement of troops and large convoys of vehicles. Nevertheless, through limited but deadly attacks and resolute resistance, they managed to block the Allied plan of advance and follow Hitler's order to "hold at any price." One of the D-Day objectives, the capture of La Fière Bridge, serves as an excellent case in point. Crossing the river Merderet not far from Utah Beach, the bridge was an essential connection between Saint-Mère-Église and Pont-l'Abbé. On June 6, the 505th PIR occupied the position, but they lost it later in the afternoon to a German counterattack. Only on June 9, after repeated massive and violent assaults, were the Americans able to gain control of this essential passageway.

JUNE 9: THE BATTLE FOR LA FIÈRE BRIDGE

The 82nd Airborne, which held the east bank of the river at the entrance to La Fière Bridge, had been under heavy shelling since 4:30 a.m. from 88s in the hamlet of Cauquigny, where the Germans were solidly dug in. The assistant division commander, Gen. James M. Gavin, ordered preliminary artillery fire fifteen minutes before the 3rd Battalion,

Infantry soldiers hole up in a barn not far from Sainte-Marie-du-Mont. *NARA*

On a farm at Foucarville, 4th Infantry Division soldiers study a hasty map sketched in the dirt. Bloated cows killed by artillery fire still lie in the farmyard. The Battle of Normandy damaged or destroyed thirty thousand of the fifty thousand farms in the region. *NARA*

325th GIR, assaulted the bridge and the kilometer-long causeway that led over to Cauquigny. Their battalion commander, Lt. Col. Charles A. Carrell, confessed to Gavin his inability to lead because of a medical condition. Colonel Harry Lewis, commander of the 325th GIR, then ordered Major Gardner to lead the assault in Carrell's place. Concerned with the unit's seeming lack of spirit, Gavin conferred with Lieutenant Colonel Maloney and Captain Robert Rae of the 507th PIR. Certain of their courage, Gavin knew he could count on Captain Rae if the 325th failed in the attack. Rae was ordered to regroup his company to act as the reserve.

At 10:30 a.m., six powerful howitzers and 75mm guns opened fire on the German lines on the opposite bank of the river. The 325th GIR had been promised a smoke screen to cover their assault, but smoke bombs were in short supply, and they were forced to advance from their positions with no protection. Charging through a gap in the stone wall surrounding the farm at La Fière Bridge, the first soldiers were mowed down as soon as they set off. At the first turn, just after the bridge, German machine gunners met their assailants, felling them right and left like bowling pins and forcing those behind them to dive for the ditches lining the causeway. The attack was effectively arrested, and the men were pinned down by fire.

Gavin then ordered Rae to take up the attack and get the paralyzed men up and moving. With the simple cry, "Let's go!" Rae took off at the head of his men, leading them past the solders of the 325th and out onto the causeway. Others rose out of the ditches, inspired by his leadership. Many fell along the way, but the strong determination of the group as a whole carried the day, permitting them to make it to the other end of the causeway and the church at Cauquigny. A battle in the surrounding graveyard ensued, but Rae continued his advance, attaining the village of Motey. Finally, divisions

General Eisenhower and his staff arrive at Omaha Beach. Eisenhower often changed CPs as he followed the course of the battle. *NARA*

General Eisenhower, accompanied by General Marshall, makes an inspection tour of Omaha Beach and surrounding areas. *NARA*

A moment of brief respite: rangers hidden by a hedgerow enjoy the company of a little dog they have adopted as their mascot. The dog, although French, seems to have had no problem in gobbling up his American rations, courtesy of the U.S. Army. *NARA*

coming off Utah Beach could now cross the Merderet River and advance on Cherbourg. The capture of the bridge was absolutely crucial, but the battle occasioned great loss of life. As one soldier of the 507th PIR later testified, there were so many bodies on the causeway, it would have been possible to walk the whole way across without ever touching the ground.

On June 7, the 506th PIR had captured Saint-Marie-du-Mont, incurring heavy losses, but it was not until June 11 that the four bridges were secured across the inundated marshes, henceforth permitting the use of RN-13 to Carentan. The Americans arrived in the city the following day, after the fighting withdrawal of the 1st Battalion, 6th Fallschirmjäger Regiment, commanded by Lieutenant Colonel von der Heydte. By the time the survivors reached Carentan, the regiment was down from an initial force of seven hundred to fewer than thirty men.

THE BATTLE OF CARENTAN

By the sixth day of the Battle of Normandy, Allied airborne divisions had achieved their initial missions and secured the flanks of the Allied beachhead. The two American divisions had overcome the handicap of widely scattered drops and inflicted heavy losses on the enemy's 709th and 91st Infantry Divisions, as well as on the 6th Fallschirmjäger Regiment. The 4th, 9th, and 90th Infantry Divisions of the U.S. Army had landed and were proceeding up to Cherbourg and west to Saint-Sauveur-le-Vicomte along routes the

Recently arrived, a member of a machine gun crew totes his weapon through a village. *NARA*

Two troopers from the 101st Airborne Division make their way through the ruins of a street in Carentan. The Germans have been forced from the city, but many enemy snipers remain behind. They will take their toll in American lives. *NARA*

Infantry soldiers who have just advanced from the beaches cross through a village in Normandy. The first soldier in the group still carries his life vest. *NARA*

The Allies have not yet captured the deep-water port at Cherbourg, but tanks are still delivered every day at beaches and artificial ports. *NARA*

This silenced German cannon has its back turned to the sea. To the right side of the distant horizon, a warship sails toward Cherbourg. *NARA*

airborne troops had opened up by capturing causeways and bridges. On June 10, the 101st Airborne Division had finished cleaning up the north bank of the river Douve. When Maj. Gen. Maxwell Taylor reported the results to his corps commander, Gen. Joe Collins replied, "Perfect! Now take Carentan!" The slow progress of American troops inland off Omaha Beach made it essential for the two American army corps to rapidly link up. Carentan was a major crossroads, the key meeting point for rail, road, and river transportation. Air surveillance showed little sign of German reinforcements, although it was suspected that elements of the 6th Fallschirmjäger Regiment still held the city. Taylor planned to send his 327th GIR southward to capture Brevands from the east, while the 502nd PIR would cross RN-13 and the railroad bridges, skirt Carentan from the west, and seize Hill 30, south of the city.

The 327th GIR encountered no resistance en route to its obejctive and began the attack from the east, but the 502nd PIR, spearheaded by the 3rd Battalion under the command of Lt. Col. Robert G. Cole, came upon fierce resistance on RN-13. Three days of ferocious combat ensued, in which the regiment, and particularly the 3rd Battalion, fought with extradinary intensity, leading to a Medal of Honor for Lieutenant Colonel Cole. Reinforced by the 501st PIR, the 327th GIR fought its way into Carentan on June 12, while the 506th PIR penetrated the city from the southwest, to discover the Germans had abandoned it, leaving behind only a few snipers. In the days that followed,

Vehicles coming off Omaha Beach wend their way through the dunes on a recently created road. *NARA*

Protected by barrage balloons, convoys off-load directly on Omaha Beach. Cranes to the right of the photo unload heavy cargo from the holds of incoming ships. *NARA*

the 101st Airborne Division repulsed a powerful counterattack by the 17th SS Panzer Grenadier Division (or "Götz von Berlichingen" Division). It hung on to its defensive positions south and southwest of Carentan until June 27, when the division moved north toward Saint-Sauveur-le-Vicomte.

SAINTE-MÈRE-ÉGLISE: CAPITAL OF THE COTENTIN PENINSULA

Once the Germans had ceased to bombard the city, Sainte-Mère-Église, restored to calm, temporarily served as the capital of the liberated portion of the Cotentin Peninsula. Refugees, evacuated by the Americans or fleeing the fall of bombs, flooded in from Montebourg, Picauville, and other villages that lay in ruins or were still the scene of combat. Hundreds of families filled the local farms, horse stables, schools, and city hall. A kitchen to feed the hungry was set up in the girls' school; supplied by area farmers and the American army, it turned out four hundred meals a day until the end of June. The Americans also established their headquarters at Sainte-Mère-Église. In a week and a half, they had built an airfield at Londe, the home of three squadrons of P-47 Thunderbolt fighter-bombers for nearly three months. In the first days of combat, they also created three temporary cemetaries around Sainte-Mère-Église to receive the remains of American solders killed in the invasion.

A rare moment of peace for German grenadiers. One holds a beer, but another still carries a flamethrower. Many among them will battle to the death defending the hilltops that dominate the Allied route of advance. *NARA*

A German paratrooper armed with a Schmeisser MP40 peers out from his post in a ruined barn. Many fallchirmjäger troops died a courageous death in Normandy. *Archives du Calvados*

German paratroopers take a break in a field. Some light up cigarettes, others amusedly milk a cow. *BA*

The cost of freedom was high for both soldiers and Norman civilians. Here, a mother waits for an American doctor to treat her injured child. *NARA*

In the center of this aerial view of the ruins of Montebourg, a vital crossroads town located in the line of Allied advance, just to the left of the main junction, the statue of Joan of Arc still stands. *NARA*

American forces in the streets of Montebourg. Before they fled the town, the Germans set fire to the few remaining houses that had not been destroyed in artillery attacks. *NARA*

THE BRITISH SECTOR: A HALT IN THE ADVANCE

Meanwhile, at the opposite end of their planned lines of attack, the Allies once again failed in the effort to capture Caen. The British 7th Armoured Division, blocked before it could enter the city, engaged in an exhaustive battle with the enemy. While the situation spelled failure for Montgomery, it could not be called a victory for the German commander either, for the absence of air and armored support prohibited him from fully exploiting his advantage.

The German responses lacked will, power, and coordination. The OKW West nevertheless possessed considerable reserves located just one or two days distant from the Normandy coast: General Feuchtinger's 21st Panzer Division, located between Caen and Saint-Pierre-sur-Dives; the 12th SS Panzer Division, commanded by Brigadeführer Witt, positioned between Evreux and Elbeuf; and the Panzer Lehr Division, under the command of General Bayerlein, between Chartres and Le Mans—a force of fifty thousand men and several hundred tanks. To the west of the landing beaches, the death of General Falley, commander of the 91st Infantry Division, and that of General Rudolph Stegmann, who commanded the 77th Infantry Division, also contributed to the disorganization of German forces.

On June 13, German units controlled a zone that stretched, on average, twenty kilometers inland. Allied reinforcements were arriving at the rate of forty thousand to

Joan of Arc still proudly displays her banner over the Montebourg square. The town center sadly is no more: only 12 out of 487 houses remain intact. *NARA*

The neighborhood around the church in Valognes. "Normandy's Little Versailles" is gone forever. *NARA*

Breakwaters consisting of scuttled ships and Phoenixes, gigantic reinforced concrete caissons, protected Mulberries from waves and currents. A Phoenix weighed from 1,600 to over 6,000 tons. *NARA*

fifty thousand a day: it was hence inconceivable that the Germans could push them back to the sea. However, the night of June 12, the first V-1s had fallen on London, greatly worrying city authorities and the high command. It was absolutely essential that the invasion forces continue to move forward.

Anxious that no foreign power assume the administration of the liberated territory, General de Gaulle arrived in Courseulles on June 14, setting foot on French soil for the first time since June 1940. The republican government was restored, and French civil authorities were made a part of Allied general planning. The liberated corridor around Bayeux and Isigny was, nevertheless, too narrow to support the Allied army, which was unable to access the infrastructure of the large ports in the region, or build the airfields planners originally envisioned to construct on the plain at Caen. Throughout the last two weeks of June, the Allies slowly continued to eat away at German positions throughout the region, but progress was most marked in the areas of American offensives.

The Panzer Lehr counteroffensive north of Caen and German resistance around Montebourg on the eastern coast reconfirmed General Bradley's opinion that a move to the southwest was the only way out of the German net in which the Allied army was currently entangled. The plan depended on penetrating German lines between

The Allies constructed Mulberries at Saint-Laurent and Arromanches. The Mulberry at Saint-Laurent, seen in the photo, was destroyed in a storm closely following its construction, but the one at Arromanches, although damaged, remained operational. *NARA*

The Mulberry at Saint-Laurent, destroyed by the terrible storm that ravaged the coast of Normandy from June 19 to 22, 1944. Until the capture of Cherbourg, it was necessary to channel all reinforcements and supplies through the artificial port at Arromanches, which suffered damage but still continued to function. *NARA*

German POWs wait on a beach for the LST that will transfer them to England. After a year or two of detention, they will be free to return to their home country. *NARA*

In July 1944, after the battle for Hill 95, Gen. Omar Bradley awards the Distinguished Service Cross to 82nd Airborne Division paratroopers. Colonel Benjamin Vandervoort, commander of the 2nd Battalion, 505th PIR, here receives his decoration. Captain Robert Rae (third to the left) and Marcus Heim (extreme right) also are part of the honored group. Captain Rae of the 507th PIR and Heim of the 505th PIR both played essential roles at the Battle of La Fière. *NARA*

Saint-Sauveur-le-Vicomte and Barneville. This would make possible a thrust toward Cherbourg, where the goal was to liquidate the thirty thousand enemy troops encircled in the northern peninsula under the command of Lt. Gen. Karl-Wilhelm von Schlieben and to seize the port. Principal efforts would then be directed south toward Saint-Lô, Coutances, and Avranches.

This maneuver, which aimed to attain the western shore of the peninsula, was successfully completed in forty-eight hours by the 9th Division of VII Corps of the U.S. Army, while the 82nd Airborne Division and the 47th and 60th Infantry Regiments undertook the mission to enlarge the area under Allied control to the north. Once again, the Allies had seized the initiative, and the offensive was in their grasp.

General James Gavin, assistant division commander of the 82nd Airborne in Normandy, was photographed at a ceremony for the 507th PIR with Col. Edson Raff, who became regimental commander of the regiment after the capture of Col. George Millett. *Dominique François*

Part IV

EXPANDING THE BEACHHEADS

★ ★ ★ ★ ★

Once the beachhead was established, the American plan called for a thrust to the north to capture Cherbourg, followed by a return south within the confines of the Department of La Manche. These actions were largely delayed because of German resistance. The Americans had, moreover, already played one of their most important cards on June 6 and no longer benefited from the effect of surprise. The Germans had recouped remarkably well and were mounting ferocious resistance to General Collins' VII Corps.

As for British objectives, Caen was still in the hands of the enemy, and it was clear from the outset that the battle was going to be long and difficult. Nevertheless, these two cities were of essential strategic importance to the Allies.

A view of Cherbourg and its harbor during the battle. The capture of Cherbourg was of paramount importance to the Allies, who needed a deep-water port to receive supplies and reinforcements. *NARA*

11

THE FIRST U.S. ARMY AND
THE CAPTURE OF CHERBOURG

THE CAPTURE OF CHERBOURG WAS of utmost importance. In the short term, the city and its surroundings would be the first large urban center to fall to the Allies since the landings on June 6, a fact which lent its capture a certain psychological importance as well. In the middle term, the control of Cherbourg would permit the Allies to concentrate all their subsequent efforts on the southern front. Finally, the possession of a deep-water port would furnish a durable logistical base for importing matériel and thousands of men. To achieve these goals, the Americans had to undergo a week of fierce, unrelenting combat with a deeply entrenched enemy.

Die Festung Cherbourg

Known to the German high command as "Fortress Cherbourg," the city possessed an extensive ensemble of impressive fortifications, which nevertheless suffered from two major faults: the heterogeneous nature of its garrisons and the fact that many of its defenses were conceived to respond to an attack by sea. The first line of defense, arranged in an arc, had the capacity to attain targets fifteen kilometers distant. Starting at Cap Levy, it passed through Maupertus, where the airfield was located, then to Gonneville, Ruffosses, Hardinvast, and so forth. Set up along multiple points of support, this first line of defense included two strong points, one at each of its two extremities. The first was situated between Carneville and L'Anse de Brick (the Osteck strong point). The second was in the sector of Grunchy-Castel-Vendon (the Westeck strong point). Both of these points were fearsomely armed and defended: the first boasted forty-five blockhouses, four 105mm cannons, four 155mm cannons, and four 240mm cannons; the latter, four 155mm cannons. The entirety was completely surrounded by minefields, antitank trenches, and barbed wire.

The second line of defense consisted of a network of batteries positioned more closely together. Beginning at Bretteville on the coast, they passed through Saint-Gabriel

Overlooking Cherbourg, the Fort du Roule on Roule Mountain was solidly equipped with artillery batteries and a network of underground tunnels in which diehard German defenders continued to fight until the city was formally surrendered. *NARA*

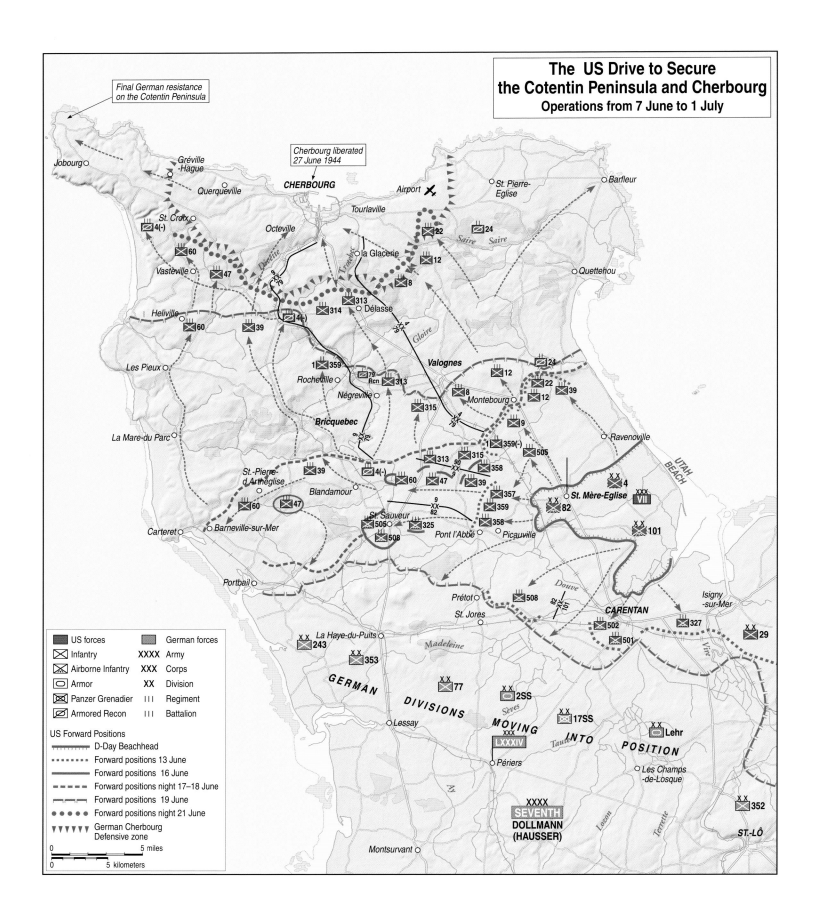

The US Drive to Secure the Cotentin Peninsula and Cherbourg
Operations from 7 June to 1 July

Final German resistance on the Cotentin Peninsula

Jobourg

Gréville-Hague

Querqueville

Cherbourg liberated 27 June 1944

CHERBOURG

Airport

St. Pierre-Eglise

Barfleur

Tourlaville

St. Croix

⬚ 4(-)

Octeville

la Glacerie

⬚ 22

Saire

⬚ 24

⬚ 60

Vasteville

⬚ 47

⬚ 12

Quettehou

⬚ 8

Divette

⬚ 313

⬚ 314

Délasse

Gloire

Heliville

⬚ 60

⬚ 39

⬚ 4(-)

⬚ 24

Valognes

⬚ 12

Les Pieux

1 ⬚ 359

⬚ 313

⬚ 22

⬚ 39

Rocheville

79 Rcn

⬚ 313

⬚ 8

Montebourg

⬚ 12

Négreville

⬚ 315

⬚ 9

Ravenoville

La Mare-du-Parc

Bricquebec

1 ⬚ 359(-)

⬚ 505

XX 4

UTAH BEACH

⬚ 39

⬚ 313

⬚ 315

90 XX 9

XXX VII

St.-Pierre-d'Artheglise

⬚ 4(-)

⬚ 60

⬚ 47

⬚ 39

⬚ 358

St. Mère-Eglise

Blandamour

⬚ 357

XX 82

⬚ 60

⬚ 47

9 XX 82

⬚ 359

XX 101

Carteret

Barneville-sur-Mer

St. Sauveur

505

⬚ 325

⬚ 358

Pont l'Abbé

Picauville

⬚ 508

Portbail

Douve

⬚ 508

Isigny-sur-Mer

Prétot

82 XX 101

CARENTAN

St. Jores

⬚ 502

⬚ 327

XX 29

La Haye-du-Puits

XX 243

Madeleine

⬚ 501

XX 353

GERMAN

DIVISIONS

Seves

XX 77

XX 2SS

Ay

XX 17SS

XX Lehr

MOVING

Lessay

XXX LXXXIV

Taute

INTO

POSITION

Périers

Les Champs-de-Losque

XXXX

SEVENTH

DOLLMANN

(HAUSSER)

Lozon

Terrette

XX 352

ST.-LÔ

Montsurvant

US forces		German forces
⊠ Infantry	XXXX	Army
⊠ Airborne Infantry	XXX	Corps
⬚ Armor	XX	Division
⊠ Panzer Grenadier	|||	Regiment
⬚ Armored Recon	|||	Battalion

US Forward Positions

- D-Day Beachhead
- Forward positions 13 June
- Forward positions 16 June
- Forward positions night 17–18 June
- Forward positions 19 June
- Forward positions night 21 June
- German Cherbourg Defensive zone

0 ————— 5 miles
0 ————— 5 kilometers

Soldiers of the 4th Infantry and 79th Infantry Division are in a slit trench on the periphery of Cherbourg. *NARA*

and La Glacerie, extending all the way to Nacqueville. Here, too, certain batteries could deliver a fearsome amount of firepower.

The third line of defense consisted mainly of fortifications that had surrounded the city since the nineteenth century: forts built to defend the harbor and other structures meant to protect the infrastructure of the port. A battery to the west, baptized "York" by the Germans, was equipped with four long-range 153mm Kriegsmarine cannons.

The Cherbourg garrison contained approximately forty thousand troops of unequal quality. Many were exhausted by previous combat. Many, of Slavic origin, pressed into combat by the Germans, had no real will to fight. Moreover, these troops knew full well that they were cornered at the tip of the peninsula, with no hope whatsoever of evacuation or reinforcements from the south when the going got rough. Nor did they benefit from air or tank support. And yet, Hitler had ordered them to resist to the last bullet!

Allied plans envisioned the fall of Cherbourg eight days after the beach invasion. Extremely well fortified, the port was one of the bastions in the Atlantic Wall. General Collins was under great pressure. The duration of German resistance had already exceeded Allied expectations, and the terrible storms that had destroyed the artificial ports off the Calvados coast, added to the urgency to capture a deep-water port. But Collins had lost

An American soldier delivers messages from one position to the next, putting an abandoned bicycle to good use. *NARA*

V-1 AND V-2 ROCKETS

BECAUSE IT LIES so close to England, the Cotentin Peninsula served as a base for German secret weapons. At the beginning of the occupation, the Germans set about installing radar stations and later installed both fixed and mobile launching sites for V-1 and V-2 weapons along the coast of the Manche. General Collins' troops discovered these secret sites after the Battle of Normandy. By lucky chance, one of the sites, located at Sottevast, was never completed and thus never served to launch V-2s.

The Americans nevertheless discovered V-1 rockets at several sites. These weapons were, in effect, small planes weighing two tons and carrying a charge of nine hundred kilograms. They were launched by jet propulsion, using a nozzle three meters long. Flying at a speed of six hundred kilometers an hour, the V-1 was mostly used to bomb southern England, and especially London.

V-2 rockets were vertically launched and intended to destroy long-distance targets. Launching required numerous complex operations, during which the rocket was exposed and susceptible to attack by Allied aircraft. The Germans thus decided to construct special bunkers in the north of France and on the Cotentin Peninsula for stocking and launching V-2 rockets. A vast underground installation at Sottevast, south of Cherbourg, was destined for this function but never completed. The first V-2 rocket attack on London was launched from Holland in September 1944. *Image credit: NARA*

Cherbourg inhabitants clear away rubble in a house destroyed by artillery fire. *NARA*

far too many men in battles among the hedgerows. On the one hand, he sought to avoid further heavy troop losses at Cherbourg; on the other, he had to act. He sent an ultimatum to von Schlieben, commander of the 709th Infantry Division at Cherbourg. When von Schlieben rejected his demands, Collins decided on an all-out attack with the heaviest means at his disposal, including support by air and sea.

Three infantry divisions would carry out the attack. The 4th Infantry Division, to the right, was charged with cutting off Val-de-Saire and thus protecting the right flank of the 79th Infantry Division, which would launch a frontal attack. This latter, in the vanguard and guided by members of the French Resistance, would proceed across the peninsula. Finally, the 9th Infantry Division would cover the left flank of the 79th and head toward La Hague.

The attack was launched on June 19, with the Americans advancing rapidly to the west. In the east, however, they soon encountered unexpected resistance, notably at Montebourg, where that evening they encountered Germans withdrawing from the town. The enemy fell back to their principal line of resistance in the Osteck bunkers along the river Saire. The central thrust by the 79th Infantry Division continued on toward Cherbourg.

By June 21, American troops were facing the lines of enemy defense. After violent combat, the 79th Infantry Division broke through the German front but on June 22, ran

A Sherman tank on a main street in Cherbourg. The artillery fire preceding the infantry attack brought down the walls of many buildings. *NARA*

An aerial view of the impressive Fort du Roule high above the city of Cherbourg, where the Germans were solidly entrenched. *NARA*

This coastal fort, known as the Ile Pelée, was constructed by Vauban and later Napoleon III to defend the port at Cherbourg. The Germans used it to good advantage, filling it with bunkers and other important defenses. *NARA*

GIs from the 79th Infantry Division pose for their portrait with a Frenchwoman. Local inhabitants traded cider and Calvados for American rations and cigarettes. *NARA*

Generals Eisenhower and Bradley are in discussion with General Collins, the greatest victor of the Battle of Cherbourg. *NARA*

up against enemy fortifications a few kilometers from the center of the city. In mid-afternoon of the same day, three successive waves of fighter-bombers and medium bombers filled the sky above Cherbourg, concentrating their attacks on the strongest points of German resistance. Field artillery took up the attack in turn and pounded enemy defenses for forty-eight hours.

Although they were not highly effective, the bomber attacks nevertheless ruptured German communication lines and liaisons, and seriously damaged enemy morale. On June 24, after rigorous fighting, the Americans finally gained control of the heights of Cherbourg. The next and final step was to seize the city and the port.

On June 23, General von Schlieben took over the command of all forces in the area. At his command was the remainder of four divisions, which had been battling on the peninsula since the invasion of June 6. His orders were to regroup his men, engage in combat, and resist the American advance to the bitter end. No reinforcements would come to his relief, but his men were determined.

Seeking to put a definitive end to German resistance, Allied naval forces engaged in a long-distance duel with Cherbourg coastal batteries on June 25. Anchored fifteen kilometers off the coast, a fleet consisting of the battleships *Nevada*, *Texas*, and *Arkansas*,

The 314th Infantry Regiment captured the principal entrance to the Fort du Roule, located on the Avenue de Paris. Kriegsmarine sailors occupied the tunnel. *NARA*

The interior of one of the tunnels where General von Schlieben and his staff held out until 2:00 p.m. on June 26. Three hundred soldiers emerged from underground. *NARA*

HÉMEVEZ: THE REVELATION OF A MASSACRE

ON THE AFTERNOON OF June 6, 1944, Roland Robiole, a worker on the Archillerie farm near the Château d'Hémevez, was asked by his employer to scout out a small nearby woods for a good place to build a shelter in case of bomb alert. There he discovered the bodies of seven American soldiers, all of whom seemed to have been executed. One of them still held a cigarette between his lips. What had really taken place?

The previous night, paratroopers from the 507th PIR had landed in the region, far from their drop zone. The group positioned itself along the road to Le Ham in the wee hours of the morning and awaited the arrival of the enemy. Later in the day, a German truck came down the road, and the Americans opened fire. Loaded with explosives, the truck was pulverized in an explosion whose force knocked the door off a nearby farmhouse. When a second truck full of German soldiers arrived, the ensuing battle raged for most of the day. Outnumbered and inferiorly equipped, the Americans were finally forced to surrender.

Hands on their heads, the Americans were marched toward Hémevez. Along the way, two of them took advantage of a moment's inattention from their guards to escape and managed to hide in a dense hedgerow at the border of a small wood. The Germans opened fire, but they neither wounded the Americans nor attempted to recapture them.

The remaining prisoners were led to a wooded area below a path close to the Hémevez church. The Germans gave their prisoners a few moments to light a cigarette and then suddenly opened fire, mowing them down one after the other. Some attempted to escape but were cut down by machine gun fire. In the smoky aftermath, a German NCO approached their bodies and delivered the coup de grace, a bullet in the nape of the neck.

Hidden nearby, the two paratroopers who had succeeded in escaping heard the sound of fire as they hunkered in their hedgerow. Waiting until nightfall, when all was calm, they approached the scene and discovered the fallen bodies of their companions.

That same day, two other paratroopers had been taken prisoner in the area, probably at Colomby, where troopers had again landed far from their drop zones. Crossing Hémevez under German escort, one of the captives flashed the V-for-victory sign at Jacques Durand, a twelve-year-old villager, who reported he thought the trooper "had a lot of nerve." Near the church, the two troopers, whose hands were free, pushed their guards off balance and fled into a wheat field. The Germans opened fire, mortally wounding one of the soldiers. The other managed to hide behind the trunk of an old oak and was never discovered, although the Germans passed right by his hiding place in their search. The body of his companion was transported to the cemetery, where it was interred next to the common grave where seven of his fellow troopers had already been buried.

On June 22, 1944, Colonel Maloney ordered a team of specialists to Hémevez to exhume the bodies of the paratroopers killed on June 6. Accompanying the team were the two troopers who had witnessed the massacre after escaping their captors. The seven bodies were found at the bottom of their common grave; the remnants of an 82nd Airborne patch were still visible on the jacket of the first body to be exhumed. Colonel Maloney heard various testimonies throughout his investigation, but the principal witnesses never appeared, for their units were already in full retreat before the Allied advance. *Image credit: NARA*

A German soldier with a white flag emerges from another tunnel to negotiate the surrender of Cherbourg. *NARA*

A very young German prisoner of war captured in the Battle of Cherbourg. *NARA*

German nurses, now prisoners of war. The French familiarly called them *les souris grises* (gray mice) because of the color of their uniform. *NARA*

The German garrison at Cherbourg consisted of approximately forty thousand men. Enormous numbers of POWs flowed into Allied prison camps after the battle. *NARA*

Some of these French citizens suspected of collaboration with the Germans will be transferred to England for interrogation and further investigation. *NARA*

and numerous cruisers and destroyers used their powerful guns to pulverize the Osteck and Westeck strong points and batteries along the dike at the port. The fort at Roule, which dominates the city, fell to the Americans after violent clashes between the GIs and German marines.

Bit by bit, the infantry invested the city, accompanied here and there by tanks, which knocked out the last nests of enemy resistance as they rolled toward the center of town. On June 26, American troops infiltrated the city from all sides, converging on the town center. At the spearhead of the attack, the 313th Infantry Regiment found itself confronting the deeply entrenched German camp located around the harbor train station. With the support of tanks and heavy mortars, the 313th was able to occupy the sector by the end of the day. For their part, the 39th Infantry Regiment had reached the area surrounding General von Schlieben's underground command post. Responding to their ultimatum, the general finally surrendered, emerging from his tunnel with a white flag, accompanied by his headquarters staff.

Although the high command had been taken prisoner, the fighting continued. Still under German fire, solders from the 39th Infantry Regiment finally reached the center of town and city hall on June 26 at 8:00 p.m. The Americans gradually continued to invest the city, all the while encountering small groups of German soldiers intent on resistance.

Liberated civilians rush to remove all sign of their former occupiers from the streets of Cherbourg. The drama of purging collaborators is about to begin. *NARA*

The maritime prefecture, where the *kommandantur* was headquartered, was also captured and was flying the French flag by 9:30 p.m. By this time, remaining resistance was centered at the marine arsenal.

The next day, elements of the 47th Infantry Regiment received the mission to assault the arsenal. Specialists from the psychological warfare section broadcast an ultimatum by loudspeaker, informing the Germans of their situation. The appearance of an American tank convinced the defenders to give up the arsenal. Nevertheless, a hundred German soldiers under the orders of frigate commander Captain Witt had taken refuge in the forts on the large dike. Only after intensive aerial bombing and shelling by American artillery did this last group of German defenders finally surrender to the Americans on June 29 and 30.

Victory came at a very high price. The Americans lost more than twenty thousand troops in the Battle for the Cotentin Peninsula. Although German losses, numbering fourteen thousand, were not as high, forty thousand men were taken prisoner. The harbor train station had been destroyed, and sunken ships obstructed the entrance to the port. It was necessary for the Americans to reconstruct the entire infrastructure of the port and clear the harbor of mines before it could receive convoys of matériel. The first shipment arrived on July 16.

The commercial port that harbored the *Queen Mary* and the *Titanic* before the war now receives Allied liberty ships delivering thousands of tons of matériel and reinforcements. *NARA*

At Saint-Martin-de-Fontenay, halfway between Lisieux and Saint-Pierre-sur-Dives, Panzer IV tankers from the 22nd Panzer Regiment stop in front of Madame Leroy's grocery store–café. *BA*

12

THE SECOND BRITISH ARMY AND THE BATTLE OF CAEN

THE CONTROL OF CAEN WAS of vital importance to the Allies. The city was key for launching operations toward the river Seine, and hence to Paris. Allied plans slated the liberation of Caen for June 6, but not until July 9 did the left bank come under Allied control, and the city was not liberated in its entirety until July 20. It took six weeks and no fewer than four offensives before the Allies were able to invest the town, after a terrible siege that cost two thousand lives. Allied tanks were unable to seize their initial advantage and lost much precious time extricating themselves from the heavily encumbered beaches and maneuvering through the narrow streets of coastal villages. Further delay was caused by the prudence of British officers like Montgomery, who were more accustomed to holding conquered territory and protecting their rear than conducting assaults in the style of General Patton. Also feeding their caution was the fear of a counterattack on June 6 by the 21st Panzer Division, commanded by General Feuchtinger, which did not arrive on the scene until that afternoon. The presence of this single division was enough to block access to Caen, and no doubt accounts for the Allied decision to bomb the city.

The capture of the city was thus imperative. It would permit the Allies to enter the plain, a flat, inland region propitious to the deployment of armored vehicles and the construction of airstrips. Most importantly of all, the control of Caen would consolidate the Allied position, which still remained at the mercy of enemy tank attack.

Seeking to gain control of the city, the British first attempted to surround it, in vain. Over a period of six weeks, they launched four successive offensives: Operations Perch (June 7–15), Epsom (June 25– July 1), Charnwood (July 4–9) and Goodwood (July 18–20).

Field Marshal Montgomery, commander of the 21st Army Group, confided the mission to the Second British Army, which totaled 150,000 men, including three tank divisions. Facing him was his old opponent from North Africa, Field Marshal Rommel, the commander of Army Group B, whose defense of the city rested on the Seventh

Hidden in a wheat field, a Grenadier armed with a Panzerfaust observes the passage of Canadian troops. *ECPA*

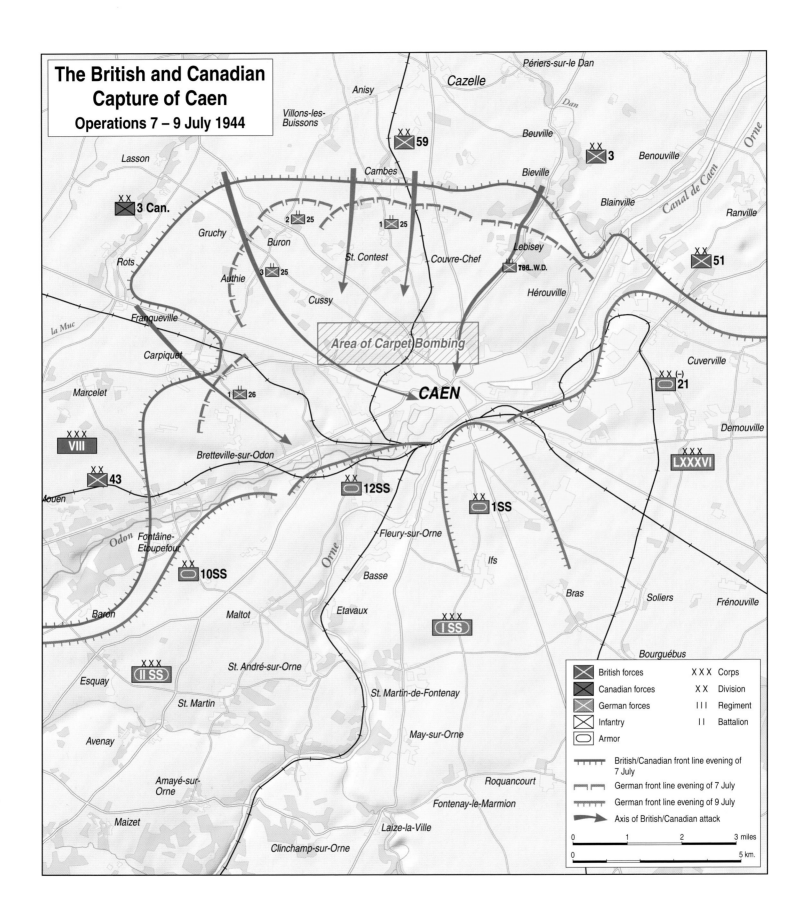

The British and Canadian
Capture of Caen
Operations 7 – 9 July 1944

Périers-sur-le Dan

Cazelle

Anisy

Villons-les-Buissons

Beuville

Benouville

Lasson

Cambes

Bieville

Blainville

Ranville

Gruchy

Buron

2 ‖ 25

1 ‖ 25

St. Contest

Couvre-Chef

Lebisey

Hé
rouville

Rots

Authie

3 ‖ 25

Cussy

786 I.W.D.

Franqueville

la Muc

Carpiquet

Area of Carpet Bombing

Cuverville

Marcelet

1 ‖ 26

CAEN

XX (–)
21

Demouville

VIII

Bretteville-sur-Odon

XX
12SS

XXX
LXXXVI

Aouen

XX
43

XX
1SS

Odon

Fontâine-
Etoupefour

Fleury-sur-Orne

Ifs

10SS

Basse

Bras

Soliers

Frénouville

Baron

Maltot

Etavaux

XXX
I SS

Bourguébus

XXX
II SS

St. André-sur-Orne

Esquay

St. Martin-de-Fontenay

St. Martin

May-sur-Orne

Avenay

Amayé-sur-
Orne

Roquancourt

Fontenay-le-Marmion

Maizet

Laize-la-Ville

Clinchamp-sur-Orne

3 Can.

3

59

51

Orne

Canal de Caen

Dan

British forces	X X X	Corps
Canadian forces	X X	Division
German forces	I I I	Regiment
Infantry	I I	Battalion
Armor		

British/Canadian front line evening of 7 July

German front line evening of 7 July

German front line evening of 9 July

Axis of British/Canadian attack

0   1   2   3 miles

0   5 km.

German Army and the western panzergruppe. His forces consisted of one hundred thousand men, including seven tank divisions. The German troops were of very uneven quality. Luftwaffe divisions assigned to rural areas and never hardened to war fought side by side with the most fearsome of German troops, such as the 12th SS Panzer Division—the dreaded Hitlerjugend.

The British launched the first attack on June 7. Operation Perch was conceived to surround the city from the west. A powerful German reaction, notably by the Panzer Lehr Division, stopped Montgomery's men at Villers-Bocage. The attack from the southwest on June 12 and 13 ended in failure: a single Tiger tank, commanded by Lieutenant Wittman, sufficed to block the advance of the 7th Armoured Division, and the ensuing battle was marked by heavy losses. On June 15, the British were forced to admit the defeat of the operation. However, another new offensive was in the planning: the capture of Caen was essential, no matter what the price.

In addition to these accumulated defeats, heavy storms at sea destroyed one of the Mulberries and damaged the other. The lack of ports also slowed down the offensive, creating difficulty in reprovisioning the troops.

Not until June 25 did Montgomery launch his new offensive. Codenamed Epsom, the offensive was designed to take Caen from the south. Although the British still were unable to completely surround the city, this new assault permitted them

Forced to steadily withdraw in the face of the Allied advance, panzergrenadiers especially fell prey to deadly air attacks. *ECPA*

Waffen-SS officers in a wheat field discuss the positions of Canadian troops. *BA*

A young Waffen-SS rifleman has camouflaged his helmet with weeds. The Waffen-SS were especially well trained, but in the end it was their fanaticism that permitted them to hold out so long against the accumulated pressure of the Allied advance. *BA*

These young Waffen-SS soldiers have just received the Iron Cross Second Class for bravery in combat. Their smiles belie the hell they have been through and the fate that will soon befall them. *BA*

to enlarge the zone under the control of the British VIII Corps and to weaken enemy defenses. The 15th Scottish Infantry Division, 11th Armoured Division, 50th Infantry Division, and 43rd Infantry Division all participated in the massive assault, which involved ninety thousand men, six hundred tanks, and seven hundred cannons. The Germans did not withdraw. The 11th Armoured Division managed to reach Hill 112 near Esquay-Notre-Dame but was forced to withdraw, bringing Operation Epsom to a close on June 29.

On July 1, west of Caen near Tilly-sur-Seulles, the Second British Army, supported by artillery, repulsed the counterattacks of the 1st SS Panzergruppe. Over the course of the battle, the Germans lost the quasi-totality of their tanks.

The extremely difficult nature of this battle, which called to mind the trench warfare of World War I, caused Allied personnel at every level, from common soldiers to the general staff, to criticize Montgomery. Montgomery defended himself by justifying

Seated on their Panzer IV, German tankers take a break to eat some bread and smoke a cigarette. In the fury of combat, many will die a fiery death, trapped in their tanks. *ECPA*

An exhausted German rifleman walks down a road with the "thousand-yard stare" in his eyes. Behind him, the wreckage of vehicles along the road testifies to violent battle. *ECPA*

A German soldier examines an inoperative Sherman tank that has just been knocked out of combat. *Archives du Calvados*

A German soldier armed with an MG-42 has set up position along a hedgerow near Caen. *BA*

the strategy, by which he aimed to keep a maximum number of enemy tanks concentrated in a fixed locality in order to facilitate American operations in the west.

Operation Charnwood began on July 4. The plan to capture Caen now depended on penetration, not encirclement. Lacking sufficient cannons, the Allies employed strategic air attacks to prepare the terrain for ground operations. Since the beginning of the invasion, the U.S. Air Force and the Royal Air Force had furnished close support as the occasion demanded, but they had never been called upon to provide large-scale direct support of ground forces. For the first time, the Allies now would employ heavy bombers directly on the battlefield. This would happen again in the American breakout during Operation Cobra.

The mission of the heavy bombers was to saturate a rectangular, suburban area north of the city. Objectives were multiple: to destroy enemy infantry and artillery positions; to cut the Germans off from their rear troops; and to demoralize the soldiers defending the

German soldiers on the alert are ready to fire a Bren gun set up in the ruins of a suburb of Caen. It would take the English six weeks to seize the capital city of Normandy, which was solidly defended by German troops. *IWM*

British troops prepare to assault an enemy position. It would require no fewer than four offensives and the loss of two thousand troops to capture Caen. *IWM*

A Sherman tank navigates a narrow village road, directed by Corp. G. Ronsky. Allied armor was unable to seize the advantage and quickly thrust toward Caen because it was so difficult to get off the beaches. *IWM*

British infantrymen advance through early-morning fog in a field on the outskirts of Caen. Contrary to their American counterparts, who were led by fearless men like Patton, the British advanced with caution, losing much time that the defenders at Caen put to excellent use. *IWM*

On July 8, soldiers from the 185th Brigade, 3rd Infantry Division, face off with the enemy near Caen. *IWM*

A moment of tension: British troops battle it out on ruined farms all around Caen. Confronting them are elite troops of the best Waffen-SS divisions. *IWM*

Two English soldiers are set to fire a PIAT, the main British platoon-level antitank weapon in World War II. The use of tanks was vital to the Battle of Caen. *IWM*

city, and hence boost the morale of the assaulting British forces. The Canadian troops kicked off the offensive on July 4, launching an advance attack that aimed to gain control of the western exit from the city. On July 7, from 9:51 to 10:30 p.m., 460 bombers of the Royal Air Force dropped nearly three thousand tons of bombs on their target.

The attack was followed by intensive shelling by British artillery; in all, 350 French civilians were found dead in the ruins. The following day, three divisions of British and Canadians assaulted the city, supported by three armored brigades.

Numerous German soldiers staggered from the ruins completely dazed. Certain regiments were wiped out and others cut off. The 16th Division of the Luftwaffe, which took the brunt of the aerial bombardment, lost three-quarters of its men. The 12th SS Panzer Division was reduced to a single battalion. In spite of these losses, the Germans refused

An English infantry soldier herds cows into Caen. The animals will furnish much-needed meat for the many refugees in the city. *IWM*

to be discouraged and continued to battle with unrelenting fierceness. Heaps of ruins and enormous craters prohibited British tanks from making rapid progress.

The evening of July 8, Rommel decided to prepare for evacuation and ordered that all heavy weapons be positioned on the south bank of the river Orne. The following day, the British and Canadians penetrated the town from both sides, reaching the Orne. The bridges had been destroyed, and the roads were choked with ruins. Unable to cross the river, the soldiers were obliged to halt their progress, but a section of Caen was finally in Montgomery's hands.

To the south, the Germans still held the city, although they were in serious disarray. On July 10, the British Second Army headed south on Montgomery's orders to the area between Caumont and Caen.

Infantrymen clear rubble from the streets of the devastated capital. Three hundred fifty Norman civilians lost their lives, crushed or buried in the ruins of their homes and shelters. *IWM*

A British soldier milks a cow on a farm outside of Caen. *IWM*

In the following weeks, "Monty" continued to hold in the face of German defenses, launching Operation Goodwood on July 18. Mounting a powerful tank assault in the east that concentrated the majority of enemy armored forces on his own position, Montgomery freed the Americans to undertake the southern offensive in the Department of La Manche and gain control of Saint-Lô. The liberation of Caen was completed on July 20, 1944.

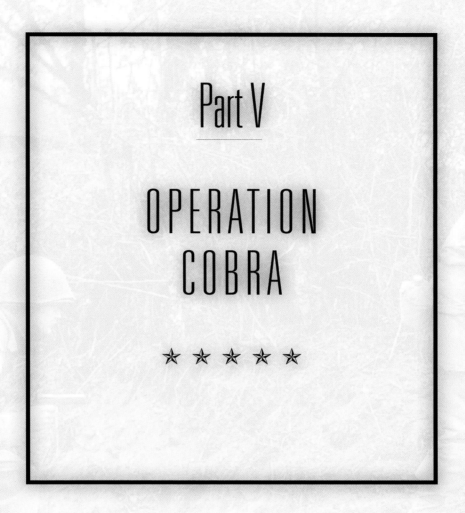

Part V

OPERATION COBRA

★ ★ ★ ★ ★

Conditions on the Normandy front are going from bad to worse.
Given the circumstances, we expect our adversaries to pierce our lines
very shortly, particularly on the front held by the Seventh Army,
and to make a deep thrust into French territory. Our soldiers
are everywhere fighting like heroes, but the unequal battle will soon be over.

—FIELD MARSHAL ERWIN ROMMEL,
message to Hitler, July 15, 1944

After the fight for the beaches, the Americans would fight for the hedgerows. It would be a war of nerves, where every bush could harbor a sniper, every orchard must be won by assault, and tanks would prove easy targets for a determined enemy. *NARA*

13
PRELIMINARIES

ONCE THE NORTH OF THE Cotentin Peninsula was liberated, the Americans turned their attention to the southern part of the Manche, with the hope of rapidly breaking out of the hedgerows. Four long weeks of exhaustive battle would be necessary to attain their goal, but the Americans finally opened the route to Brittany at the end of July, and two weeks later completely liberated the Department of La Manche. Before this victory took place, however, thousands of GIs would lose their lives in the Battle of the Hedgerows.

Since the capture of Carentan by paratroopers on June 12, frontlines in the sector had not budged an inch. The Americans had concentrated all their efforts on Cherbourg. Meanwhile, farther east, troops who had debarked on Omaha Beach were ground to a standstill in the battle for Saint-Lô.

Bradley launched his attack with vastly superior forces that seemed likely to crush the enemy quickly—at least on paper. Over the range of a seventy-kilometer front, four American army corps faced six German divisions, some of which were down to a single regiment. General Middleton's VIII Corps set out on July 3 with the objective of taking Lessay and Coutances but was forced to battle for a week against the well-established defenses of General Mählmann at La Haye-du-Puits. To reach Coutances, the Americans first had to break the deadlock at La Haye-du-Puits, whose surrounding hills the Germans had heavily fortified. The terribly bloody struggle to seize the monts or hilltops lasted ten long days. This struggle was the indispensable preliminary to Operation Cobra.

The southward path of the Allied army depended on the capture of La Haye-du-Puits because it was an important crossroads for routes to Cherbourg, Carentan, Barneville, and Coutances. To the west of the city lay

Vehicles and armor of every sort attempting to navigate narrow country roads often bogged down in muddy quagmires. *NARA*

The Americans pushed back the Germans field by field, hedgerow by hedgerow. Each field was a bastion that could only be seized at enormous cost. Throughout the entire month of July, pouring rain turned unpaved country roads and lanes into muddy messes, causing many Allied delays. *NARA*

the estuary of Ay; to the east were the marshlands—both difficult terrains to master. Breaking the deadlock was thus first necessary to seize the high ground; this, in turn, would permit the southern passage of Patton's tanks over the valley roads.

In the final days of June, General Mählmann had positioned his 353rd Infantry Division in the hills defending the northern approach to La Haye-du-Puits: Mont-de-Doville, Mont-Castre, and Mont-Etenclin (Hills 131 and 95). The 353rd had transformed each of these points into solidly entrenched encampments. With relatively modest means of defense—no bunkers, only trenches, foxholes, and a few small batteries and machine gun positions—Mählmann had achieved a model tactical position. Well ensconced on the heights, the Germans dominated the entire region, eliminating all possibility of surprise attack and obliging their enemy to pass through the jaws of a deadly trap.

General Middleton's VIII Corps launched the offensive on July 3 and immediately confronted Mählmann's forces in a terrible bloodbath. Artillery duels, infantry charges, hand-to-hand combat, counterattacks, and aerial bombardment continued for ten days.

On July 3, Mont-de-Doville fell to the Americans of the 79th Infantry Division. Not long later, paratroopers from the 82nd Airborne Division seized Mont-Etenclin at

Americans use a captured SS panzer division soldier as a human shield, placing him on the hood of their jeep to dissuade enemy snipers from opening fire as they drive through the winding country roads. *NARA*

dawn on Independence Day, July 4, 1944. This was the last battle in Normandy for General Ridgway's All Americans, who subsequently embarked for England to prepare for Operation Market-Garden, the upcoming invasion of Holland.

By July 6, the 79th Infantry Division had conquered the hills dominating the route to La-Haye-du-Puits. At Mont-Castre the same scenario played out: launching its attack on July 3, the 90th Infantry Division battled ferociously until one of its battalions was finally able to reach the summit on July 6. On July 8, fighting again broke out on Mont-Castre; not until the 12th were the Americans able to lay claim to the hill entirely, after engaging in heavy confrontations with the SS Division Das Reich—responsible for massacring the village of Oradour-sur-Glâne in central France—and a regiment of para-troopers brought in as reinforcements from Brittany.

Meanwhile, the 79th Infantry Division and the 8th Infantry Division were slowly advancing toward La Haye-du-Puits. Deserted by its population on June 7, the city now lay in ruins. The following day, the Americans had numerous confrontations with enemy soldiers hidden among the ruins as the GIs carried out the murderous and painstaking work of cleaning out the town, street by street, house by house. On July 9, La Haye-du-Puits was finally liberated.

After a dozen days of bloody combat between General Collins' VII Corps and General Mählmann's grenadiers, La Haye-du-Puits was liberated on July 9. Seizing control of the hills to the north of the town was a vital preliminary to Operation Cobra. *NARA*

A 79th Infantry Division outpost at the entrance to Lessay. The Germans have now withdrawn to their third line of defense (the *wassersterlung*, or positions at the waterline), relying on the rivers Ay, Sèves, Taute, and Terrette as natural barriers. *NARA*

The Americans had advanced eleven kilometers in ten days, but their casualties numbered ten thousand men killed or wounded, including three thousand for the 79th Infantry alone. Only at the successful conclusion of these preliminary battles could Operation Cobra be put into effect.

The American war machine bogged down in the hedgerows, where its tanks did not have enough room to maneuver in the hollow lanes. With no direct observation of enemy positions, their artillery was obliged to fire thousands of rounds, just to permit the infantry to cautiously creep a few feet forward. Meanwhile the air force was nailed to the ground, unable to fly because of adverse weather. In such conditions, the terrible task of taking five kilometers of ground and capturing Sainteny fell squarely on the frontline infantry soldier. In the space of one week, seven thousand Americans became casualties of war.

The situation was very grave: by mid-July, the Allies had already delivered to Normandy almost a million and a half men, just as many tons of matériel, and three hundred thousand vehicles—all of which were now backed up in a bridgehead of narrow perimeter that was already full to overflowing. Whatever the price, the pressure to expand required an immediate breakout from the hedgerows.

Riflemen from the 2nd Armored Division dressed in camouflage are positioned in a hollow lane to the west of Port-Broccard. They are wearing two-piece herringbone twill camouflage jungle suits, which were little used in Normandy for fear they would be confused with the camouflaged fatigues of the Waffen-SS. *NARA*

On July 29, troops in Coutances pass by shelled-out buildings and the wreckage of German vehicles on the Boulevard Alsace-Lorraine, marching south in the drive to Avranches. *NARA*

The walking wounded: these men are the lucky ones. Operation Cobra succeeded only at a staggering price in human lives. In two weeks of combat, the Americans advanced only five to six kilometers and lost seven thousand men. *NARA*

Long weeks of battling through the hedgerows exhausted American and German forces alike. The Americans slowly gained territory, advancing yard by yard. On July 18, 28th Infantry Division soldiers managed to seize the road junction at the entrance to Saint-Lô, the crossroads for the routes to Torigni, Bayeux, and Isigny. *NARA*

14

THE BREAKTHROUGH AT SAINT-LÔ

★ ★ ★ ★ ★

FILLED WITH HOPE ON JUNE 6, the inhabitants of Saint-Lô were plunged into despair and suffering only a few hours later when Allied bombing began. Saint-Lô was bombarded for several weeks on end, until the martyred city was finally liberated on July 18.

On the morning of June 6, the joyous news traveled through the city like a lighted fuse: the Americans have landed! They are only thirty kilometers away! The most cautious of the city's inhabitants replenished their stock of provisions, put their money in the bank, or even left town. But the vast majority remained in the city, commenting on events and waiting for further news.

The first alert sounded at 10:00 a.m.: a small group of Allied planes dropped four bombs on the Agneaux electrical plant, then returned a quarter of an hour later to finish up the job. A second alert took place at 4:40 p.m., when the Saint-Lô train station was bombed and strafed by machine gun. Shortly after 8:00 p.m., events took a fatal turn. Seated at the family dinner table, the inhabitants of Saint-Lô heard a droning in the sky. The curious who rose from the table to investigate witnessed a terrifying spectacle: three formations of B-26 Marauders were raining bombs straight down on their city, and several neighborhoods already had sprung up in flames.

Emergency efforts were rapidly organized, but few means were at hand: a few days earlier, the Germans had requisitioned the only two motorized water pumps in the city. Rescuers armed with nothing but courage and personal strength desperately searched for survivors among the ruins. The population fled to the neighboring countryside, passing in droves through the hollow lanes among the hedgerows. It was lucky they did so, for around 12:30 a.m., Saint-Lô was surprised by a second bombing attack. In the space of ten minutes, approximately fifty bombers

A soldier identified as Ralph Reese drives an M28 cargo carrier baptized the *Saint-Lô Special* down one of the many narrow roads lined with hedgerows in the sector. *NARA*

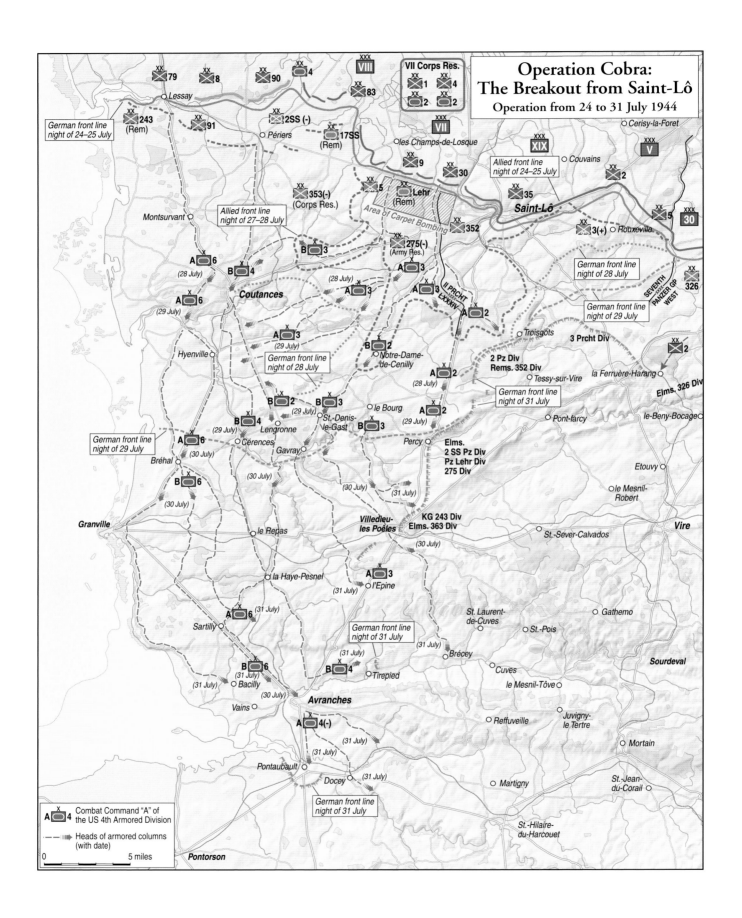

**Operation Cobra:
The Breakout from Saint-Lô**

Operation from 24 to 31 July 1944

VII Corps Res.

XXX
VIII

XX 79
XX 8
XX 90
XX 4
XXX
1
XXX
4
XXX
2
XXX
2
XXX
83

XX 243 (Rem)
XX 91
XX 2SS (-)
XX 17SS (Rem)
Lessay
Périers
les Champs-de-Losque
o Cerisy-la-Foret
XXX
VII
XXX
XIX
XXX
V
o Couvains

*German front line
night of 24–25 July*

XX 9
XX 30
*Allied front line
night of 24–25 July*
XXX
2

XX 353(-)
(Corps Res.)
XX 5
Lehr
(Rem)
XX 35
Saint-Lô
XXX
5
XXX
30

Montsurvant o
*Allied front line
night of 27–28 July*
Area of Carpet Bombing
XX 352
XX 3(+) o Rouxeville

A X 6
B X 4
(28 July)
B 3
XX 275(-)
(Army Res.)
A 3
A 3
A 3
A 2
II PRCHT
LXXXIV
*German front line
night of 28 July*
*German front line
night of 29 July*
SEVENTH PANZER GP WEST
XX 326

Coutances
(28 July)

A X 6
(29 July)
A 3
(29 July)
A 3
o Troisgots
3 Prcht Div
XX 2

Hyenville o
*German front line
night of 28 July*
B 2
o Notre-Dame-de-Cenilly
**2 Pz Div
Rems. 352 Div**
o Tessy-sur-Vire
la Ferruère-Harang o

A 2
(28 July)
*German front line
night of 31 July*
Elms. 326 Div

B 2
B 3
o le Bourg
A 2
o le Mesnil-Robert

B 4
(29 July)
St-Denis-le-Gast
B 3
(29 July)
Percy o
**Elms.
2 SS Pz Div
Pz Lehr Div
275 Div**
o Etouvy

Lengronne
*German front line
night of 29 July*
A X 6
(30 July)
o Cérences
Gavray o
o Pont-farcy
le-Beny-Bocage o

Bréhal o
B X 6
o St.-Sever-Calvados
o **Vire**

(30 July)
o le Repas
*Villedieu-
les Poêles*
**KG 243 Div
Elms. 363 Div**
o St. Laurent-de-Cuves
o **Sourdeval**

Granville
(30 July)

o la Haye-Pesnel
A 3
o l'Epine
o St.-Pois
o Gathemo

A X 6
(31 July)
Sartilly o
*German front line
night of 31 July*
(31 July)
o Brécey
o Cuves
o le Mesnil-Tôve
o Juvigny-le Tertre

B X 6
(31 July)
o Bacilly
B 4
o Tirepied
(31 July)
o Reffuveille
o Mortain

(30 July)
o Vains
Avranches
A 4(-)
(31 July)
St.-Jean-du-Corail o

o Pontaubault
(31 July)
o Docey
(31 July)
o Martigny

*German front line
night of 31 July*
o St.-Hilaire-du-Harcouet

Legend

A X 4 — Combat Command "A" of
the US 4th Armored Division

— Heads of armored columns
(with date)

0 ————— 5 miles

Pontorson

emptied their holds over the city in a raid more massive than the last. The survivors witnessed an apocalyptic vision as their city was devoured in flames before their eyes—a vision which only worsened later that night when Allied planes finished up their mission, passing over the city several times yet again. Saint-Lô collapsed in a fiery inferno to the sound of explosions, screams, cries for help, and sobs.

By the close of June 15, the Americans had advanced to within a few kilometers of Saint-Lô. It would nevertheless take a month of ferocious combat before they could finally liberate the city. The 29th Infantry Division and the 35th Infantry Division ground to a standstill due to a lack of air support: adverse weather conditions once again prevented fighter-bombers from participating in the mission.

In any case, the Germans were too well hidden deep in the hedgerows to fear an Allied air attack. The forces of the Reich largely consisted of the Seventh Army, under the orders of SS Gen. Paul Hausser. The hedgerow country or *bocage* so foreign to American troops was crisscrossed with thick hedges and cut by hollow lanes propitious to guerilla warfare and surprise attack. Unable to advance through the muddy labyrinth, tanks were sitting ducks for Panzerfaust attacks by German patrols determined to fight on. Such conditions rendered it impossible for the Americans to conduct the kind of massive offensive at which they so excelled.

On the German side, just a few dozen meters from the American lines, soldiers took advantage of every defensive opportunity the terrain could possibly offer, establishing

On a death-strewn road, soldiers from the 29th Infantry Division pass the body of a German soldier and the wreckage of an enemy vehicle. *NARA*

Two American tankers examine a damaged Panzer IV tank along a road at Saint-Denis. *NARA*

An American medic attends to a German soldier with a grievous facial wound. *NARA*

A German convoy decimated on a road near Saint- Lô. The Allies controlled the airspace over Normandy and interdicted enemy convoys during the hours of daylight. *NARA*

Progress is very slow, for every hedgerow may hide an enemy sniper who can hold up an advance for several hours. *NARA*

On July 25, Pont-Hébert, to the north of Saint-Lô was also subjected to bombing. The city was later completely rebuilt. *NARA*

dominant positions that were easily defended on the hills around Saint-Lô, Villiers-Frossard and Saint-André de l'Epine, and in the marshes at Sainteny. The Battle of the Hedgerows, so detested by the Allied soldiers, actually consisted of many small-unit battles, where the collective courage of the group, the determination and experience of a lieutenant, or the initiative of a single private could all determine the outcome of a battle.

Bogged down in the mud, American forces were torn to shreds all throughout the region. When they managed to capture a farm or a country road at the end of an exhausting day of battle, an official communiqué announced the victory as a reward for their superhuman efforts. But victory at what price? Every advance of one hundred meters cost one hundred men. To capture Sainteny, ferociously defended by an SS division with tank support from Das Reich, General Collins' VII Corps battled steadily for two full weeks, from July 1 to 14. On a single day of the battle, July 5, the 83rd Infantry Division managed to advance two hundred meters and take a few prisoners. The price of doing so was 1,500 men wounded or killed in action. After two weeks of fighting at Sainteny, the Americans had advanced five to six kilometers at the sacrifice of seven thousand soldiers.

The Germans defended every village on the approach to Saint-Lô as ferociously as if the entire war depended on it. On the outskirts of the city, casualty rates soared: between July 7 and 22, the 35th Infantry Division lost more than 2,000 men; the 29th lost 3,700; and the 30th lost no fewer than 3,900. Faced with the sacrifice of so many

On the road from Couvains, GIs encounter a German soldier with a white flag less than seven hundred meters from the entrance to Saint-Lô. *NARA*

"Saint-Lô, Capital of Ruins": G.I.s file through the rubble toward Notre-Dame de Saint-Lô. The damaged church rising from the ruins symbolizes the horror the city has endured since June 6. *NARA*

Taking a minute's rest next to the sign for Saint-Lô, just outside the city limits, is a soldier identified as A. Landbish, an MP with the 29th Infantry Division. *NARA*

men, the American high command changed tactics and called for massive artillery support. On July 15, 35th Infantry Division artillery fired eleven thousand shells and seven thousand white phosphorus mortar rounds in a deluge that destroyed targeted villages and the entire surrounding countryside.

Battling for the hedgerows exhausted American forces, but the Germans were no less depleted. Slowly, yard by yard, the Americans gained ground. On July 18, elements of the 29th Infantry managed to seize the crossroads for the routes to Torigni, Bayeux, and Isigny at the entry to Saint-Lô, giving the Americans a view of the city at last. German planes bombarded this strategic position but did not succeed in wresting it from the Americans. Partially surrounded inside Saint-Lô, Seventh Army officers requested permission to withdraw. Their command post relayed the request to Army Group B, under Rommel's command, only to discover headquarters in a panic. The field marshal had just been wounded by machine gun, caught on the road in the sights of an English fighter-bomber. Rommel was evacuated and soon replaced by General von Kluge.

It was during this uncertain period that the defenders at Saint-Lô received the response to their request to withdraw. Contrary to Hitler's orders to "fight to the last man," Army Group B Headquarters authorized the Seventh Army to establish a new line of defense behind the city. In the night of 17–18 July, the Germans gradually disengaged and quietly withdrew from the city.

Arriving from the north, a U.S. convoy enters a shattered Saint-Lô. The struggle is nevertheless not yet over: although the Germans have vacated the city, the snipers they have left behind will cost American lives over the following days. *NARA*

A tanker armed with a Colt .45 examines enemy positions through his binoculars at Saint-Lô. Meanwhile, his photographer takes cover behind the Sherman. *NARA*

The body of a German soldier lies at the foot of the plateau. Entrenched to the west and southwest, the Germans continued to plunder the city. *NARA*

Americans crossing Saint-Lô pass by the ancient château, damaged in the bombing. The city's luckiest citizens were able to take shelter in a tunnel in the plateau (unseen, to the left of the photograph). *NARA*

The post office at Saint-Lô was ravaged by bombing in the heart of the city on June 6. *NARA*

A jeep stops at the foot of the Château de Saint-Lô. The tunnel used as a bomb shelter durning the horrific bombardment of the city is located in the imposing rock wall to the left. *NARA*

American P-47 pilots visit the front lines to inspect a German Panther tank, destroyed on July 19 at Saint-Lô. *NARA*

The struggle for Saint-Lô was nevertheless not over. Although the vast majority of the Germans had withdrawn, the city nevertheless remained a warren for enemy snipers who claimed the lives of American soldiers over the following days. The main body of German troops was not far away. Entrenched to the southeast and west of Saint-Lô, they continued to shell the city until the area was finally completely cleared during Operation Cobra.

THE BREAKOUT

After the capture of Saint-Lô on July 18, General Bradley and General Collins focused on one idea: to be over and done with the damned battle for the hedgerows and stop the sacrifice of thousands of their men. Not even considering the delay in the original schedule planned before the landings, Avranches, fifty kilometers beyond Saint-Lô, should have been in American hands since June 26. It was out of the question to take another month, and maybe even more, to liberate the entire Department of La Manche. It was time to change tactics.

Bradley and Collins decided to pull out all the stops and completely annihilate enemy resistance by concentrating every force at their disposal on a single narrow sector

Two Panthers destroyed near Dézert on July 13. The tanks belonged to 1st Company, Panzer-Lehr Regiment 130, which attacked the 3rd Armored Division. Sights like this were common during Operation Cobra. *NARA*

A soldier with Combat Command B, 2nd U.S. Armored Division, takes a coffee break at Port-Broccard on July 29. *NARA*

to create a breach in enemy lines. Armored units then would rapidly pass through the gap in a southern thrust to quickly wipe out German positions.

The commander of the First U.S. Army, Bradley, laid out the plans for Operation Cobra with his general staff in mid-July. Designed to put an end to costly and interminable static infantry battles, Cobra was based on a single idea: to rupture the enemy front by concentrating maximum force on a limited area, including simultaneous air and artillery attacks, followed by a ruthless ground campaign. In an exception to past operations, for once the Americans would massively employ saturation bombing to the immediate benefit of the infantry.

The sector chosen for the operation was a swath of land seven by three kilometers large, located south of RN-800 between Hébécrevon and Mesnil-Vigot. At the disposition of the Army were 1,800 heavy bombers from the U.S. Eighth Air Force and 1,100 medium bombers from the U.S. Ninth Air Force. On the ground, VII Corps would carry out the principal effort, reinforced by an artillery brigade and the firepower of VIII Corps and XIX Corps, on its west and east flanks, respectively—a combined force of over one thousand artillery pieces. The air force would simultaneously carry out a tactical bombing mission to the rear of the area to prohibit the

A motorcycle MP is positioned to check convoys on the route to Saint-Lô. *NARA*

COUTANCES

ON JULY 26, the Americans liberated Coutances after heavy combat, but the city was in ruins. The ancient capital of the Cotentin Peninsula, Coutances was built on the site of the Roman city of Cosedia. The bombings on July 6, 7, and 14 left the city three-quarters destroyed. By miracle, the splendid eleventh- and thirteenth-century cathedral was largely spared, left standing in the midst of ruins heaped about its very walls. The *cathédrale de fierté*, the pride and joy of its city, was damaged but repairable: its elegant nave was still standing, and although the lead had melted from its dome, its vaults were still intact. Close by, the fifteenth-century Church of Saint-Nicholas could no longer be used, and the bishop's palace had burned to the ground. In all, 1,900 houses were damaged, 612 of which were reduced to rubble, and two thousand families were burned out of their homes. Three hundred fifty civilians died in the bombing. *Image credit: NARA*

arrival of German reinforcements. The success of the operation demanded that the bombing be extremely precise, to ensure the safety of Allied troops who would necessarily be positioned very near the targeted area in order to guarantee immediate follow-up. Directly preceding the ground assault, ninety minutes of unrelenting heavy artillery fire and saturation aerial bombardment of the zone was planned to remove all major obstacles to an immediate breakout by the infantry; a follow-up thrust by armored units would take place the following day. The concentration of firepower was extremely intense: VII Corps would concentrate its entire attack on an area reduced to a mere seven kilometers, the size of the targeted zone.

Set to launch on July 20, the operation was delayed for several days. There was another attempt to begin the attack on July 24, but rain and a low ceiling caused Bradley to call it off in extremis, although the first wave of bombers had already taken off. They mistakenly dropped their bombs on American frontlines, causing 150 casualties.

Bradley relaunched the offensive on July 25. Again, bombing errors occurred, amounting to one hundred dead and five hundred wounded. But the bombs also fell on German forces. In the restricted locality of Saint-Gilles, Marigny, and Hébécrevon, not a square meter of land was spared from Allied attack. The Panzer Lehr Division was

Mail Call! For the first time since the battle began, 29th Infantry Division GIs in the Saint-Lô sector receive their mail. *NARA*

The temporary grave of German General Erich Marcks, whose command post was at Saint-Lô. Commander of the LXXXIV Army Corps, he was mortally wounded by a fighter-bomber on June 12 near Hébécrevon. *NARA*

An MP indicates the remains of the Chapelle-en-Juger church. *NARA*

completely decimated at Chapelle-en-Juger during the maelstrom. General Bayerlein, the commander of the unit, later declared: "My frontline was cratered like the moon, and at least 70 percent of my men were wiped out—dead, wounded, or in a state of severe shock"

The following day, Operation Cobra claimed its initial victory: the first American armored division raced through the breach between Saint-Gilles and Marigny, with three other divisions close on its heels. To the west, Lessay was finally liberated. July 27 saw the liberation of Périers. The following day, the Germans were definitively routed from the area, abandoning a vast amount of territory to American control. The Allies had again seized the initiative.

On July 28, Patton, who had heretofore remained out of sight at his secret command post at Nehou, took command of the armored offensive. The burden of the ground mission, so far confided to VII Corps, now passed to VIII Corps. The cadence of the

War correspondents interview a captured German officer in the Saint-Lô area. *NARA*

Two well-known figures of American journalism, Robert Capa (left) and Ernest Hemingway (right), pose with a young tanker at Port-Broccard on July 30. *NARA*

An American soldier shows off a Fallchirmjägergewehr 42, used by German paratroopers. Other weapons captured at Saint-Lô are stacked behind him to the right. *NARA*

mission accelerated under Patton: the order of the day was "Advance!" Thrusting ever more quickly into enemy-held territory, Patton operated on the principle that tactical mobility was the best protection for an armored division. With the benefit of constant air support, he pushed his tanks onward to Coutances, which was liberated on July 29 just before his arrival.

In just three days, the Americans had advanced twenty-four kilometers. From this point on, nothing could stop the amazing progress of Collins' men. On July 29, a German convoy of a hundred vehicles combining the remnants of two SS divisions and von der Heydte's 6th Fallschirmjäger Regiment was trapped in the village of Roncey, southeast of Coutances. All afternoon, fighter-bomber and incessant Allied artillery attacks reduced the convoy to cinders. Surviving enemy troops fought fiercely, most notably at Saint-Denis and Cèrences, in the effort to rejoin their forces, which were already in full rout.

After Roncey, the Germans no longer resisted American forces. From this point on, they had but two desires: to escape by any means possible or surrender. Taking prisoners by the thousands, the Americans rapidly moved through the Manche. On July 29 they reached Hambye and Orval; on July 30, they took Bréhal, Lengronne, La Haye-Pesnel, and Montchaton. Finally, on July 31, they liberated Granville and Avranches. That afternoon, the bridge at Pontaubault was secured without resistance, thus opening up the road to Brittany. Patton now could truly unleash the armored fury of his Third Army. Seven divisions sped through the bottleneck at Pontaubault in the space of seventy-two hours. Freed at last from the confines of the hedgerows, Patton's tanks could finally deploy in the open. In a single week, the Americans progressed from a static war to a war of dynamic movement. Operation Cobra had been a total success.

In the countryside outside Saint-Lô, an old woman mourns her damaged house, which has partially been destroyed in the fighting. By the time the Battle of Normandy was over, sixty thousand houses had been burned, damaged in combat, or destroyed by bombing. *NARA*

Part VI

NORMANDY'S STALINGRAD

★ ★ ★ ★ ★

There will be no withdrawals with rearguard actions,
nor any disengagement to establish new frontlines.
Every man will fight and fall, there where he stands.

—Adolf Hitler,
message to General Hausser

On August 8 and 9, ferocious battles took place between German and American troops over farms, lanes, and crossroads throughout the area around Mortain. The photograph depicts houses at the entrance to the town. *NARA*

15

THE COUNTERATTACK
AT MORTAIN

THE EUPHORIA OF THE RAPID American drive toward the south of the Manche gave hope to the inhabitants of Mortain and surrounding areas that they soon would be liberated and would suffer no damage to their region. Unfortunately, their fate was nothing of the sort. Little did they know that their city was instead soon to become the linchpin of an enemy counteroffensive, Operation Lüttich. Launched in mid-July, the battle raged in the region for a week, as the Germans played their last card in the attempt to recapture Avranches.

Hoping to cut Patton off from his rear troops by attacking his flank, Hitler ordered von Kluge to assemble all available armored forces for an attack on Avranches, passing though Mortain. Rapidly arriving at the Seventh Army command post at Mortain, General von Kluge sent a message to the German high command stating the urgent need for fresh troops. He concluded that it was still too early to know whether the enemy could be stopped in its tracks.

General von Kuge told SS-Obergruppenführer Hausser, commander of the Seventh Army, that he intended to reestablish the continuity of the front all the way to the western shore of the Cotentin Peninsula. He believed the counterattack should be launched with as little delay as possible. The first step was to pull all valid forces from the current front, then reassemble them in a single place for a virulent offensive on Avranches, the keystone to German defenses in the area. When necessary, the army would be supported by units of the German Fifth Panzer Army and elements of the Fifteenth and Nineteenth Armies.

Hausser explained to von Kluge that it initially would be necessary to seal the gap as much as possible by concentrating troops in a line of defense to the south, west, and southeast of Avranches. He hoped to launch a simultaneous counterattack in the direction of the city, carving out a depth of thirty kilometers. The terrain would be used to maximum advantage to protect his armor during the engagement.

Waffen-SS soldiers prepare to mount combat. All wear the speckled camouflage characteristic of elite SS units. *NARA*

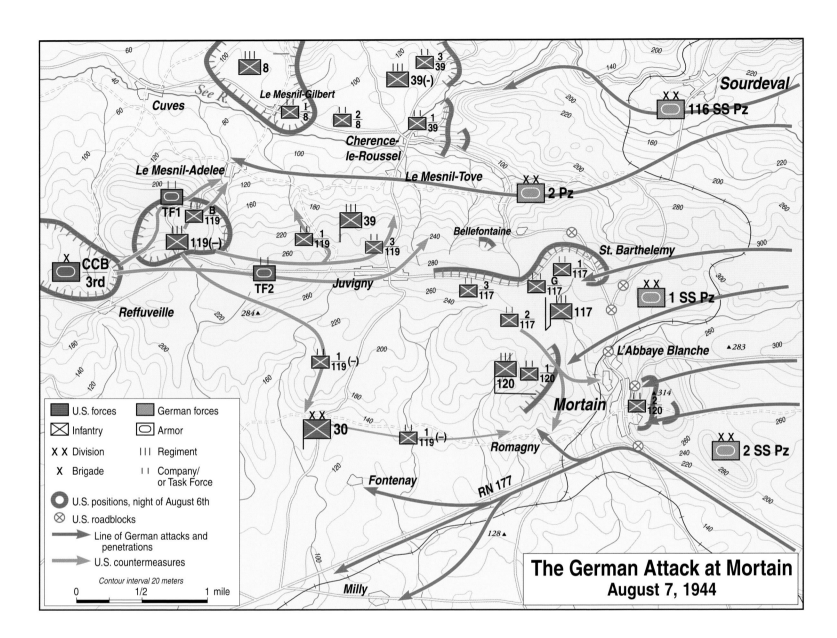

The German Attack at Mortain
August 7, 1944

Legend:
- U.S. forces
- German forces
- Infantry
- Armor
- X X Division
- III Regiment
- X Brigade
- II Company/ or Task Force
- U.S. positions, night of August 6th
- U.S. roadblocks
- Line of German attacks and penetrations
- U.S. countermeasures

Contour interval 20 meters

0   1/2   1 mile

At approximately 11:00 p.m. on August 6, General von Kluge led three divisions from XLVII Corps, including 147 tanks, under cover of heavy fog in a successful counterattack on Mortain. He retook the city at daybreak on August 7, and was soon poised to overrun Saint-Hilaire-du-Harcouët.

At midnight, the 2nd SS Panzer Division engaged American units, earning a rapid victory. For the Germans, all proceeded according to plan. Seizing Mortain close to 4:00 a.m., they rapidly moved on, leaving a few pockets of resistance that continued

American artillerymen have set up an M5 3-inch gun at a crossroads near Mortain. *NARA*

The wreckage of an American convoy in the main street of Mortain on August 12. *NARA*

A light armored car traverses the flaming streets of Mortain on August 12, after a round of fierce combat. *NARA*

SS-OBERGRUPPENFÜHRER PAUL HAUSSER (1880–1972)

THE SON OF an officer, Paul Hausser joined the Prussian army at age nineteen after several years as a military cadet. During World War I, he fought with the 155th Regiment in Romania, becoming a commander by the end of the war.

A talented officer, he was promoted to division general in 1932. In World War II, he commanded the new SS Das Reich Division, which fought under his command in Holland and Belgium. Battles in France followed in the cities of Reims, Orléans, and Bordeaux, which he reached in June 1940. After fighting in the Balkans, with the capture of Belgrade, the division received heavy weapons.

In June 1941, the Das Reich Division fought on the eastern front, participating in the battles of Smolensk and Kiev, for which Hausser was awarded the Knight's Cross of the Iron Cross. His division next fought on the outskirts of Moscow, where he was severely wounded by shrapnel and lost an eye.

In November 1942, General Hausser took command of II Corps of the Waffen-SS, which occupied southern France that month. In January 1943, II SS-Panzerkorps was sent to defend Kharkov in the Ukraine, where General Hausser acted on personal initiative to save several German divisions. Having acted against Hitler's orders, he expected to be relieved of his command, but this did not occur. In summer 1943, he led his armored corps into battle at Kursk, the largest tank battle of the war, commanding three armored divisions consisting of over a thousand tanks at the Battle of Prochorowka.

When the Allies invaded Normandy in June 1944, the II SS-Panzerkorps returned to France, where it fought against the British VIII Corps' offensive to break through German left-flank defenses at Caen. Hausser took command of the Seventh Army, which after the German counteroffensive at Mortain was forced continually to retreat before the Allied advance.

At the end of the war, General Hausser defended the cities of Mannheim, Heidelberg, and Karlsruhe. He was taken prisoner May 8, 1945, and remained in prison until 1949. In 1972, Paul Hausser died at the age of ninety-two in Ludwigsburg. *Image credit: Dominique François*

The Americans discover heavy artillery on railway lines around Mortain. *NARA*

A villager passes by the remains of the church and the wreckage of a German convoy in Mortain on August 12, 1944. *NARA*

A GI examines the remains of a destroyed German convoy. The vehicle in the foreground was most likely a reconnaissance vehicle belonging to the 2nd SS Panzer Division "Das Reich," and in the background to the right is a Kettenkrad. *NARA*

to harass their rearguard troops. By 5:00 a.m., still according to plan, the division occupied Romagny. However, the Americans had no intention of allowing the Germans to retake Avranches. Southeast of Mortain on Hill 317, a battalion of the U.S. 30th Infantry Division refused to surrender. Completely isolated, they nevertheless fiercely resisted German attack for six days and six nights, creating an island of resistance that deterred enemy progress. In a stroke of good fortune for the Allies, the weather briefly cleared, creating a window of opportunity for the U.S. Army Air Forces to attack the German tanks.

The three hundred bombers the Luftwaffe had promised as support never materialized. German infantry and armored units were unexpectedly forced to make do on the battlefield with no aerial protection, just as the Allied air force arrived on the scene in tight formation. Attacking with unprecedented brutality, Allied planes totally paralyzed the German plan of action, grinding the attackers to a halt.

By the night of August 7, it was clear that Operation Lüttich had already failed. Nevertheless, the battle was far from over.

During the night of August 7–8, the Allies called up their reserves. At the break of dawn, they launched a counterattack with massive aerial support to retake Saint-Barthélemy and Mesnil-Tôve. After the initial shock, the two adversaries reestablished

Normans on their way to the hay field indifferently pass the remains of a German staff car. The incinerated body of a German officer can be seen entangled in the wreckage. *NARA*

The counter-offensive at Mortain was the Germans' last substantial backlash against the Americans and the prelude to their crushing defeat in the Falaise Pocket. The Allied air forces systematically decimated enemy convoys. *NARA*

A young Luftwaffe soldier in a prisoner of war (POW) camp reads a notice informing German soldiers of the plot against Hitler by members of his staff. *NARA*

their lines, with the Germans now on the defensive. By nightfall on the 8th, the northern German front threatened to crack. Continuity could no longer be guaranteed, for participating units were depleted, and lines were stretched to their furthest possible limit.

On August 8 and 9, Germans and Americans fought viciously throughout the Mortain area, battling it out over every farmhouse, lane, and crossroads. By August 10, the Americans had contained the Germans and launched a new assault. Over the night of the 11th to 12th, they massed in the foothills around Mortain in preparation for a final attack. By 10:00 a.m. they were once again in control of the town.

The Germans had just played their last card in Normandy. Pushed back to their original line of departure, the remnants of the three armored divisions that participated in Operation Lüttich received the order to withdraw east on August 12. But it was already too late: the Americans had decided to move in the same direction. Their objective was to encircle swiftly the German troops that had advanced too far in the drive to capture Avranches, and thus entrap them in a pincer movement, with the Americans to the south and the British and Canadians to the north. The trap at Falaise now was about to be set.

The faces of these tankers from the 130th Panzer-Lehr Division wear the haggard, worried look of men who no longer have any illusions about their fate. Their division would shortly be completely decimated in the Falaise Pocket. *ECPA*

16

THE FALAISE POCKET: THE ROAD OF DEATH
(Todesgang)

★ ★ ★ ★ ★

IT WAS ON THE WESTERN part of the front, in the Manche, that the Battle of Calvados would finally play out. Advancing from Saint-Lô on July 25, Patton raced toward Avranches, reaching the city on July 31 and opening in one fell swoop the road to Brittany, the Mayenne, and the Loire. To cover their advance, the Americans launched Operation Bluecoat, liberating Vire on August 8, after three days of difficult combat. Concurrently, Montgomery launched the Falaise assault, Operation Totalize, on August 7. On the German side, some generals had begun to suggest an organized retreat in order to give themselves enough time to establish a solid line of defense behind the Seine. But Hitler would hear of no such talk. Worse yet, he ordered the Mortain counterattack in the attempt to cut Patton off from his rear guard. The attempt failed, leaving German positions blocked too far to the west. Such, in brief, was the situation on the Normandy front during the first days of August.

Studying the maps, Bradley discovered an important enemy weak point. On August 8, he proposed to Eisenhower a plan to entrap the German Seventh Army in a pocket around Falaise. To the north were situated the English, the Canadians, and an armored division of Poles. To the south, a portion of Patton's army and the Free French 2nd Armored Division led by Gen. Jacques-Philippe Leclerc would make an eastern thrust to quickly overwhelm the Germans and trap them in the pocket. According to General Bradley, only once in a hundred years did an army commander have the chance to seize so great an opportunity.

But the lines of the 12th SS Panzer Division held firm. German cannons, the much-dreaded 88s, ravaged eight attacking American columns as if they had been lined up

The wreckage of a German tank and tracked vehicle in the streets of Chambois on August 21.
NARA

261

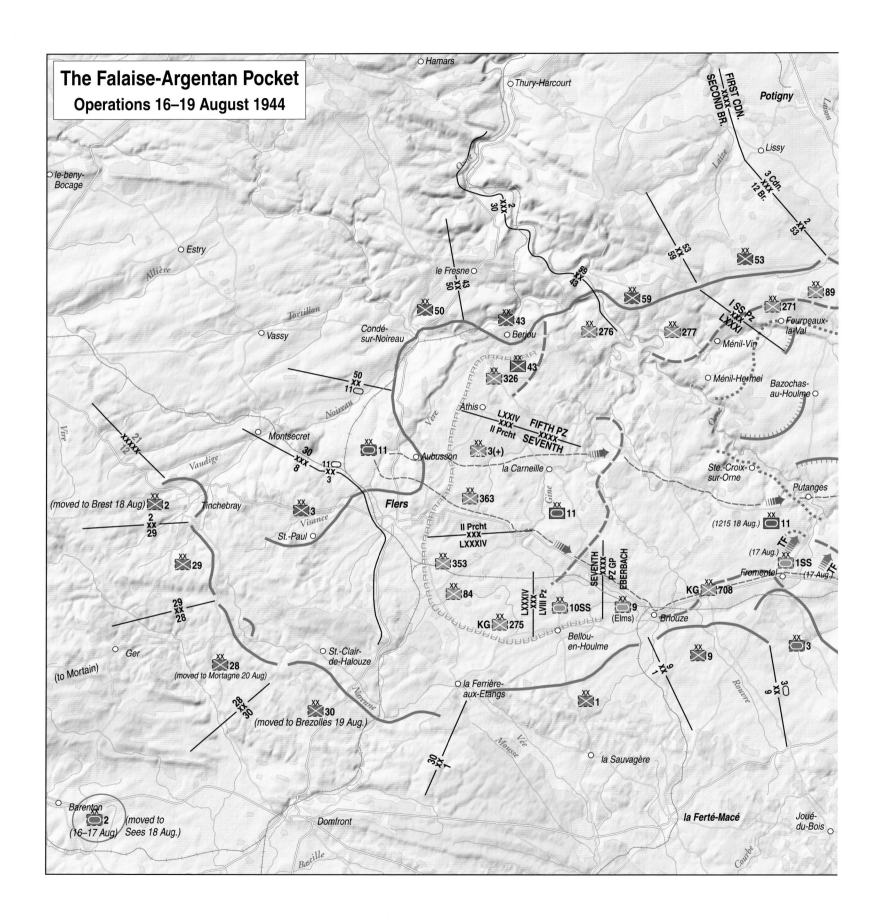

The Falaise-Argentan Pocket
Operations 16–19 August 1944

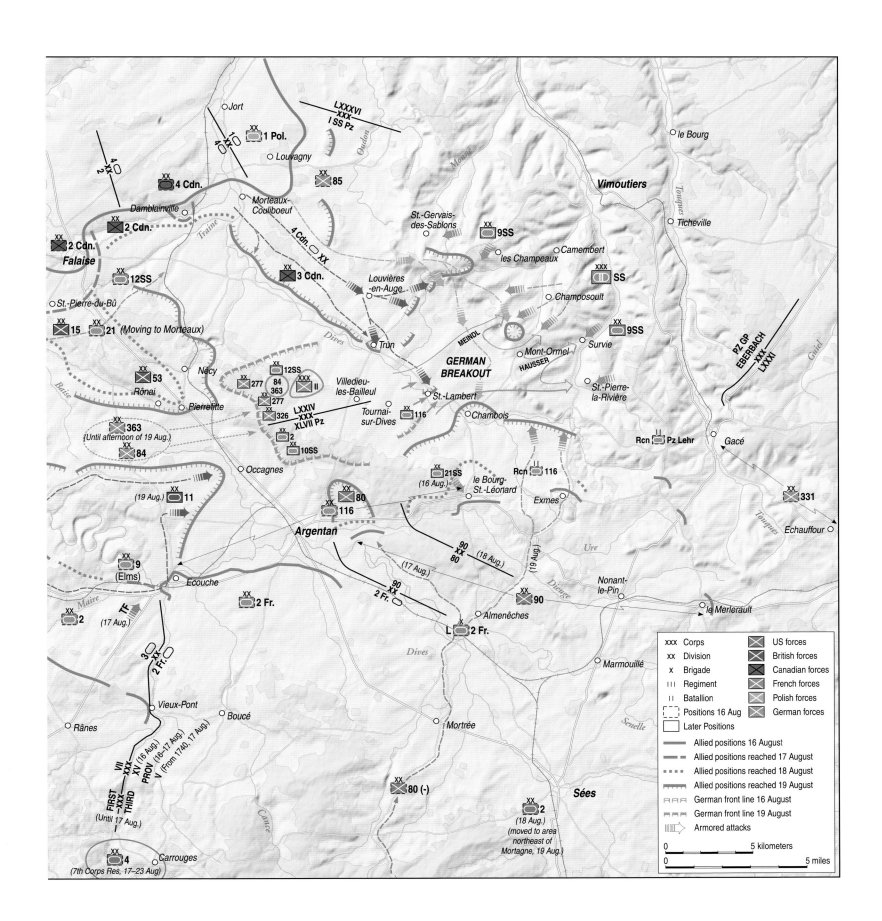

Jort

LXXXVI
XXX
I SS Pz

le Bourg

XX 1 Pol.

Louvagny

Oudon

Vimoutiers

Ticheville

XX 85

XX 4 Cdn.

Morteaux-Couliboeuf

St.-Gervais-des-Sablons

Camembert

Damblainville

XX 2 Cdn.

4 Cdn. XX

les Champeaux

XX 9SS

XXX SS

XX 2 Cdn.

Falaise

Traine

XX 3 Cdn.

Louvières-en-Auge

Champosoult

XX 12SS

Dives

Trun

MEINDL

Mont-Ormel

HAUSSER

Survie

St.-Pierre-la-Rivière

XX 9SS

St.-Pierre-du-Bû

GERMAN BREAKOUT

XX 15   XX 21   (Moving to Morteaux)

Nécy

XX 12SS

XXX 84 363

II

Villedieu-les-Bailleul

St.-Lambert

PZ GP EBERBACH
XXX
LXXXI

Guiel

XX 53

Rônai

XX 277

XX 277

Baise

Pierrefitte

XX 326

LXXIV
XXX
XLVII Pz

Tournai-sur-Dives

XX 116

Chambois

Gacé

XX 363

(Until afternoon of 19 Aug.)

XX 2

XX 84

Occagnes

XX 10SS

Rcn Pz Lehr

XX 21SS

(16 Aug.)

le Bourg-St.-Léonard

Rcn 116

XX 331

(19 Aug.) XX 11

XX 80

Exmes

Toques

XX 116

Echauffour

Argentan

Ure

XX 9

(Elms)

Ecouche

90 XX 80   (18 Aug.)

(17 Aug.)

(19 Aug.)

Dreuge

Nonant-le-Pin

Maire

TF

(17 Aug.)

XX 2 Fr.

90 XX 2 Fr.

XX 90

le Merlerault

XX 2

Almenêches

Rânes

3 XX 2 Fr.

L 2 Fr.

Dives

Marmouillé

Vieux-Pont

Boucé

Mortrée

Senelle

VII
XXX
XV (16 Aug.)
PROV (16–17 Aug.)
V (From 1740, 17 Aug.)

FIRST
XXX
THIRD

(Until 17 Aug.)

XX 80 (-)

Sées

Cance

XX 2

(18 Aug.)
(moved to area
northeast of
Mortagne, 19 Aug.)

XX 4

Carrouges

(7th Corps Res, 17–23 Aug)

Symbol	Meaning		Force
xxx	Corps		US forces
xx	Division		British forces
x	Brigade		Canadian forces
III	Regiment		French forces
II	Batallion		Polish forces
	Positions 16 Aug		German forces
	Later Positions		

Allied positions 16 August
Allied positions reached 17 August
Allied positions reached 18 August
Allied positions reached 19 August
German front line 16 August
German front line 19 August
Armored attacks

0   5 kilometers
0   5 miles

Wounded Germans are delivered to an American medical station during the fighting in Chambois. The SdKfz 251 carrying the wounded formerly belonged to the 2nd Panzer Division. *NARA*

A long column of light armored German vehicles has been stopped dead in its tracks by P-47 fighter planes. *NARA*

Abandoned German helmets and equipment litter a hay field near Chambois, left behind by POWs who have joined the long lines of prisoners marching to the rear. *NARA*

on parade. Renewing and readapting their ambitions, the Allies launched a new plan, Operation Tractable, on August 14. The same day, further south, the Third Army reached the route to Argentan at Bourg-Saint-Léonard. Only thirty-five kilometers now separated the two Allied forces as they approached each other from opposing cardinal directions.

It took ten days to close the jaws of the trap on the Germans. Although the Americans and the French advanced rapidly in the north (with Leclerc's forces liberating Alençon on August 12), the Canadians were seriously held up at the entry to Falaise. Entrenched on the last hill defending the city, five hundred German solders, a couple of dozen tanks, and a few cannons kept the 2nd Canadian Infantry Division at a respectful distance for two days, allowing the time for thousands of German troops to escape. When Falaise was finally seized on the 18th, it was nothing but ruins. This time, it was the Americans who showed up late, having stopped to mop up pockets of resistance around Argentan. The Germans propelled themselves through the remaining thirty-kilometer gap with the energy of despair.

The meeting point—the place the Allies chose to close the loop—would determine the size of the net, and hence the size of the catch. The parameters were not all that simple, however. To choose a point far to the east—the Seine or its environs, for example—would probably stretch Allied lines too thin, and thus diminish their pressure. To the contrary,

On August 20, Field Marshal Walther Model gave the Fifth Panzer Army the mission of holding a pocket of land on the left bank of the river Seine. As the sky fills with "Jabos" (as the Germans nicknamed the Allied fighter-bombers, an SdKfz 251 from the 9th SS Panzer Division "Hohenstaufen" takes concealment in a wooded area. Although the faces of these young soldiers are still full of confidence, the anxious looks they cast at the sky betray their fear of the dreaded enemy planes. *All images: NARA*

to close the net far to the west—at the Orne, for example—would allow those units already beyond the area to escape, and thus diminish the number of enemy captured. Finally, the choice was the sleepy village of Chambois, located not too far from either front. Moreover, Chambois was ideally situated as a perfect crossroads town, the junction for routes from the Canadian front to the west, the Polish to the northwest, the French to the northeast, and the American to the south. Meanwhile, in the northwest, the British army, which had just successfully completed its own breakout in the capture of Mont-Pinçon, would serve to steamroll operations in its sector. The night of August 19, the "Tough Ombres" of the U.S. 90th Infantry Division passed through the dense forest at Gouffern and into the Dives River plain, which was swarming with units of the Reich flowing back from Mortain. The fall of Falaise had left the Germans with a sole route for withdrawal, obliging them to pass through Argentan and Vimoutiers.

On August 19, the Americans and the Poles linked up. What the Germans came to call "das Stalingrad der Normandie"—Normandy's Stalingrad—was about to begin. But the enemy refused to be trapped. The infernal battle lasted for three whole days, totally depleting both adversaries. Exhausted and parched, they still fought on, led at

The Germans retreat to the Seine. Once crossed, the Seine was the last natural barrier in France that offered the Germans a chance of survival. All the vehicles have been camouflaged with leafy branches in the hope of escaping the deathly eye of the many Jabos on the hunt for enemy troops. *ECPA*

times by officers in confusion, who could do no more than shout "Advance!" in the absence of further orders. On August 20, the Germans, hunted down by plane, dazed by artillery, and massacred by Allied infantry and tanks, still continued to escape through the cracks. On August 21, the Allies completed and sealed their encirclement, winning final victories in the vicinity of Saint-Lambert and Chambois. Not until the morning of August 22 did the battle finally stop.

Describing his inspection of the battlefield in his memoir, *Crusade in Europe*, Eisenhower painted a grotesque vision that told of the bitterest of combats: "Forty-eight hours after the closing of the gap I was conducted through it on foot, to encounter scenes that could be described only by Dante. It was literally possible to walk for hundreds of yards at a time, stepping on nothing but dead and decaying flesh."

For Bradley, more than seventy thousand demoralized Germans were killed or captured in the Falaise Pocket, breaking the back of the better part of nineteen enemy divisions. Between twenty and forty thousand Germans managed to escape. For Gen. Heinrich Eberbach, commander of the Fifth Panzer Army, an estimated twenty thousand troops broke through the net, and thirty thousand were killed in the fighting from August 10 through 22. For Gen. Hans Speidel, chief of staff for Army Group B, one hundred tanks were all that remained of six armored divisions. For Field Marshal Walther Model, five decimated divisions would return to Germany.

On August 19, Montgomery took a tally of German losses in Normandy to date. Even before the heavy German losses incurred in the Falaise Pocket, the figures included twenty enemy commanders killed or captured; two army commanders wounded; two commanders in chief replaced (von Rundstedt and then von Kluge, who committed suicide on August 19); forty divisions eliminated or seriously mauled; two hundred thousand casualties, at minimum; three thousand cannons captured or destroyed; and over one thousand tanks destroyed.

THE RETREAT TO THE SEINE

As the Germans were escaping through the holes in the Falaise Pocket, the British entered the town of Lisieux, the scene of a decisive battle that would open the road to Paris. The

Soldiers with grim expressions direct the German retreat at Rouen. The only hope remaining is to get across the Seine. *ECPA*

A GI contemplates a convoy of German horse-drawn wagons destroyed by Allied air attack in the Chambois countryside on August 19. *NARA*

GENERAL PHILIPPE DE HAUTECLOQUE, *NOM DE GUERRE:* LECLERC (1902—1947)

PHILIPPE DE HAUTECLOQUE was born to a noble family from Picardy, the son of Adrien, Count of Hauteclocque. Like many of his generation, he began his military career at Saint-Cyr. He later commanded a native armored cavalry unit of Spahis in North Africa and attained the rank of captain. In 1938, he graduated from the Ecole Supérieure de Guerre.

Under his French Resistance alias, Gen. Jacques-Philippe Leclerc's bravura and exemplary conduct in the 2nd Armored Division during the "phony war" early earned him a favorable reputation. Wounded, he escaped from the Germans and decided to join the Free French after hearing de Gaulle's radio message on June 18. Passing through Spain and Portugal, he joined de Gaulle in

London on July 25. De Gaulle promoted him from captain to major (commandant).

Having former colonial experience, he was first sent to French Equatorial Africa as governor of French Cameroon. Leclerc's reputation grew in popularity at Fort Lamy in Chad. Attacking the Italians, he seized Koufra, Libya, on February 28, 1941. He used the occasion to throw down the glove anew, making the famous vow that he would never stop fighting until he had captured Strasbourg.

Leclerc's forces were integrated into the British Eighth Army and renamed the 2nd Light Division in May 1943. At the end of that year, Leclerc was promoted to major general and formed the Free French 2nd Armored Division.

Image credit: NARA

A few troops attempt to hold up the Allies as they now thrust eastward to Paris. *ECPA*

Achieving an incredible exploit, all the German troops that reached the Seine managed to cross successfully, taking with them 90 percent of their vehicles and 70 percent of their tanks. Losses were limited to four thousand vehicles, abandoned for want of gas on the banks of the river, and approximately fifty destroyed and abandoned tanks. *ECPA*

A camouflaged convoy has just been spotted by an American P-47. German troops dive for cover in ditches along the road in the face of fearsome enemy attack from the sky. *Both images: ECPA*

British 144th Armoured Division had set out for Lisieux on August 22. The first two attempts at approach ended in failure, causing numerous Allied casualties. At morning's end, the Germans still held control of the town. Elements of the 5th Queen's Regiment next took up the battle cry but were repulsed on their first attempt. The Scots of that regiment next tried to pass along the right bank of the Touques River, which they followed all the way into the suburbs. Here, isolated fire from marksmen and machine guns denied them access to the city.

Attempting to reach the train station, tanks from the 144th Armoured Regiment followed the railroad tracks, where they were pounded by constant mortar fire. Scots from the 5th Queen's engaged in the same direction, taking control of all the neighboring streets, one by one, under constant threat of ambush by a hidden enemy. As night fell, their progression slowed; the Scots maintained their positions, but the Germans still dominated the heights.

After two days of unrelenting battle in the ruins of the town, the Germans surrendered. The costs were sobering: the Allies had lost six hundred men, while the Germans had sacrificed almost four thousand in their effort to defend the town.

One of the last pockets of resistance on the route to Paris had just fallen, and the Allies could again proceed. Meanwhile, fighting in the streets of Paris had already begun in anticipation of the Allied arrival. Paris was the next objective.

With all of their lines in Normandy decimated, the Germans were left with a single option: to head east. Thousands of men would succeed in the incredible exploit of escaping the net surrounding them—between twenty thousand and forty thousand, according to various estimates. The roads were littered with the wrecks of ten thousand vehicles, five hundred tanks burnt to cinders by Allied air attack, and the carcasses of five

Two Waffen-SS soldiers hidden in a field observe an Allied tank passing by their position. *ECPA*

thousand horses, giving off the nauseating stench of death as they slowly disintegrated in the hot summer sun.

Pushed by the Allied advance on one side and slowed by the twists and turns of the Seine on the other, hundreds of thousands of fleeing German soldiers were positioned to be caught in one of the largest traps of all times. Huge columns of men and vehicles clogged every route leading to the Seine, offering easy, immobile targets to Allied planes.

Except for two railroad bridges, one at Rouen and the other at Elbeuf, there was no viable bridge downstream from Paris. It thus was necessary for German engineers to repair the ferries, which had suffered severe strafing by the U.S. Army Air Forces, and to locate barges or anything at all that could possibly serve as a raft.

The Germans nevertheless managed a miracle: at Elbeuf, over one hundred thousand men and sixteen thousand vehicles successfully crossed the Seine, employing the railroad bridge and the ferries at Duclair, Caudebec, and Villequier. Rouen, where all bridges had now been destroyed, was completely choked with vehicles, creating a natural trap.

A *feldgendarme* (German military policeman) takes a brief nap in a sidecar, exhausted by constant combat. *ECPA*

Entirely surrounded, panzergrenadiers attempt to break through an area under Allied control. The Germans later dubbed this battle "Normandy's Stalingrad." *ECPA*

Three on a match? Waffen-SS soldiers light up along a country road. They are about to establish a defensive position intended to delay the American advance. *ECPA*

When adverse weather grounded Allied planes for two days and six nights, thousands of Germans took advantage of the reprieve to cross the Seine. In the photograph, a car in a German column passing through Rouen races down a boulevard bordering the Seine. *ECPA*

Retreating Germans, attempting to cross by any means, took their chances in small barks and on rafts under constant threat of Allied air attack.

Yet, in spite of all these difficulties, the German crossing was a success. Unbelievably, not only did all the troops who made it to the Seine manage to get across, but they further saved 90 percent of their vehicles and 70 percent of their tanks. Losses were limited to four thousand vehicles abandoned on the banks of the river for lack of gas and approximately fifty tanks, all of which had been destroyed and then abandoned. A total of 240,000 Germans managed to cross the Seine.

Although they had accomplished an incredible exploit, the state of the troops who assembled on the east bank of the Seine was nevertheless far from brilliant. Their units were scattered all along the river. Exhausted, the average German infantry soldier possessed no more than his personal weapon.

The thousand-yard stare. Fatigue and worry line the face of a retreating German soldier. He knows, like thousands of others, that nothing now can stop the Allies, and the war has already been lost. *ECPA*

British Prime Minister Winston Churchill and General Omar Bradley in a field command post. The time has come to make the momentous decision to liberate Paris. *NARA*

17

THE RACE TO PARIS

ON AUGUST 7, GEN. DIETRICH von Choltitz was appointed to govern the garrison of approximately twenty thousand troops stationed in Paris. His orders were to defend the capital and—something the Allies did not yet know—to destroy it if it proved impossible to defend. Pressured by General de Gaulle as the leader of the Free French, General Leclerc, and the French Resistance—which had just mounted an insurrection in Paris on the night of August 18—Eisenhower finally agreed that the Allied thrust should not attempt to skirt Paris, as the Americans had already begun to do on August 19 at Mantes and Fontainebleau. The Parisians had taken control of the Hôtel de Police, and German troops in the capital were weak. Taking advantage of the situation, Eisenhower made his move to wrest Paris from the occupier. He confided the mission to General Leclerc's 2nd Armored Division, V Corps, and the U.S. 4th Infantry Division.

Arriving at Mantes-la-Jolie, thirty kilometers outside of Paris, the 79th Infantry Division under General Wyche was the first Allied unit to cross the Seine. A reconnaissance patrol on the left bank reported that it was indeed possible to cross the river from Rolleboise, using the dam at Mericourt. The night of August 19, the 313th Infantry Regiment crossed the dam to the right bank of the Seine, with the 314th and 315th Infantry Regiments following on August 20. The 79th seized the occasion to capture German headquarters at Roche-Guyon, which Rommel had previously used and which von Kluge had just evacuated two days prior to the Allied arrival. About thirty kilometers downstream, the little town of Vernon, crucially located at an obligatory point of passage on the Seine, fell to the Gaullist Resistance movement, the Force Française de l'Intérieur (FFI), which blew the bridge to prohibit retreating German troops from passing over to the north bank of the river.

August 1, 1944: the 2nd French Armored Division, commanded by General Leclerc, lands at Saint-Martin-de-Varreville near Utah Beach. His division will participate in the Battle of Alençon and the liberation of Paris. *NARA*

GENERAL JOSEPH LAWTON COLLINS (1896–1987)

AN INFANTRY OFFICER and graduate of West Point, Collins was a genuine war leader. At the time of the Normandy invasion, he commanded VII Corps, the American forces that landed on Utah Beach and liberated Carentan on June 12, Barneville on June 18, Valognes on June 20, Cherbourg on June 26, and Saint-Lô on July 19. He then took part in Operation Cobra, leading VII Corps from Coutances to Villedieu-les-Poêles, and then against the Falaise Pocket.

Image credit: NARA

For several days, the bulk of the effort fell to American forces in XV Corps. On August 21, XII and XX Corps set out, spearheaded by troops departing from Orléans, who reached and captured Sens on that same day.

On August 23, the Free French 2nd Armored Division reached Rambouillet on a drive with a sole objective: the liberation of Paris. General Leclerc was determined to be the first to arrive at the Place de la Concorde, the very heart of Paris. On the 24th, his division was at Arpajon. That evening, the first of his tanks reached the Hôtel de Ville, the magnificent town hall of Paris, where the prefect welcomed the capital's first liberators.

Late in the morning of August 25, Leclerc entered Paris by the Porte d'Orléans, surrounded by his bodyguards and general staff. The 4th Infantry, entering by the Porte d'Italie, proceeded to clean out the east side of the city. The same day, General von Choltitz received an ultimatum to which he did not respond. He shortly capitulated when German headquarters at the Hôtel Meurice, Place de l'Opéra, were taken by assault. The surrender of Paris was signed at noon, and von Choltitz was escorted to remaining German positions later in the day to give the order to cease fire. Paris was liberated!

The Free French 2nd Armored Division estimated it took fifteen thousand prisoners and killed 3,200 Germans during the Normandy Campaign, at a cost of 630 casualties among its men. On August 26, the Allies made their triumphal entry into Paris. The Free French 2nd Armored Division, followed by American units that took part in the liberation of the capital, paraded down the Champs Elysées.

General Leclerc and his general staff triumphantly enter the streets of Paris. *NARA*

Parisians revolted against their occupier and constructed barricades in the major boulevards in defiance of the German troops in the city, as evidenced by this photo of the Place de la Concorde. Here, German snipers wreak havoc in the crowds welcoming their Allied liberators. *NARA*

The Resistance took up arms and constructed barricades in the boulevards of Paris. General de Gaulle insisted that the capital be liberated by the French and quickly return to its former functions as the centralized seat of government and administration. *NARA*

Surrounded by his bodyguards and preceded by his general staff, Leclerc entered Paris through the Porte d'Orléans late in the morning of August 25. The U.S. 4th Infantry Division entered by the Porte d'Italie and proceeded to clear out the east end of the city. *NARA*

Tanks belonging to Leclerc's 2nd Armored
Division are aligned at the foot of Notre Dame.
NARA

The surrender of Paris is signed on August 25, 1944. That afternoon, General
von Choltitz is escorted to the remaining German positions in the city to order
a ceasefire. *NARA*

Generals de Gaulle, Koenig, and Leclerc lead the ceremonies on the way to
the Tomb of the Unknown Soldier beneath the Arc de Triomphe. *NARA*

THE PURGES

PURGING BEGAN ONCE the Germans were forced to withdraw from France in the summer of 1944. They started in Paris but took place on a grand scale throughout all of France, in an effort to "purify" the country by expressly condemning collaborators under the German occupation. Nothing of similar fury had been seen in France since the Commune of 1871.

It cannot be stated too strongly that France emerged from the war completely traumatized by four years of suffering, humiliation, restriction, and privation, a trauma that was also born of the tension between French Resistance and the fear of a conquered populace that had lived under Nazi domination since 1940. To exorcise the accumulated frustrations, resentments, and anger that had built up during the occupation, it was necessary to find someone to blame and publicly designate as guilty. When the Liberation arrived, including all the excesses found in periods of insurrection, it unleashed an era of revenge. The frenzied rush to settle old scores, an *épuration sauvage*, or brutal purge, as it was later termed, was carried out with primeval savagery.

The reigning climate of chaos left no place for the rule of law. Men and women were summarily seized and subjected to judgment by popular decree and ad-hoc tribunals. Denouncement and defamation abounded, as collaborators were judged, condemned, and executed in the public squares. Fueled by four terrible years of occupation, the French clamored for the heads of those they blamed for their suffering.

The significance of such persecutions should be considered as inherent in the human psyche, for they traditionally perform an important social function. Their role is to free a population of its obsessions by designating a "scapegoat" that is charged with the collective sins of an entire society.

When social tension follows a period of grave moral or economic crisis and threatens to tear a community apart, the community can only reorganize, go forward, and reclaim its innocence if it designates a sacrificial victim from within its own circle. The common action against the "guilty culprit" appeases social anguish and unites the group.

Image credit: NARA

General de Gaulle had much to make him satisfied. The evidence of victory was overwhelming. After Bayeux and the triumphal road from Cherbourg to Rambouillet, Paris gave de Gaulle, leader of the Free French government and "Fighting France," a grandiose welcome worthy of his stature. The populace now considered de Gaulle the guardian of legitimacy, the guarantor of national unity, and the leader most apt to restore the French Republic.

After four years of occupation and submission, France had regained its freedom and its honor. General de Gaulle delivered a speech, famous in the annals of history: "Paris outraged, Paris martyred, but Paris, Paris liberated by its people, with the help of the armies of France, and the support and help of the entire French nation!"

Monsieur le Général GOERING. son Confident ;
Monsieur Pierre LAVAL. son Frère :
Monsieur HIMLER. son Beau-Frère ;
Monsieur le Docteur GŒBBELS. son Valet :
MM. DE BRINON, FLANDIN. DÉAT. DORIOT. ses Amis
Messieurs DE LA ROQUE. DEGRELLE. DARNAN et BUCARD
ses Elèves ;

Ont la profonde douleur de vous faire part de la mort tant souhaitée de leur Fürher qui vous a dégoûté et vous prient d'assister aux funérailles de

Adolphe HITLER

Grand Chevalier de l'Espace Vital

décédé a la suite d'un faux pas au dessus de la Manche. en voulant soulager les Ouvriers Anglais tyrannisés.

La Messe de Requiem sera chantée par les célèbres MACARONIS qui interprèteront La Fuite d'Afrique et Le Replis d'Albanie. sous la direction de leur chef bien-aimé Benito MUSSOLINI.

Un défile grandiose aura lieu sous l'Arc de Triomphe. sous la conduite de Messieurs CHURCHILL. ROOSEVELT. et du Général DE GAULLE. installés dans le wagon mémorable de Compiègne-Berlin le plus vite et au plus tard demain.

Ni fleurs, ni couronnes.
Seules les musiques de danses seront permises.

DE PROFUNDIS !

Les Anglais et Américains auront la victoire.
Les Français auront la gloire.
Les Italiens seront la poire.
Mais pour que rien ne se perde
Les Allemands auront la M......

A sarcastic notice announcing the death of Hitler. *Dominique François*

Translation:

Monsieur le General GOERING, his Confidant,
Monsieur Pierre LAVAL, his Brother,
Monsieur HIMLER, his Brother-in-law,
Monsieur le Docteur GOEBBELS, his Valet,
Messieurs de la ROQUE, DEGRELLE, DARNAN and BUCARD, his Pupils

(SWASTICA)

Have the deep sorrow to announce the greatly desired death of their disgusting Führer, and invite you to attend the funeral of

ADOLPH HITLER

Grand Knight of Lebensraum

Deceased due to a misstep over the Channel in the attempt to relieve the plight of English Workers living in tyranny.

The Requiem Mass will be sung by the celebrated MACARONIS, who will interpret "Flight from Africa" and "The Albanian Withdrawal," under the direction of their much-beloved conductor, Benito MUSSOLINI.

A grandiose procession to the Arc de Triomphe, led by Messieurs CHURCHILL and ROOSEVELT and General de GAULLE in the Compiègne-Berlin memorial hearse will take place as quickly as possible, and at latest tomorrow.

No flowers or wreathes are accepted.
Only music and dancing is permitted.

DE PROFUNDIS!

The English and Americans get the victory.
The French get the glory.
The Italians just look sorry.
And lest we ever forget,
The Germans get the S….

Nevertheless, much remained to be done. First of all, the war was far from over. De Gaulle was faced with a huge task as the front moved north of the capital, with battles taking place just ten kilometers from the center of Paris.

The joyous celebration in the Paris streets made it hard to believe a war was going on. For hundreds of thousands of Parisians, the liberation was one gigantic party, a *fête populaire* or national holiday akin to Bastille Day, July 14. Allied soldiers and all the youth of Paris thronged the bars. The dancing in the streets went on for hours.

PRISONERS OF WAR

Shortly after the Allied landings, prisoner of war camps sprung up along the coast near the landing beaches. While both sides executed numerous prisoners in the first hours of battle, the arrival of military police soon enforced respect for the Geneva Conventions, at least on the Allied side. Accounts of German massacres abound, like the instance at Hémevez, where Wehrmacht soldiers shot in cold blood seven paratroopers from the 507th Parachute Infantry Regiment; or the atrocity at Graignes, where the SS brutally murdered twelve wounded paratroopers and their battalion surgeon. But the first wave of Allied troops, commanded to take no prisoners in the first hours of battle, also killed their prisoners. The furious onslaught of the titanic battle left little room for compassion for one's enemy.

Meanwhile, in the brasseries and bistros of the capital, American soldiers are busy meeting French girls, happy to have a short reprieve before rejoining the front. Paris may be liberated, but the war is far from over. *NARA*

The first American prisoners of war were paratroopers from the 82nd and 101st Airborne Divisions. They were subsequently transferred to stalags (prisoner of war camps) in Germany. *ECPA*

A German officer and interpreter gives instructions to hungry prisoners much more interested in eating their meal than in listening to his pronouncements. The POWs in the photograph are all American paratroopers. *ECPA*

On June 6 or 7, the first American POWs are marched to Cherbourg. The soldiers in this group will have the good fortune to be liberated at the end of the month by VII Corps. *Dominique François*

The Germans also captured many British paratroopers who landed far from their drop zones. They soon would join their American counterparts in stalags and oflags (POW camps for officers). *ECPA*

At a barracks in Saint-Lô, American paratroopers, their faces full of disappointment, wait to be transferred to POW camps in Germany. *ECPA*

SHORN WOMEN

Women accused of having a relationship with a German soldier are paraded in an open truck through the streets of Cherbourg to the mocking sound of drum rolls. The sign reads: "The Float for Female Collaborators." *NARA*

THE LIBERATION UNLEASHED a wave of resentment and the drive to settle old scores. Many men took advantage of the atmosphere of revolt to institute a witch hunt, in which any French woman accused of involvement with a German solider was fair game for punishment.

The men who participated in these actions had not been soldiers themselves. Often referred to as *les résistants de la dernière heure*—last-minute resistants—many had demonstrated an ambiguous attitude during the occupation and now sought to prove their loyalty by punishing women accused of "horizontal collaboration." Over twenty thousand women had their heads publicly shorn for having had a relationship with a German.

While some of the accused did indeed enter into such relationships, others were innocent of any such action. Humiliated and publicly shorn of their hair, sometimes beaten or raped, many were forced to leave their communities in disgrace and attempt to build another life elsewhere.

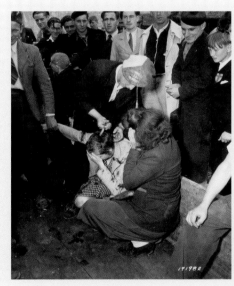

A woman accused of "horizontal collaboration" has her head shaved in Cherbourg, a scene of humiliation all too frequent in July 1944. *NARA*

Stripped to her slip, a woman is shaved before a jeering crowd on a hastily constructed scaffold in a Paris square. *NARA*

Although they may be POWs, the faces of these young Waffen-SS solders still express the defiance and fanaticism that was always the mark of their unit. *NARA*

At the end of the Normandy campaign, overwhelming numbers of German POWs forced the Allies to hastily construct new camps and transfer many prisoners to England and North America. *NARA*

Thousands of POWs flowed into the southern part of the Manche after the Battle of the Falaise Pocket. By the end of July 1944, more than sixty thousand German soldiers had been taken prisoner. *NARA*

At Foucarville, near Sainte-Mère-Église, a large POW camp was established under American administration where nearly ten thousand German soldiers were detained before being shipped to England. Later, other camps were constructed at Valognes, Formigny, Saint-Jean-de-Daye, Saint-Jores, and Tourlaville. At the end of the Normandy Campaign, POW camps in the region held sixty thousand German prisoners, of whom fifty-five thousand would be transferred to England. German POWs were used to dig graves and as manual labor in the various camps and field hospitals. They later were employed as agricultural workers or assigned to help rebuild farms throughout the devastated countryside. They also worked to clear the beaches of mines, where some were killed by antipersonnel mines planted by their own camp.

As for Allied POWs, some of the earliest captured American soldiers were shipped to the northern part of the peninsula. The Pasteur Hospital in Cherbourg received the first cases of American soldiers wounded too badly to be transported: these were freed at the end of June when VII Corps liberated the city. Less lucky were the Allied prisoners trucked to Saint-Lô for processing. The lightly wounded then were transferred to Rennes. The rest were shipped east via Paris to Germany, where their long detention in stalags and oflags would only come to an end when Soviet units liberated their camps in the westward drive for Berlin.

EPILOGUE

THE WAR DID NOT END with the Battle of Normandy. Moreover, the end of combat did not put an end to German hostilities in the region. During the Christmas holidays in 1944, a troop-transport ship, the converted steamship *Léopoldville*, was sunk by German submarine at the mouth of Cherbourg Harbor. In spring 1945, the German occupiers of the Channel Islands (Jersey, Guernsey, and Alderney) carried out two fairly successful commando raids on Granville and Cherbourg. German mines in Norman fields and beaches also continued to do their dirty work, killing Allied soldiers and hapless civilians. Finally, there were the French survivors of German prison camps, some of whom had been held since 1940, who began to return home in spring 1945.

Over twenty thousand French civilians died in the Battle of Normandy, killed in air raids or during combat.

On the German side, fifty-five thousand were killed between June 6 and August 29. Total casualties combining killed, wounded, and missing amounted to four hundred thousand men.

On the Allied side, there were thirty-seven thousand deaths, 153,000 wounded, and twenty thousand missing—over two hundred thousand casualties in all.

Ravaged by combat, the Department of La Manche emerged from the war horribly mutilated. The process of reconstruction would be long and difficult, fraught by many seemingly insoluble problems. For twenty years, the region would mourn the disappearance of dozens of cities and villages, razed to the ground in the summer of 1944. Five thousand inhabitants of the Manche perished in the battle.

Of the 647 *communes* (administrative districts) in Normandy, 390 suffered war damage. Sixty thousand buildings were destroyed, and thirty thousand out of fifty thousand farms were affected by combat. A third of all cattle and other farm animals perished, and cadavers of German soldiers and animals killed by artillery fire long covered the fields. Three hundred churches, including several of the most historic and beautiful in France, were destroyed or damaged.

Two women place flowers on the freshly dug grave of an American paratrooper who died in the battle for Carentan. The people of Normandy today still express eternal gratitude to the brave young men who gave their lives to liberate them from oppression. *NARA*

After four years of German occupation, American troops liberated Mont-Saint-Michel, the crowning glory of Normandy's cultural heritage. The dragon was finally slain. *NARA*

Joseph, Jules, and Fernand were orphaned by the Allied bombing that also destroyed their home in the little village of Saint-Marcouf. Nonetheless, the boys greatly enjoyed the company and kindness of American soldiers, who showered them with rations, chocolate, and chewing gum and rode them around in their jeeps. *Dominique François*

Normandy, and most particularly the region of the Manche, had gone up in flames, sacrificed to the grandeur of the Liberation. However, at the village of Saint-Marcouf, three little boys—Joseph, aged fourteen; Jules, twelve; and Fernand, ten—were having the time of their lives, despite the recent death of their father and the destruction of their house. "Adopted" by compassionate GIs, the three little orphans were living the life of Riley at the temporary airfield the soldiers had constructed at Fontenay. After four years of deprivation, the children discovered the marvels and delights of vitamin-packed chocolate bars, chewing gum, K-rations, baseball, and jeep rides. The blithe nature so typical of children, combined with the care of their new American friends, helped them to forget, at least a bit, the tragedy that had struck their family.

Throughout their entire lives, they never uttered a bitter phrase or word, or even thought a bitter thought against the Allies. They always understood that freedom and the destruction of the Nazi regime could only be won at a terrible price—a price that was paid in the Battle of Normandy.

Appendix A

THE BATTLEFIELD:
THEN
AND NOW

★ ★ ★ ★ ★

Saint-Sauveur-le-Vicomte, French 2nd Armored Division, August 2, 1944. *NARA*

Today. *D. Roussey*

Sainte-Marie-du-Mont, June 6, 1944. *NARA*

Today. *D. Roussey*

Cherbourg, June 28, 1944. *NARA*

Today. *D. Roussey*

Valognes, June 21, 1944. *NARA*

Today. *D. Roussey*

Sainte-Marie-du-Mont, June 6, 1944. *NARA*

Today. *D. Roussey*

WN-65 at Omaha Beach. *NARA*

Today. *D. Roussey*

Picauville: Château de Bernaville, visit of Rommel, April 1944. *D. Roussey*

Today. *D. Roussey*

Appendix B

UNIT INSIGNIA

★ ★ ★ ★ ★

101st Airborne Division "Screaming Eagles"

82nd Airborne Division "All American"

501st Parachute Infantry Regiment
101st Airborne Division

502nd Parachute Infantry Regiment
101st Airborne Division

Seabees

1st Infantry Division "Big Red One"

VIIth Corps

1st U.S..Army

8th Infantry Division "Golden Arrow"

28th Infantry Division "Keystone"

29th Infantry Division "The Blue and Gray"

80th Infantry Division "The Blue Ridge"

83rd Infantry Division "The Thunderbolt"

British Commando

Kriegsmarine

Luftwaffe

506th Parachute Infantry Regiment
101st Airborne Division

507th Parachute Infantry Regiment
82nd Airborne Division

508th Parachute Infantry Regiment
82nd Airborne Division

British Airborne Wing

2nd Infantry Division "Indian Head"

5th Infantry Division "Red Diamond"

4th Infantry Division "Ivy"

90th Infantry Division "The Tough 'ombres"

79th Infantry Division "The Cross of Lorraine"

9th Infantry Division
"The Varsity and the Old Reliables"

35th Infantry Division "The Santa Fe"

Heer

Luftwaffe

Airborne Cap Badge
All U.S. Parachute Infantry Regiments

Note: While this is not a complete collection of unit insignia for the Battle of Normandy, an effort was made to be as inclusive as possible. Regrettably, some rare but important insignia were unavailable to include.

BIBLIOGRAPHY

Ambrose, Stephen E. *D-Day, June 6, 1944.* New York: Simon & Schuster, 1994.

Dawson, Forrest. *Saga of the All American.* Atlanta: Albert Love Enterprises, 1946.

Desquesnes Rémy. *Le Mur de l'Atlantique en Normandie.* Caen: Mémorial de Caen, 1976.

Carrel, Paul. *Ils arrivent!* Paris: Robert Laffont, 1994.

Gavin, James M. *On to Berlin.* New York: Bantam Book, 1978.

Griesser, Volker. *Les lions de Carentan.* Bayeux: Heimdal, 2006.

Goldstein, D. M., Katherine V. Dillon, and J. Michael Wenger. *D-Day Normandy: The Story and Photographs.* Fayetteville: University of Arkansas Press, 1992.

Hogg, Ian V. *The American Arsenal.* London: Greenhill Books, 2001.

Keegan, John. *Six Armies in Normandy.* New York: Penguin Press, 1982.

Kurowski, Frank. *Die Panzer-Lehr-Division.* Bad Nauheim: Podzun, 1964.

Marshall, George C. *Night Drop.* Nashville: Battery Press, 1962.

Marshall, George C. "The Winning of the War in Europe and the Pacific." Report to the United States War Department, 1945.

Master, Charles J. *Glidermen of Neptune.* Carbondale: Southern Illinois University Press, 1995.

Van der Vat, Dan. *D-Day, the Greatest Invasion.* Toronto: Madison Press Book, 2003.

Weidinger, Otto. *Division Das Reich im Bild.* Osnabrueck: Munin Verlag, 1981.

INDEX

Company Q, 173
Troop B, 173
Troop X, 173
Troop Y, 173
43rd Infantry Division, 173–174, 222
59th Infantry Division, 177
197th Brigade, 177
26th Armoured Engineers, 177–178
90th Field Artillery Regiment, 173
144th Armoured Division, 267
144th Armoured Regiment, 269

Canadian Forces

North Shore (New Brunswick) Regiment, 179
Queen's Own Rifles, 179
Company A, 179
Company B, 179
Regiment de La Chaudière, 179
2nd Canadian Armoured Brigade, 102
2nd Canadian Infantry Division, 264
3rd Canadian Division, 102, 166, 176, 179
Regina Rifles, 177
Company A, 177
Company B, 177–178
Company C, 177–178
Company D, 177
Royal Winnipeg Rifles, 178
Company B ("Black Devils"), 178

French Forces

Force Française de l'Intérieur (FFI), 24, 273
2nd Armored Division (Free French), 237, 261,
268, 273–274, 276, 286
Combat Command B, 248
2nd Light Division, 268

German Forces

Afrika Korps, 75
Flak Abteilung 32, 143
Kriegsmarine (German navy), 44, 179, 209, 213
Oberkommando der Wehrmacht (OKW), 43–
44, 47, 136, 183
Waffen-SS, 27, 30–31, 41, 47, 59, 63, 118,
221–222, 227, 235, 237, 243, 252, 255, 269–
270, 279, 282
II SS-Panzerkorps, 257
1st SS Panzergruppe, 222
9th SS Panzer Division, 265
SS Charlemagne (1st French), 30
33rd Waffen Grenadier Division, 30
SS Das Reich Division, 235, 243, 257

Wehrmacht, 17, 19, 33, 42–43, 47–48, 63, 65,
191, 279
Luftwaffe, 20, 35, 44–45, 52, 59, 61–64,
66–67, 68, 97, 181, 187, 221, 228, 258–
259
6th Fallschirmjäger Regiment ("Lions"),
66–67, 188, 195, 197, 252
16th Division, 228
91st Infantry-Air Landing Division, 62,
66–67, 82, 112–115, 195, 201
Third Air Fleet, 66
Oberbefehlshaber West (OB West), 48–49,
60, 201
Army Group B, 49, 57, 59–61, 63, 105,
219, 244, 267
LXIII Rommel Panzerkorps, 63
I SS Tank Corps, 63
1st Panzer Division, 63
2nd Panzer Division, 63,
258, 264
12th SS Panzer Division
(Hitlerjungend Division), 63–64, 201, 221,
228, 261
21st Panzer Division, 63,
123, 181, 201, 219
Panzerjager-
Abteilung 200, 167
116th Panzer Division, 63
Panzer Lehr Division, 63,
201–202, 221, 247, 249
Regiment 130, 247, 260
1st Company, 247
9th Panzer Division, 63
11th Panzer Division, 63
17th SS Panzergrenadier
Division, 63, 118, 198
Seventh Army, 17, 21, 57, 59–61,
66, 68, 105, 219, 221, 231, 241,
244, 255, 257, 261
XXV Corps, 60
LXXIV Corps, 60
LXXXIV Corps, 60, 250
Fifteenth Army, 55, 57, 59–60, 105,
183, 255
LXVII Corps, 60
LXXXI Corps, 60
LXXXII Corps, 60
LXXXIX Corps, 60
Army Group G, 60
First Army, 60
Nineteenth Army, 60, 255
Fifth Panzer Army, 255, 265, 267
77th Infantry Division, 115, 201
243rd Infantry Division, 115

306th Infantry Division, 115
319th Infantry Division, 62
325th Infantry Division, 167
1/916, 167, 171
346th Infantry Division, 176
857th Regiment, 176
6th Company, 176
352nd Infantry Division, 62, 115, 135–136,
138–139, 143
1st Artillery Group, 136
4th Artillery Group, 136
353rd Infantry Division, 234
709th Infantry Division, 195, 210
716th Infantry Division, 62, 135–136, 138–
139, 166
736th Infantry Regiment, 166, 176, 179
761st Infantry Division, 165
II/914, 143
3/341, 167
4/441 Ost.Abt., 166
9/726, 143
22nd Panzer Regiment, 218
84th Armored Flak Battalion, 115
155th Regiment, 257
1716th Artillery Regiment, 179
642nd Ost Battalion, 179
3rd Company, 179
795th Battalion, 113

Italian Forces

Fourth Army, 48

GENERAL INDEX

Abwehr, 104, 105
Aisne River, 21
Albany mission, 85, 112
Albemarle planes, 123
Alderney, 45, 283
Aldis lamp, 92
Alençon, France, 264
Allied forces, 19, 24, 29, 31, 33, 38–39, 41–43,
45–46, 48–51, 55–56, 60, 62, 64–68, 71,
74–76, 79–80, 83, 88–90, 95–107, 109, 114,
134, 136–138, 142, 147–148, 152–153, 169,
178–179, 181, 183–184, 187–188, 190,
192–193, 196, 199–200, 202–207, 209–210,
213–217, 219, 221–222, 224, 226, 233–234,
237, 239, 241–243, 249–250, 252, 257–259,
264–271, 273, 275, 279, 282–284
Amfreville, France, 111, 115, 192
Amiens, France, 63
Angers, France, 103
Angoville, France, 110

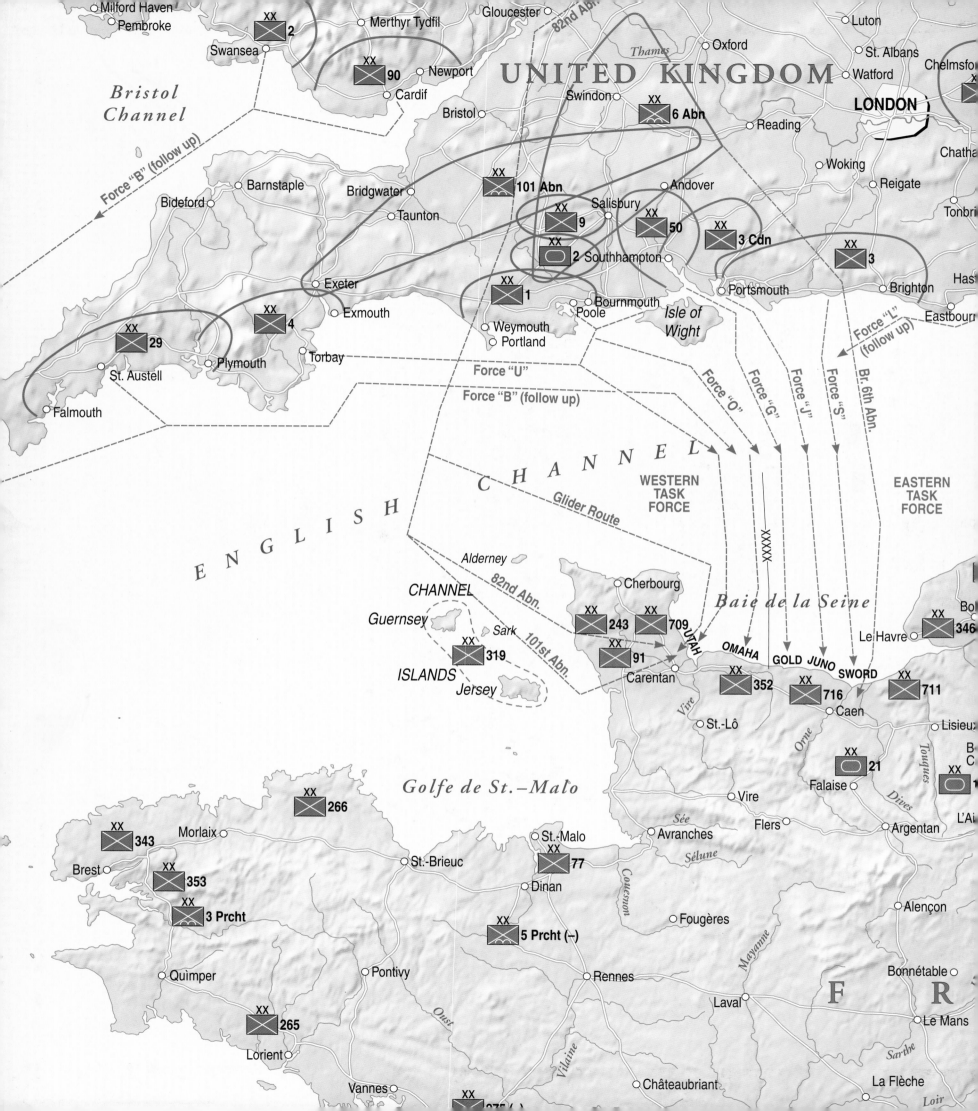

Milford Haven
Pembroke
XX 2
Swansea
Merthyr Tydfil
Gloucester
82nd Abn.
Luton
St. Albans
Chelms
UNITED KINGDOM
XX 90
Newport
Cardif
Swindon
Oxford
LONDON
Chatha
Bristol
Channel
Bristol
XX 6 Abn
Reading
Woking
Reigate
Tonbri
Barnstaple
Bridgwater
XX 101 Abn
Salisbury
Andover
Bideford
Taunton
XX 9
XX 50
XX 3 Cdn
XX 3
Hastin
Exeter
XX 2 Southhampton
Portsmouth
Brighton
Eastbour
Force "B" (follow up)
Exmouth
XX 1
Bournmouth
Poole
Isle of Wight
Force "L" (follow up)
XX 4
XX 29
Weymouth
Portland
Br. 6th Abn.
St. Austell
Plymouth
Torbay
Force "U"
Falmouth
Force "B" (follow up)
ENGLISH CHANNEL
WESTERN TASK FORCE
Force "O"
Force "G"
Force "J"
Force "S"
EASTERN TASK FORCE
Glider Route
XXXXX
Alderney
82nd Abn.
Cherbourg
Baie de la Seine
CHANNEL
Guernsey
Sark
101st Abn.
XX 243
XX 709
UTAH
OMAHA
GOLD
JUNO
SWORD
Le Havre
XX 346
XX 319
XX 91
Carentan
XX 352
XX 716
Caen
XX 711
ISLANDS
Jersey
Vire
St.-Lô
Lisieux
Golfe de St.-Malo
XX 21
Falaise
Touques
XX B C
XX 266
Vire
Dives
L'Ai
XX 343
Morlaix
Sée
Avranches
Flers
Argentan
Brest
St.-Malo
Sé; lune
XX 353
St.-Brieuc
XX 77
Alençon
XX 3 Prcht
Dinan
Coue non
Fougères
Mayenne
XX 5 Prcht (--)
Rennes
Bonnétable
Quimper
Pontivy
Laval
Le Mans
FR
XX 265
Oust
Vilaine
Sarthe
Lorient
Vannes
Châteaubriant
Loir
La Flèche